Advances in Information Systems
and Management Science

Band 20

Advances in Information Systems and Management Science

Band 20

Herausgegeben von

Prof. Dr. Jörg Becker
Prof. Dr. Heinz Lothar Grob
Prof. Dr. Stefan Klein
Prof. Dr. Herbert Kuchen
Prof. Dr. Ulrich Müller-Funk
Prof. Dr. Gottfried Vossen

Peter Westerkamp

Flexible Elearning Platforms: A Service-Oriented Approach

Logos Verlag Berlin

Advances in Information Systems and Management Science

Herausgegeben von

Prof. Dr. Jörg Becker, Prof. Dr. Heinz Lothar Grob,
Prof. Dr. Stefan Klein, Prof. Dr. Herbert Kuchen,
Prof. Dr. Ulrich Müller-Funk, Prof. Dr. Gottfried Vossen.

Westfälische Wilhelms-Universität Münster
Institut für Wirtschaftsinformatik
Leonardo-Campus 3
D-48149 Münster

Tel.: +49 (0)251 / 83 - 3 81 00
Fax: +49 (0)251 / 83 - 3 81 09
http://www.wi.uni-muenster.de

Bibliografische Information Der Deutschen Bibliothek

Die Deutsche Bibliothek verzeichnet diese Publikation in der
Deutschen Nationalbibliografie; detaillierte bibliografische Daten
sind im Internet über http://dnb.ddb.de abrufbar.

ISBN 3-8325-1117-2
ISSN 1611-3101

D 6 2005

Logos Verlag Berlin
Comeniushof, Gubener Str. 47
10243 Berlin

Tel.: +49 (0)30 / 42 85 10 90
Fax: +49 (0)30 / 42 85 10 92
http://www.logos-verlag.de

Geleitwort

Elektronisches Lernen, in moderner Diktion heute zumeist mit E-Learning abgekürzt, hat sich dank der immer billiger werdenden Hard- und Software von Computern innerhalb von etwa 10 Jahren in allen Formen von Aus- und Weiterbildung flächendeckend durchgesetzt. Während anfangs noch sehr genau differenziert wurde, was nun zu E-Learning dazu gerechnet werden darf und was nicht („ist eine Powerpoint-Show bereits E-Learning?"), ist man mittlerweile fast soweit, das „E" wieder entfallen zu lassen, da Formen der elektronischen Unterstützung von Lehrenden und Lernen bzw. von Lernszenarien heute so selbstverständlich geworden sind. E-Learning hat viele Facetten: Aus einer (software-) technischen Sicht wird E-Learning typischerweise über ein System bzw. eine rechnergestützte Plattform abgewickelt, in welchem bzw. welcher sich der einzelne Benutzer identifiziert und dann seiner Rolle (Lernende, Tutor, Lehrer, Autor usw.) entsprechend bestimmte Funktionalität nutzen kann; in der vorliegenden Arbeit steht diese Sicht im Vordergrund. Daneben gibt es didaktische und pädagogische Aspekte, es gibt rechtliche sowie organisatorische Gesichtspunkte, um nur einige der weiteren Facetten zu nennen. Heutige E-Learning-Softwaresysteme sind typischerweise *geschlossene* Systeme mit fest vorgegebener Funktionalität (wie Chat-Room, Email-Funktion, Helpdesk, Suchfunktion, eigentliche Lernumgebung usw.), mit denen oft auch große Gemeinschaften von Lernenden durch einzelne oder viele Kurse begleitet werden können. Die Hersteller solcher Systeme, aber auch die Autoren von Inhalten (typischerweise von Kursen, aber auch von kleineren Einheiten, die in diesem Zusammenhang oft als „Lernobjekte" bezeichnet werden) haben frühzeitig erkannt, dass gerade der Austausch von Inhalten („Content") zwischen Systemen aus verschiedenen Gründen wünschenswert ist, und haben in der Folge eine Reihe von Standards (wie SCORM oder LOM) entwickelt, an die man sich halten muss, wenn man tatsächlich eine Wiederverwendbarkeit von *Material* erreichen will (an Wiederverwendung von Funktionalität ist dabei noch gar nicht gedacht).

Nun gibt es eine Reihe von Lernszenarien, in denen solche geschlossenen Systeme wenig hilfreich sind, in denen man aber dennoch elektronische Unterstützung beim Lernen gewähren oder benutzen möchte. Ein typisches Beispiel ist die betriebliche Fortbildung, etwa bei der Vorbereitung der Einführung eines neuen Produkts, bei der Einarbeitung von neuen Mitarbeitern in die Prozesse eines Unternehmens oder bei der Weiterqualifikation von Mitarbeitern hinsichtlich einer bestimmten Spezialisierung, die eine Zertifizierung erfordert. Hier ist meist der oder die Lernende gefordert, von sich aus aktiv zu werden, nach Content-Anbietern zu suchen, ggfs. Kurse oder Lerneinheiten zu „buchen" und diese zu bearbeiten bis hin zu abschließenden Tests und Prüfungen. An einem derartigen Szenario setzt die Arbeit von Peter Westerkamp an mit der Überlegung, sich für die adäquate Unterstützung solcher und ähnlicher Lernsituationen das in den letzten Jahren populär gewordene Informatik-Konzept der (Web-) *Service-Orientierung* zunutze zu machen. Er setzt sich somit das anspruchsvolle Ziel, Service-Orientierung, ein zunächst völlig technisches Konzept basierend auf Standards wie SOAP oder WSDL, in angemessener Form in E-Learning-Umgebungen hineinzutragen, um damit letztlich für bestimmte Lernsituationen flexiblere Lösungen bieten zu können, als dies mit heutigen monolithischen Systemen möglich ist. Dass es bei der Entwicklung einer völlig neuen Generation eines bestimmten Systemtypus der Bewältigung eines umfangreichen Arbeitsprogramms bedarf, versteht sich am Rande; der Autor stellt sich hier also einer umfassenden Herausforderung.

Die von Peter Westerkamp vorgelegte Arbeit kombiniert in eindrucksvoller Weise Informatiktechniken mit organisatorischen und wirtschaftlichen Überlegungen und stellt damit ein Paradebeispiel für eine Dissertation der Wirtschaftsinformatik dar. Die gesetzten Ziele werden in vollem Umfang und mit einem eindrucksvollen Instrumentarium erreicht, das von VOFI auf der einen bis hin zu Web-Standards und deren technische Nutzung auf der anderen Seite reicht: Da werden Prozessmodelle zur genauen Ablaufbeschreibung herangezogen, ein Datenmodell für ein Repository entworfen oder eine Ontologie herangezogen, wenn semantische Hilfe beim Suchen nach Diensten nötig wird. Der Autor konzipiert dabei ein umfassendes System ausgehend von einer Kritik an bestehenden Systemen und einer kritischen Analyse vorhandener Möglichkeiten. Die Entscheidung, Web Services als Grundlage einer Neuentwicklung heranzuziehen ist mutig, stellt sich aber nach so gründlicher Durchdringung als neuartig, richtig und zukunftsweisend heraus, und sie führt sogar dazu, dass etablierte E-Learning-Standards in ihrer heutigen Form am Ende in Frage gestellt werden.

Die in englischer Sprache abgefasste Arbeit hat in der Fachwelt bereits internationale Anerkennung gefunden. Peter Westerkamp konnte diverse Beiträge in internationalen Konferenzen rund um den Globus platzieren und wurde mehrfach aufgefordert, Konferenzpapiere zu Zeitschriftenartikeln auszuarbeiten. Allerdings hat er hier nicht einfach diverse Papiere zusammengefasst, sondern sich erfolgreich um einen klaren Kontext und eine durchgehende Entwicklung mit großer Liebe zum Detail bemüht; die Arbeit erhält vieles Unveröffentlichte und ist damit ein hervorragender (vorläufiger) Abschluss seiner

Arbeiten auf diesem Gebiet. Ich wünsche der Arbeit auch im deutschsprachigen Raum eine breite Leserschaft, was durch die Veröffentlichung in dieser Reihe zumindest vorbereitet wird.

Münster, im Dezember 2005

Prof. Dr. Gottfried Vossen

Preface

Throughout this thesis a service-oriented environment called LearnServe will be developed. There is no connection between the former company Learnserve Ltd., Ireland, (now Northgate Information Systems), its Learnserve RM system providing IT support for primary schools, and the LearnServe environment developed here. Moreover, there is no connection to the Intercosmos Media Group, which registered the Internet domains http://learnserve.com and http://www.learnserve.org at the end of 2004. At press time, details about their fully-fledged, SCORM-compliant elearning platform could not be found on the Internet. Apart from these IT companies, there is no connection between the work presented here and the LearnServe projects to foster education in developing countries (particularly in Paraguay and Ethiopia).

Internet search engines also provide hits for the keyword "LearnServe" that result from the use of this term as a short form of other phrases used in the Internet addresses (URLs) of documents. This concerns particularly the "Service Learning in the Northwest" program, which has no elearning background.

Additional information on the LearnServe project presented in this thesis can be found on the Internet at:

http://www.learnserve.de

Acknowledgments

I would like to express my thanks to my advisor Prof. Dr. Gottfried Vossen for his continuous support, motivation, and advice during the work on this thesis and my stay in Münster. He also gave me the opportunity to visit scientific conferences in Europe, North America, Asia, and Australia to discuss my ideas with experts from all over the world.

I would like to thank Prof. Dr. Heinz Lothar Grob for his willingness to act as second reviewer and Prof. Dr. Jörg Becker for his willingness to act as third examiner in the disputation.

I would like to extend my grateful thanks to Carolin Letz, Daniel Dahl, Sebastian Eichholz, Stephan Hagemann, Dr. Bodo Hüsemann, Dr. Jens Lechtenbörger, and Joachim Schwieren for all the discussions on issues covered within this thesis. In addition, I would like to thank Barbara Wicher for her administrative and Ralf Farke for his technical assistance. All of the latter including Prof. Dr. Gottfried Vossen contribute to the outstanding working atmosphere and human relations at the European Research Center for Information Systems (ERCIS) in Münster from which I extremely benefited during the last years.

I am also very grateful to my family for their continuous support at any time. Above all, I am particularly grateful to my girlfriend Frauke Fuchslocher who cheered me up so many times and provided a lot of help and encouragement while I was working on this thesis.

Münster, December 2005

Peter Westerkamp

Contents

Chapter 1

Introduction

Electronic learning applications offer possibilities for learners to enhance their knowledge in a computer-supported, self-directed, time- and location-independent way. The variety of manufacturers in the field of electronic learning (or elearning for short) is huge and includes, for example, platform providers, content providers, and consulting companies. Current surveys offer comparisons of elearning platforms and include mostly descriptions of up to 100 platforms (see, for example, [HK03], [GL05], or the Brandon Hall Web site[1]). However, the market is much bigger, and, by the end of 2005, [Hal05] will publish an overview listing more than 1,000 organizations selling elearning products or offering elearning services. Currently, most elearning platforms are incapable of exchanging content and learner profiles [Vos04] with other elearning platforms or enterprise systems [ALF+01, AFL+01]. Moreover, reusing functionalities is a problem for most elearning platforms [Mor04]. Although standards in the elearning field intend to address the reusability of content, many systems do still not adhere to these standards. As a consequence, it is very costly to transfer content offered by these proprietary systems to other elearning platforms if it is possible at all. The situation is even worse for the reuse of functionalities offered by elearning platforms. Some platforms provide functionalities that are helpful for many learners, but none of them can either be deployed independently of the platform or provide any integration interfaces to be used by other systems. It goes without saying that there are also a couple of functionalities that each elearning platform implements, for example, a user management, but reusing these functionalities is nowadays rather uncommon in the field of elearning. In addition, an inclusion of new tools into most platforms at the moment when they become available is difficult [LHS+03, Atw04] because systems are not implemented in a modular way with well-defined interfaces.

---

[1]http://www.brandonhall.com

The development of elearning products is presently characterized by high costs, particularly for realizing platforms and contents. Owing to these high costs, the critical mass of learners for an economically justifiable development of offerings in elearning is higher than compared to the one in traditional forms of learning. From an economical perspective, a reuse in the area of elearning is consequently an important factor to reach the critical mass. However, elearning platforms and content cannot be offered as mass products and must be adaptable and usable in many environments in order to respond to the needs of various types of learners [AP02].

A strategy to open traditionally closed elearning platforms and to sell access to elearning content and functionalities on the Web which are independent of a full-fledged elearning system would increase the target group for both content and functionalities to reach the critical mass. At the same time it would offer the flexibility to adapt both the content and the platforms for individual learners and, therefore, fosters the reuse of elearning offerings. To provide access to the latter over the Web, elearning platforms have to be implemented in a different manner than nowadays common. Instead of offering elearning solutions in the form of closed systems trying to implement the entire functionality typically covered by elearning platforms, parts of elearning applications have to be offered publicly on the Web as stand-alone applications with well-defined interfaces. This way elearning platforms and courses can be plugged together by offerings from a huge variety of manufacturers and authors. This includes elearning content and elearning application functionality.

An elearning market study [Mas05] published on the portal of the European Union[2] underscores the development of these stand-alone applications. It comes to the conclusion that most manufacturers of elearning products in Europe have less than ten employees. They usually act nationally on the markets of the educational and workplace segments. The study predicts that many of them will cease to exist because a lot of companies are too small to compete successfully against the big multinational providers, in particular against those from the United States. To survive, companies have to change their strategies and choose between the following options [Mas05]:

- they can offer solutions that sell access to learning content and services;

- they can also offer their products as an open source solution and sell integration services;

- they can expand into other national markets.

An offering of access to content and services on the Web is, of course, in line with an expansion into other national markets.

---

[2]http://europa.eu.int

1.1 Courses and Learners in Tertiary Education

Many institutions are currently offering courses for tertiary education or workplace education. In order to pass a course, participants typically receive checklists that describe the content of teaching. Based on these descriptions, learners can freely choose content from various providers. Some courses may end in exams, which can be taken at different institutions. Normally, there is a well-defined order of taking exams of each course unit, but the order of sub-unit exams and even the combination of these exams may not be fixed (for example, take two out of four).

Figure 1.1 shows the structure of a course preparing to become a "Certified Internet Application Developer, Oracle Forms Developer Rel. 6/6i" offered by the Oracle University[3] [Ora05]. In this case, the course has a simple structure as it consists of only four exams to be passed; they can be taken in any order. For two of the exams, there is a choice of which content to include. [Ora05] also offers a checklist that identifies the topics to be learned in order to pass the exams. Although it references books from the Oracle Press, it states that these books can only be seen as additional preparation for the exams. Furthermore, courses and books are recommended to be studied before the exam is taken. Moreover, job experience, job practice, and self-studying are the best ways to prepare for the exams. The way of preparing for exams can be customized according to the learner's budget. Every exam can be taken at Oracle University or at any authorized test center. The exam "1Z0-001" can already be taken online on a platform offered by Oracle University.

The course described above is typically taken by employees to deepen their knowledge about the subject matters to improve their skills for their employer (workplace education) or by people to increase their chances for a new job while learning in their spare time. Both types of learners opt for participating in tertiary education. Their situation is characterized by the necessity of life-long learning and by a high need for specialization in a certain subject. These types of learners are also the main target groups of publicly-available elearning offerings as they have to participate in courses like the one described above. However, there are also fields of application in other areas of education, for example, in universities, as will be explained later.

In future, preparations for exams in tertiary education will be developed by third parties that will offer their content on the Web. Learners will then be able to choose from many offerings to prepare for their exams. Merely the exams themselves will still have to be taken at an authorized institution. The independent third parties will be able to offer an

---

[3]http://www.oracle.com/education/

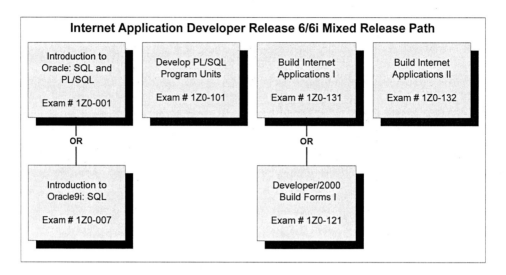

Figure 1.1: A sample course (according to [Ora05]).

added value for learners, for example, a competent population of checklists with content. In addition, they will be able to offer extra functionalities for certain learners, for example, a simulation of the job training or access to systems in order to gain hands-on experience.

The course "Certified Internet Application Developer" (CIAD) shown in Figure 1.1 will be referenced in the following chapters to clarify matters and to establish a running example throughout the entire text. It is assumed that this course is taken by learners in tertiary education; they study in their spare time. Although the preparation for this course can currently still be taken in different forms including classroom teaching, the learners want to prepare for the exams by consuming online content only.

1.2   Thesis Objective

Traditional elearning platforms do not provide the flexibility learners need in tertiary education. Platforms are normally centralized and offer courses with well-defined content instead of checklists. Learners do not have the ability to choose from content offered by different authors and styles within a course; and, moreover, the content is usually neither selected nor adapted to learners' needs. Normally, it is also impossible for learners to import content because of several reasons, which will be explained in Chapter 2.

The need to offer learning flexibility, the demand for reuse, and an independent offering of content and functionality lead to the development of stand-alone elearning components as described above. Although it is possible to link Web applications from different providers to build an application from offerings of several remote servers, elearning components have to be integrated to provide useful functionalities and a uniform look-and-feel. This cannot be achieved by simply linking Web pages. Consequently, the approach must go far beyond that which is possible with an integration of this form.

The implementation of remote functionalities as components to be included into other platforms is well known from the field of distributed systems. The main objective of this thesis is to transfer this approach to elearning environments and define and realize distributed elearning components based on well-known techniques to offer flexible elearning environments. It particularly addresses the following aspects:

1. Which approach and technology is best suited to implement elearning offerings in a distributed way? How can learners plug components (in particular remote content components) into a running system on their own?

2. What are reasonable elearning components to be offered remotely? Does an integration of these components match existing elearning-architecture standards? How can elearning components be discovered?

3. What does the internal and external architecture of the environment look like? What does the communication between the components look like?

4. How can elearning content be transferred from remote servers on demand as intended by the author?

5. How can a tracking of user activities be managed in a distributed system?

6. How can a single-sign-on be realized?

7. The organization of content as remote service is different from traditional content packages. There is only one copy of the content and there is no physical distribution of the latter. Are there any changes in business models which component providers have to consider?

8. Which organizational aspects have to be taken into consideration for the use of remote elearning components in different environments?

All elearning components ought to adhere to common standards and specifications as far as possible. This includes both elearning and specifications of the chosen distributed-systems technique. The concepts are implemented in form of a prototype called *LearnServe*. It is composed of several remote servers that interact in the way as specified throughout this thesis. Some of the servers have to be realized in order to provide the new services, but LearnServe also uses remote functionalities already offered by other manufacturers on the Web.

1.3 Structure of the Thesis

To address the aspects mentioned before, the thesis is structured as will be described next and as shown in Figure 1.2. After the motivation of remote elearning components and an introduction of a small sample scenario given in this section, Chapter 2.1 will provide an overview of the field of elearning. It will start with major historical perspectives and will introduce common terms used in the field of elearning. Afterwards, Chapter 2.2 will sketch common elearning standards used today. As there are particularly three very important initiatives that also cooperate, the presentation will concentrate on the work of the IEEE[4] Learning Technology Standards Committee, IMS Global Learning Consortium, and the Advanced Distributed Learning (ADL) Initiative. These standardization efforts frequently have a major influence on the implementation of modern elearning platforms that can be realized by being based on different architectures. These architectures and common distribution models will be explained in Chapter 2.4. The chapter will conclude with an analysis of shortcomings in traditional, centralized elearning systems and will give additional reasons for the necessity of distributed elearning platforms.

Several well-known approaches can be used to implement a distributed elearning system. They will be introduced in Chapter 3. The chapter will concentrate on techniques that are conceptually independent of platforms and programming languages. Most of them are evolutions of the Remote Procedure Call paradigm described in Chapter 3.1 and include Transaction Processing Monitors (Chapter 3.2), object-based middleware (Chapter 3.3), and message-oriented middleware (Chapter 3.4). The limitations of these conventional middleware approaches for the use in distributed elearning applications will be explained in Chapter 3.5. The argumentation will underline the necessity of a special form of message-based systems called Web services in general and also in the particular elearning case. Web services will be introduced in Chapter 3.6.

The basic concepts of the elearning and Web-service fields will be combined in Chapter 4. It will present a top-down division of a common, but hypothetical elearning platform into several stand-alone applications that can be offered as Web services. Afterwards,

---

[4]IEEE is a short form for: Institute of Electrical and Electronics Engineers, Inc.

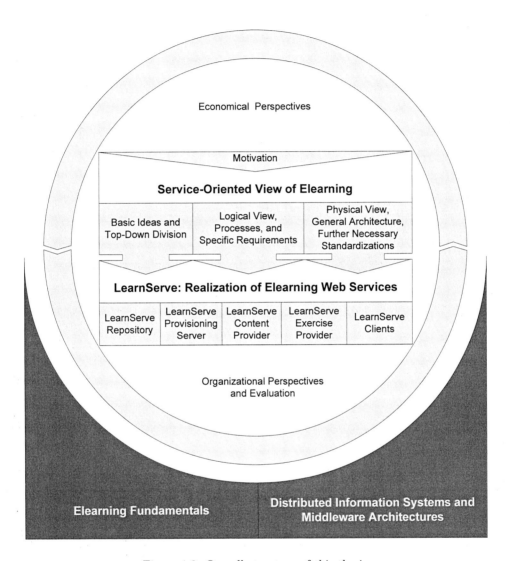

Figure 1.2: Overall structure of this thesis.

the service-oriented concept will be mapped to the IEEE Learning Technology Systems Architecture (LTSA) standard to show that it still meets the requirements of the latter standard. LTSA is regarded as a framework to design a range of elearning systems over the years, not as a blue print for designing a single system. However, the LTSA specification will have to be extended in order to realize the service-oriented concept. The external message flow of the communication between the servers taking part in the entire environment will be shown in Chapter 4.2.1 for the most likely activities in an elearning platform. This will include content presentation, exercises, discovery services, as well as tracking and feedback processing. As there are a lot of authoring tools that can be used to create content and as authoring is not part of the IEEE LTSA standard, it will not be stressed in this thesis.

The elearning data and the physical view of the services depend on the particular implementation of a specific provider and will consequently only be sketched in Chapter 4 and will be explained in detail in Chapter 5. Before, a couple of specific requirements that have to be met in order to realize a Web-services-based elearning environment will be discussed in Chapter 4.2.3.

Chapter 5 will describe the "LearnServe" realization of elearning Web services based on the concepts of the previous chapters. This environment will comprise the LearnServe Repository (Chapter 5.1), the LearnServe Provisioning Server (Chapter 5.2), the LearnServe Content Provider (Chapter 5.3), the exercise server in form of a wrapper of an existing system (Chapter 5.4), and the LearnServe Consumer and client platforms (Chapter 5.5). In addition, Chapter 5 will discuss an extension of the open source platform OpenUSS to be used as LearnServe Consumer and will illustrate the use of services from a learner's perspective. It will also discuss advantages and disadvantages of the realized LearnServe environment.

Chapter 6 will stress different perspectives of the realization of elearning Web services; this will be, on the one hand, the economical aspect and, on the other hand, the organizational aspect. The thesis will take a closer look at new business models that will have to be developed for the elearning services. Additionally, organizational aspects for offering services will be explained, which will finally be followed by a conclusion in Chapter 7.

Chapter 2

Elearning Fundamentals

"Elearning" is a modern term for the use of computers in teaching and learning. Since the idea of supporting learners by computers has not emerged only recently, a short overview of important development steps and recent activities will be given in this chapter. First, Chapter 2.1 will take a closer look at the use of computers in teaching, learning, and education. It will explain several terms used in the field of elearning today and will particularly define the term "elearning" in the way it will be used in this thesis to give a clear understanding of it. The development of elearning is characterized by the development of elearning standards, at which Chapter 2.2 will take a closer look. These standards have an influence on the implementation of modern elearning platforms. Some of the latter will be discussed in Chapter 2.4, and Chapter 2.5 will conclude this chapter with a description of challenges still not met by modern elearning platform implementations.

2.1 A Historical Perspective of Elearning - Some Terminology

About five decades ago, SKINNER [Ski54] argued that teaching can be systematized by arranging content in small and progressive granules to present them in a well-defined process to learners, and he called this theory "Programmed Instruction". The key characteristics of this concept are very similar to those which learning platforms currently provide:

- small granules of instruction,

- self-pacing for learners,

- active learner response to questions, and

- immediate feedback to the response.

SKINNER suggested that the process could be supported by a "Teaching Machine" as an instructional tool that could improve student learning.

The first "Teaching Machines" were mainframe systems, and learners used terminals to access these learning platforms. The entire application logic was provided by the mainframe because terminals did not have any processing power at that time [Col02, Bar02]. One of the most famous systems was PLATO[1] (Programmed Logic for Automatic Teaching Operations [Ker01a]), which was able to present both text-based learning units and multimedia content on special multimedia teaching stations. It used a special-purpose authoring language called TUTOR to produce courseware. Apart from the mainframe systems, several non-computer-based improvements have made teaching easier. These systems, for example, are learning programs on TV, learning videos, audio tapes, or education via radio [Hip03].

An important technical improvement to support the "Programmed Instruction" has been the development of microcomputers (also called personal computers, "PCs"), which have made it possible to use computers even at home because prices for these machines have become acceptable to private buyers. First, well-priced systems by Commodore and Apple were commonly preferred; they were able to present multimedia content. The improved infrastructure has led to the development of the "Computer Based Training" (CBT) [Dit03], which can be used at home and is still in use today. Often CBTs try to substitute the teacher by multimedia [AP02]. Today, CBT courses are usually distributed on compact discs (CDs) [JOV03] or digital versatile discs (DVDs, sometimes also called digital video discs). CBT courses are mostly closed applications that do not provide links to content resources outside of the course. They merely have to be inserted into the corresponding drive and then started. In addition to simple texts, graphics, and simple multimedia building blocks used for teaching purposes, the high capacities of CDs and DVDs also allow the use of high quality videos in courses. One of the major drawbacks of CBTs is the fact that there is no interaction with other learners because the computers do not have to be connected to a network. Although there may be an interaction with the system by providing immediate (programmed) feedback to the input of learners, there is no learning community on a single machine. In addition, an update of content is only possible by distributing new volumes. This is particularly difficult if CBTs have to be bought in shops.

---

[1]http://www.plato.com

Another major step in the development of elearning systems has been the emerge of Intranets, the Internet and, in particular, the World Wide Web (WWW). Enterprises using networks make it possible to access CBTs via the Intranet. This form of elearning is sometimes called "Network Based Training" (NTB)[2]; it solves the problem of updates since the content has to be changed only once for all employees of the company. Today, the distribution of learning content via the Internet and the WWW is more important. Particularly, the use of hyperlinks and the Hypertext Markup Language (HTML)[3] makes it more comfortable to create and structure content. Content created by means of HTML can include texts, pictures, video files, audio files, and further formats like FLASH [BH03c] animations. The use of the WWW for this type of learning system is known as "Web-based Training" (WBT). Today, advanced server technologies and programming languages provide mechanisms to support collaborative work and discussions of learners in closed communities. Strictly speaking, the term WBT does not include the transfer of files and the use of emails in a learning environment. That is why the term "Internet Based Training" (IBT) has emerged. The latter includes all services of the Internet (e.g., File Transfer Protocol, Newsgroups, Emails) [Han02]. However, there is no clear definition of these terms; and, moreover, most "Web-based" elearning platforms support the transfer of files, emails, etc. Thus, there is no clear distinction between the use of the terms IBT and that of WBT as they are often regarded as synonyms.

Several other terms exist in the field of computer-supported learning and teaching [JOV03], for example, "Computer Based Learning (CBL)", "Computer Assisted Learning (CAL)" and "Computer Assisted Teaching (CAT)" [Gro95], "Computer Aided Instruction (CAI)", "Computer Managed Instruction (CMI)" [PH02], "Computer Based Instruction" [AT01], "Web Based Learning (WBL)" [Leu99], and "Computer Supported Learning (CSL)" [GSW03]. They will not be discussed and classified here. However, it is of high importance to realize that software or computers are used in the teaching and learning processes and that they can also be implemented in form of CBTs or WBTs (resp. IBTs). Merely the perspective of how to describe the support of the computer is different.

Like most of the terms in the field of electronic learning, the term *elearning* itself is not clearly specified either. Some authors refer to elearning as the generic term for the forms of computer supported learning already mentioned above, also including learning tapes, interactive TV etc. For example, [Bac03] presents a definition that includes all of these aspects:

---

[2]From Open Lexicon, see http://www.community4you.de/lexikon/de/c4u/open-eis/Network_Based _Training.html

[3]http://www.w3.org/MarkUp/

"Elearning is a broader concept ..., encompassing a wide set of applications and processes which use all available electronic media to deliver vocational education and training more flexibly. The term elearning is now used in the framework to capture the general intent to support a broad range of electronic media (Internet, intranets, extranets, satellite broadcast, audio/video tape, interactive TV and CD-ROM) to make vocational learning more flexible for clients."

Nonetheless, others use the term elearning still in a broad sense; however, for them, it does not include audio/video tapes, interactive TV, and satellite broadcast and, therefore, focuses on the use of information and communication technologies (ICT). Audio/video tapes, interactive TV, and satellite broadcast are here classified as a part of what is known as "teleteaching" (see, for example, [AK99]). One of these wide definitions is given by [Mer02]:

"Elearning is the process of learning that is supported by information and communication technologies and particularly uses special forms of learning technologies and learning systems."

According to this definition, elearning includes all technical systems that use software and information and communication technology to support the learning process and thus describes elearning as the generic term mentioned above. Although the definition seems to focus on computers using special learning systems, the phrase "information and communication technology" is not defined explicitly. More narrow definitions of the term elearning only include systems that use Internet-based or Web-based technologies. These definitions have a comparable understanding of the "e" to that which is meant in the definitions of ecommerce (electronic commerce, see, for example, [Kle01, Mer02]) and egovernment (electronic-government, see, for instance, [KBS03]). The definition given by [JOV03] focuses on these technologies and is also used as working definition throughout this thesis:

"Elearning is location-independent and time-independent learning that is self-organized and controlled to the greatest possible extent. Learning and gathering knowledge is performed by using the Web or by using Web-based technologies based on adaptable curricula, navigation structures, and learning content to achieve a certain learning target[4]."

---

[4] Translated from the German original.

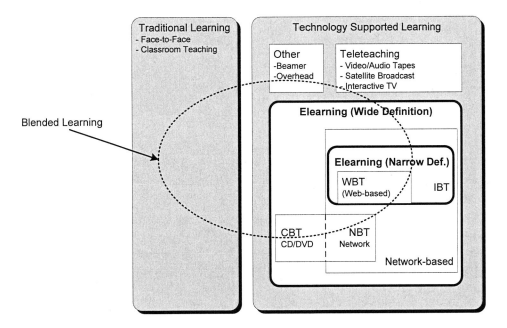

Figure 2.1: Correlation of elearning terms.

Figure 2.1 gives an overview of the correlation of some terms mentioned above. In addition, the term "Blended Learning" describes a concept combining traditional classroom teaching and the use of computers to support the learning process.

In the following, the focus will be on Web-based learning systems. They build the starting point for the implementation of a distributed elearning system that operates over the Web. Web-based learning systems have certain user groups and system components no matter if they are used in primary, secondary, or tertiary education [JOV03, IMS01a]. As shown in Figure 2.2, an elearning system consists of an *Authoring System* to create content, a *Learning Management System* (LMS) to integrate and maintain content as well as to store information about the users that access the system, and a *Run-Time System* that can be accessed by learners to consume content and interact with the LMS and other learners.

Some authors (see, for example, [BR02]) distinguish between *Course Management Systems* and Learning Management Systems. Course Management Systems support the maintenance and publication of learning material for people without a profound technical knowledge. The systems even combine material for new courses and can enrich courses with additional files. In addition, they provide a closed user community, password-

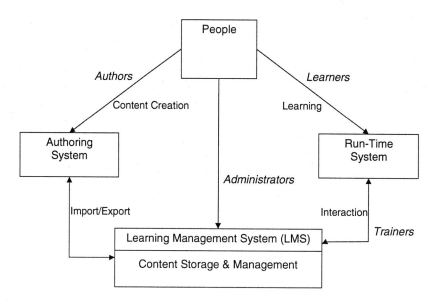

Figure 2.2: Global (logical) organization of an elearning platform [VJO02].

protected access mechanisms, and collaboration tools. Famous representatives for these systems are WebCT[5] and CourseInfo[6] from Blackboard. LMSs provide a broader range of functionalities like tracking and scheduling mechanisms for the learning activities. Sometimes they incorporate financial features and the integration of third-party systems (see [HLV+02, VW04, SVW05] for examples of integrating third-party systems into learning platforms). However, as there is no clear definition of what constitutes a Course Management System and what constitutes a Learning Management System, this thesis uses the more comprehensive term of LMS.

The courses managed by these LMSs can vary for different groups of learners. Particularly, the order of the content as well as the amount of content to be learned about a topic can be changed for individual learners. This can depend, for example, on particular characteristics of the users. These LMSs are sometimes called *adaptive systems* [ACP02]. A second type of system, the *adaptable systems*, changes its look-and-feel according to the different learners. It enables the user to configure parameters of the application. Thus, in adaptable systems, users initiate the actions, whereas, in adaptive systems, the systems themselves initiate changes.

---

[5]http://www.webct.com/
[6]http://courseinfo.com/

According to Figure 2.2, users of an elearning platform can be subdivided into four groups having different roles:

1. **Learners** use presented material to improve their knowledge about certain subjects. Apart from using the presented material, the learning process can be fostered by interactions between learners, and between learners and tutors. In addition, learners can take tests and do exercises to check the success of their learning process.

2. **Authors** are responsible for creating and structuring content to be learned by learners. They are experts on the subjects. Making content available can be a complex task and often needs collaboration between experts, didacts, programmers, and designers in the authoring process [Vos04].

3. **Trainers** coach learners and answer questions concerning content. They also ought to be able to answer technical questions about the learning system used. Consequently, they must have pedagogical experiences and, at the same time, they must be experts on the corresponding subjects [Vos04].

4. **Administrators** maintain the systems. This includes technical work as well as the maintenance of users and content if necessary. They do not have to be qualified in terms of the content that is provided to the learners.

A user has at least one role, but can also have many roles. In particular, the author role and the trainer role are often connected and adopted by one person. It is worth mentioning that the exact labeling of the roles varies, see, for example, [RV03, ACP02, Vos04, Sch02a]. However, the main categories of roles exist in almost all systems.

In the (technically oriented) elearning community, there is a shift from big educational building blocks (for example, in the form of CBTs) to reusable content components [Col02]. The latter are maintained and stored by LMSs, consumed by learners, and created by authors. They are usually organized, exchanged, and handled by using units of *learning objects* (LO). Although there is no clear definition of a LO, several authors [VJ02, IEE02, BL00] see LOs intuitively as units of content that can be consumed in one learning session. The LOs can be accessed dynamically, for example, over the Web [VJ02]. Ideally, LOs can be reused by different LMSs and plugged together to build classes that are intended to serve a particular purpose or goal. Accordingly, LOs need to be *context-free*, which means that they have to carry useful description information on the type and context in which they may be used. Several classes can be plugged together to build course programs. Recalling the sample course from Figure 1.1, the course CIAD consists of at least four classes. Here, a class can be interpreted as a unit that ends up in an exam, for example, the unit "Introduction to Oracle: SQL and PL/SQL". These classes can contain several learning sessions which are represented by one learning object each.

Several authors have given overviews of different definitions and have discussed what constitutes a learning object (see, for instance, [IMC01, Wil00, VJ02, GNR00, MB02]). This discussion will not be taken any further at this point owing to the following reasons:

- In the distributed organization of an elearning platform as it will be constructed in the following chapters, content will not be delivered in form of physical learning objects, but in form of presentation services. This means that content will be called on demand from a remote server by a learner and content will be stored only once[7]. In contrast, in traditionally organized platforms, an author or administrator copies learning objects to the content storage of an LMS. Owing to this physical view, traditional definitions of learning objects and their reuse are often based on the notion of physical files. In the new distributed environment, the reuse of content is achieved by including remote presentation functionalities.

- For a technical construction of presentation services, it does not matter what kind of content is delivered. Therefore, content services can still be units of study, exercise, or practice and represent reusable granules (in form of services).

- As will be shown, presentation services can be combined to build classes and courses. Learners will not recognize the difference between the traditional and the new form of content presentation.

To enable a usage of content in different LMSs, several standardization efforts try to foster the idea of content reuse. Some of the most important approaches will be described in the following subsection because the construction of the distributed elearning environment explained in Chapters 4 and 5 will use some of these standards as far as possible. A couple of these efforts have a broader view on content, others have a closer one. Although the terminology used by the institutions for similar concepts varies, the idea of reusability and the use of content in different LMSs is always the main objective. Learning objects are sometimes called "resource", "SCO", or "content object", but the actual approaches are always comparable.

---

[7]Owing to technical reasons, it may be useful to have redundant copies of presentation services for the same content. This may be the case, for example, to achieve a load-balancing or owing to backup and reliability reasons.

2.2   Elearning Standardization

Using standards is important for an economic application of elearning. Although the development and distribution of standards lead to increasing costs in the beginning, the main advantage of its use is a higher compatibility of products, which, on the other hand, results in lower costs once the standard is accepted widely by developers and users. The benefits of a standard increase with the number of its users (Network Effect Theory [WWW00]). Standards are used in several industrial sectors and can be seen as a unification and formalization of products, services, or processes in form of rules, guidelines, and specifications and simplify matters for developers and users. Standards for information systems define rules for processing, storing, and exchanging information to simplify interactions between systems [Mer02].

Learning software development was often fostered by individual ideas and initiatives in former times [CET04]. It has been taken progress without the developers having the rapid changes in technology in mind. Today, even some of the older high quality learning materials cannot be read on modern systems anymore owing to changes of operating systems, hardware, etc. In addition, no consistent formats existed to describe the content. This was counterproductive to the reusing of content. Other data stored in learning systems like students records, course descriptions, and administrative data could not be exchanged easily either.

Since the beginning of 1997, interoperability standards which address most of these areas have been developed. In addition to technical standards like graphics interchange formats, learning content also needs formats for the processes which handle the packaging, sequencing, and other management so that the content can be transferred from one learning system to another. Furthermore, standard ways of describing learning content have been developed so that they can easily be searched for and located [Paw05, CET04]. Several organizations work on standards for elearning following different main focuses. All of the organizations, which will be mentioned in the following, are committed to collaboration to establish learning technology interoperability standards.

Several institutions have become involved in the development of learning-technology standards. Some of their activities will be described in the following. Apart from those activities described here, there are a couple of other similar but partially different standards or definitions that are not as widely adopted in the field of elearning as the ones discussed here, for example, in the area of metadata or the definition of course structures. Overviews for many standards in the field of elearning are presented, for example, by

the Learning Technology Standards Observatory[8] (LTSO) and AICTEC[9]. The leading
organizations speeding up the developments are IEEE, IMS, the Dublin Core Metadata
Initiative, and the European CEN/ISSS and Prometeus initiative as well as the American
Aircraft Industry (AICC), and the Department of Defense's Advanced Distributed Learning program (ADL). The most valuable parts of the AICC models have been taken by
ADL in their own development. Consequently, AICC activities will not be explained here
as separate development approaches. Several aspects covered by the work of these initiatives are related to each other. Although the work of each initiative has made substantial
progresses, the entire work was initially not connected to each other. ADL has changed
this situation and has worked with many of these organizations to build a common reference model for the foundation of Web-based learning called SCORM (Sharable Content
Object Reference Model). The structure of the working group currently makes SCORM
the most promising standardization activity [Paw01, JOV03, Jon02b]. SCORM provides
foundations that will be used throughout the development of the distributed elearning
platform in this thesis. In fact, SCORM bundles some of the most accepted approaches
to a reference model. Accordingly, activities having a strong influence on SCORM will be
explained in detail in the following. Some general additional activities having an influence
on the development of the distributed elearning environment will also be sketched below,
in particular, the IEEE LTSA standardization. Very specialized activities from CEN/ISSS
(e.g., the Simple Querying Interface) and IMS (e.g., the IMS Enterprise Web Services and
IMS General Web Service specifications) related to very specific functionalities of the
distributed elearning environment will be explained in the respective chapters.

Several corresponding institutions also have an impact on the development of standards
in the field of learning technology because they provide more general standards. The
most important ones are OASIS (Organization for the Advancement of Structured Information Standards)[10] and the World Wide Web Consortium (W3C), which develops
interoperable technologies to make the Web realize its full potential[11]. They are involved
in the standardization processes for XML (eXtensible Markup Language [BPS+04]), Web-
service-related standards, and several additional ones.

---

[8]http://www.cen-ltso.net/

[9]http://www.standards.edna.edu.au/

[10]http://www.oasis-open.org/

[11]Self description on http://www.w3c.org

2.2.1   Dublin Core Initiative

The Dublin Core Metadata Initiative[12] (DCMI) is an open forum engaged in the specification of interoperable online metadata standards. DCMI defines a domain-independent metadata model with 15 core elements. It tries to give an easy description of resources - not a comprehensive one [IM02]. The Dublin Core standard covers attributes describing the content of a resource (title, subject, description), intellectual properties of the resource (creator, publisher, contributor, rights), and information related to the document (date, type, format, identifier, source, language, relation, coverage).

2.2.2   IEEE LTSC Standards

The IEEE [13] Learning Technology Standards Committee (LTSC) is one of the main competitors in the development of learning standards. This committee tries to create technical standards, recommendations, and guidelines for tools, technologies, and methods in the area of elearning [AP02] to support the development, maintenance, and interoperability of learning systems. Their activities are based on the "Learning Technology Systems Architecture" (LTSA), which is extended by the standards "Learning Object Metadata" (LOM), "Public and Private Information" (PAPI), "Standard Computer Managed Instruction" (CMI), and others. Owing to their high relevance for this thesis, LTSA and LOM will be described in the following.

Learning Technology Systems Architecture (LTSA)
LTSA is an architecture for IT-based learning systems. It is regarded as a framework to design a range of systems over the years, not as a blue print for designing a single system. Neither does it address implementation and platform details (concerning programming languages, authoring tools, operating systems) to build the system components nor the management components (user administration, access control, etc.) necessary to manage a learning system. The LTSA specification is designed in a pedagogical-neutral, content-neutral, cultural-neutral, and platform-neutral way; and neither is it prescriptive nor exclusive [IEE03].

Figure 2.3 shows the five layers of the specification. Merely Layer 3 has a normative character; the other four layers are informative. Thus, the core of a learning system is described in Layer 3. In the following, a short overview of all layers will be presented [IEE03]:

---

[12]http://www.dublincore.org/
[13]IEEE is a short form for: Institute of Electrical and Electronics Engineers, Inc.

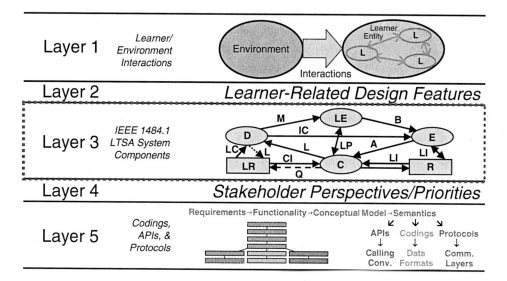

Figure 2.3: The LTSA Abstraction-Implementation Layers. Only Layer 3 (System Components) is normative in this standard [IEE03].

- **Layer 1 (Learner and Environment Interactions)** builds the top layer of LTSA and is a very general architectural refinement layer called "Learner-Environment Interactions". It defines the relationship between the learner and the system. The diagram illustrates how a learner acquires additional knowledge by interacting with the (learning) environment and other learners.

- **Layer 2** covers **Learner-Related Design Features**. The design of the lower layers of the architecture is affected by the learners' needs and particularly by nature of the human learning process. The details of the learners' effects on the system design are not explained in the standard.

- **Layer 3 (System Components)** describes the component-based architecture and builds the core of the specification. It defines four processes, two stores, and thirteen information flows. This layer will also build the conceptual foundation for the decomposition of the centralized elearning platform into several stand-alone applications (see Chapter 4.2).

- **Layer 4 (Implementation Perspective and Priorities)** describes examples of LTSA system implementations from a variety of perspectives.

- **Layer 5 (Operational Components and Interoperability - Codings, APIs, Protocols)** gives an overview of how technical standards can be related to LTSA and the development process. The specification of actual coding, API, protocol, etc., standards is not part of the LTSA specification.

As the specification gives a framework how to implement learning systems and as, in particular, Layer 3 describes core functionalities that must be included into a learning system, Chapter 4.2 will give more details about this layer and its impact on the development of a distributed elearning system. It builds the foundation for the identification and definition of possible remote components.

Learning Object Metadata (LOM)

The LOM metadata specification is to describe digital and non-digital resources that can be used in computer-supported learning. These resources, which can roughly be seen as the counterparts of learning objects, can be courses, software tools, single learning units, and multimedia objects as well as human teachers. In LOM, a metadata instance for a LO describes relevant characteristics of the LO to which it applies. Such characteristics may be grouped into general, life cycle, meta-metadata, educational, technical, educational, rights, relation, annotation, and classification categories [IEE02]. Apart from this conceptual data schema, the standard defines bindings of this schema in ISO/IEC11404[14], XML[15], and RDF[16] respectively.

A description of a resource according to LOM is uniquely to identify the resource [AP02]. The LOM specification defines basic entities and attributes, which can be extended if necessary [Paw01]. [Paw01] also points out that the LOM specification can be interpreted as the fundamental basis of most other activities. Other metadata specifications for learning objects (IMS, ARIADNE, DCMI) have had an influence on the development of LOM and are thus in parts equal or comparable to LOM. For example, LOM uses attributes from DCMI.

LOM is already widely accepted for the implementation of learning systems and can be seen as de facto standard for the implementation of elearning platforms [AFL+01]. Table 2.1 offers an overview of the categories covered by LOM. It also gives a short description and some sample attributes.

---

[14]http://standards.mackido.com/ie1/iec-standards24_view_79.html
[15]http://www.w3.org/XML/
[16]http://www.w3.org/RDF/

Table 2.1: LOM overview.

Learning Object Metadata Overview		
Typ	**Description**	**Sample Attributes**
General	Groups the general information that describes the LO as a whole.	Identifier, Catalog, Title, Language, Keywords
Life Cycle	Describes the history and current state of the LO and these entities that have affected this LO during its evolution.	Status, Author, Role
Meta-Metadata	Describes the metadata record itself (rather than the LO).	Catalog, Author
Technical	Describes the technical requirements and characteristics of the LO.	Format, Size, Location, Requirements
Educational	Describes the key educational or pedagogic characteristics of the LO.	Learning Resource Type, Interactivity Level, Intended End User Role
Rights	Describes the intellectual property rights and conditions of use for the LO.	Cost, Copyright
Relation	Defines the relationship between the LO and other LOs if any.	Kind of relationship, Resource, Identifier
Annotation	Provides comments on the educational use of the LO, and information on when and by whom the comments were created.	Entity, Date
Classification	Describes where the LO falls within a particular classification system.	Purpose, Taxon Path

2.2.3   IMS Global Learning Consortium Specifications

The IMS Global Learning Consortium[17] is a worldwide non-profit organization with more than 50 members and affiliates, which come from every sector of the global elearning com-

---

[17]IMS originally was a short form for "Instructional Management Systems", but over time this term was too imprecise. They changed their official name to the short form. Details about the organization can be found at http://www.imsglobal.org/.

munity. It develops and launches open technical specifications for interoperable learning technologies. Several IMS specifications have become worldwide de facto standards in the field of elearning. IMS specifications and related publications are made available to the public at no charge, and no fee has to be paid to implement the specifications. The IMS provides an own metadata standard to describe learning resources. As mentioned above, it had a decisive influence on the development of LOM. Today, there are only minor differences between the IMS Learning Resource Meta-data Specification and LOM as the new version of the IMS specification is now based on LOM. Thus, this thesis does not describe the IMS Learning Resource Meta-data Specification. Details can be found in [IMS04a]. The most important activities of the IMS will be sketched in the following. Two additional activities related to Web services will be presented in Chapter 4.

IMS Content Packaging

Content for elearning can be composed of miscellaneous items such as text, pictures, videos, animations, diagrams, XML and HTML files, etc. Content ought to be designed in such a way that it can be exchanged between different learning management systems in order to enable an efficient reuse. The IMS *Content Packaging Information Model* specifies a technique for storing and exchanging content using XML and a suitable bundling of files. The objective of the IMS Content Packaging Information Model is to define a standardized set of structures that can be used to exchange content. These structures provide the basis for standardized data bindings that enable software developers and implementors to create instructional materials that interoperate across authoring tools, LMSs, and runtime environments that have been developed independently by various software developers [IMS01b, IMS01a]. There are just three steps to be taken when processing given content so that it can easily be exchanged: first, a so-called *Manifest* document is created, which is an XML document; this document is validated in the second step; finally, this XML document is bundled with the physical files, which contain the actual content, to form a *package*.

An IMS Package represents a unit of (re-)usable content and can be combined with other packages. It consists of two major elements: the Manifest file describing the content organization, metadata and resources in a package, and the physical files being described by the Manifest file. A package in this sense is a logical directory which contains the specially named XML file (the Manifest, always called "`imsmanifest.xml`") together with any XML control document it references, and subdirectories containing the physical files. This logical directory can be incorporated into a single file (using standard archive formats like zip, jar, cab) for an easier exchange and storage and is henceforth called "Package Interchange File" (PIF). PIFs can be sent via the Internet or be exchanged via

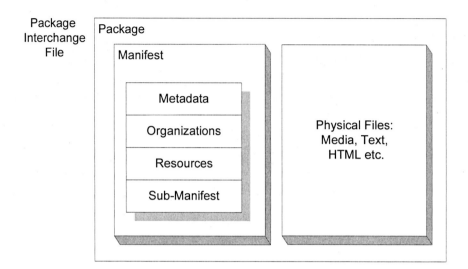

Figure 2.4: Logical structure of a "Package Interchange File".

CD-ROM. Figure 2.4 shows the logical structure of a PIF.

The Manifest can include an identifier for labeling purpose and a version which refers to the IMS Content Packaging version number. The Manifest is subdivided into four parts which contain a *metadata* section, an *organizations* section, and a *resources* section as well as an optionally additional *submanifest*:

- The metadata of the learning content in the **metadata section** is embedded into a metadata tag and follows the specifications of the IMS Meta-Data Information Model [IMS01c]. The metadata describes the Manifest (and thus the content) as a whole.

- The **organization segment** contains information describing the structure of the content in the package, for instance, the table of contents or a custom structure.

- The **resources** refer to the actual content. This can be a physical file in the package or even a reference to another Manifest file. Each resource can be additionally described by metadata following the specification of the IMS Meta-Data Information Model [IMS01c].

- Any **nested submanifest** describes the content at the level to which it is scoped, such as a course, instructional object, or other.

A PIF of the LO on the "Introduction to Orcale9i: SQL" used within the CIAD course can include various HTML files to explain the different SQL statements in a descriptive way. It can also include some Flash animations to demonstrate the different kinds of join operations (left, right, outer, and inner joins). Incorporating these files and the Manifest document into a ZIP file leads to a PIF for SQL.

IMS Simple Sequencing Specification

The IMS Simple Sequencing Specification [IMS03a, IMS03b, IMS03c] is to describe the intended behavior of an authored learning experience. Based on the representation used by the simple sequencing, any elearning system can sequence discrete learning activities in a consistent way. The specification defines the required behaviors and functionalities that systems must implement in order to be compatible with the specification. It defines an XML binding and is related to the IMS Content Packaging, but also to other IMS specifications.

The specification extends the IMS Content Packaging to embed additional order information. To achieve this, it defines a unique namespace to arrange the items. IMS Simple Sequencing elements should be included in the *organization* element of the IMS Content Packaging. A *sequencing* element in the Manifest document indicates that a sequencing process will be required to deliver the content in a consistent manner. The IMS Simple Sequencing is based upon the concept of a learning activity that describes a pedagogical-neutral unit of instruction, knowledge assessment etc. and is delivered only once at a time to the learner. Activities are organized in a hierarchical structure by defining sub-activities. Content resources (for example, learning objects or simple HTML files) can only be associated with leaf nodes. Thus, the entire numbers of managed activities build an activity tree that can be used by an LMS to determine which activity must be delivered to the learner. The IMS Simple Sequencing Specification defines a default traversal of the activity tree as pre-order traversal. It can be changed through the association of sequencing rules by the author of the content. The sequencing rules are evaluated at runtime. They can be conditionally based on the tracking status of a learner who can trigger the order of activities by a navigation through the content. Rules are always defined for clusters of activities (nodes and their immediate children). The scope of a rule never extends beyond its cluster. The two basic control modes that define the order of the activity in the cluster are *choice* and *flow*. One of these parameters has to be activated in order to tell the LMS whether a learner is allowed to choose between the sub-activities or be guided. If both are activated at the same time, the user can choose any activity or can also be guided. Detailed information about the rules and conditions are given in [IMS03a].

If IMS Simple Sequencing is used to define the CIAD course, a choice element is needed to define that the learner can choose between "Introduction to Oracle: SQL and PL/SQL" and "Introduction to Oracle9i: SQL". Within these classes, several rules and further definitions can be made in order to guide the learners.

IMS Learner Information Packaging Specification
The IMS Learner Information Packaging Specification (IMS LIP) specification defines how learner data can be packaged and exchanged between compatible LMSs. It is the system which is responsible for enabling the learner to define what part of the learner information can be shared with other systems. The core structures of the IMS LIP are: accessibilities, activities, affiliations, competencies, goals, identifications, interests, qualifications, certifications and licenses, relationship, security keys, and transcripts [IMS01d].

2.2.4   ADL SCORM

The Advanced Distributed Learning (ADL) Initiative[18], sponsored by the Office of the Secretary of Defense (OSD), is a collaboration between government, industry, and academia. The effort is to establish a new, distributed learning environment model to foster the interoperability of learning tools and course content on a global scale. ADL's objective is to give access to the highest quality education and training, tailored to individual needs, delivered cost-effectively anywhere and anytime.

As already shown before, several organizations have been working on standards and guidelines in the field of elearning technologies. ADL has worked with many of these organizations to build a common reference model for the foundation of Web-based learning called SCORM (Sharable Content Object Reference Model). It describes a "Content Aggregation Model", a "Run-Time Environment", and a "Sequencing and Navigation", and provides an overview document that covers the broad picture of SCORM (see Figure 2.5). Several existing standards have had an influence or have been taken completely or partly over in SCORM. This applies in particular for the following models:

- Content Aggregation Model includes:

    Metadata (from IEEE LOM 1484.12)

    Content Structure (derived from AICC)

    Content Packaging (from IMS)

    Sequencing Information (from IMS)

---

[18]http://www.adlnet.org/

- Run-Time Environment includes:

    IEEE API 1484.11.2

    IEEE Data Model 1484.11.1

- Sequencing and Navigation includes:

    Sequencing Information and Behavior (from IMS)

ADL's "-ilities" build the conceptual starting points and define high-level requirements for all SCORM-based elearning environments. They are the foundation for all changes and additions [ADL04a]:

- **Accessibility:** the ability to locate and access instructional components from one remote location and deliver the latter to many other locations.

- **Adaptability:** the ability to tailor instruction to individual and organizational needs.

- **Affordability:** the ability to increase efficiency and productivity by reducing time and costs involved in delivering instruction.

- **Durability:** the ability to withstand technology evolution and changes without costly redesign, reconfiguration, or recording.

- **Interoperability:** the ability to take instructional components developed in one location with one set of tools or platform and to use them in another location with a different platform or set of tools.

- **Reusability:** the flexibility to incorporate instructional components in multiple applications and contexts.

In addition to these requirements, ADL is based on the assumption that the Web provides the best opportunity to maximize both access to and the reuse of learning content. The overall objective of SCORM is to make content objects reusable and interoperable across multiple LMSs [ADL04c].

In SCORM, learning content is composed of small, reusable content objects that can be aggregated to form units of instruction like courses, modules, chapters, etc. The content objects do not have a context and are designed to be reused in multiple contexts. The aggregation of the content objects provides the context and supports the learning experience. In addition, content objects do not carry information about other content

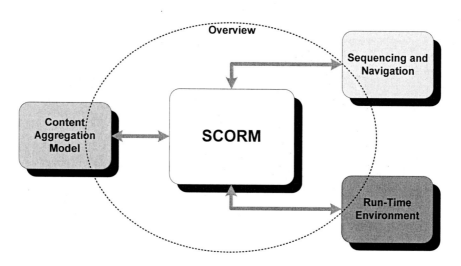

Figure 2.5: SCORM organization according to [ADL04a].

objects. Instead, sequencing is defined by rules in the aggregation to retain a maximum of flexibility. These rules have to be interpreted by LMSs.

As pictured in Figure 2.5, SCORM is a bundle of technical definitions comprising existing standards and specifications. Nearly all of them have been taken from other organizations [ADL04a]. Enhancements of the existing SCORM reference model are achieved either by adding new definitions in future or changing existing ones. Each part is intended to stay on its own. However, there are some overlapping features. The subparts are presently grouped under the topics "Content Aggregation Model (CAM)" [ADL04b], "Run-Time Environment (RTE)" [ADL04c], and "Sequencing and Navigation (SN)" [ADL04d]. In addition, the overview document [ADL04a] describes a high-level view of SCORM. Except for the overview document, a short explanation and its relation to existing standards and specifications for each subpart are presented in the following.

SCORM CAM [ADL04b] defines the components a learning unit can consist of (SCORM Content Model) and how to package (SCORM Content Packages) and describe these components (SCORM Meta-data) to enable a discovery and exchange mechanism. In addition, sequencing information for components is part of SCORM CAM, but only as an overlapping part of SCORM SN. Thus, sequencing information will be described in detail in SCORM SN. The SCORM Content Model defines an Asset as the most basic form of a learning resource. An Asset is an electronic building block and can be a text, image (e.g., JPG), sound (e.g., MP3, WAV), or any piece of data that can be rendered by

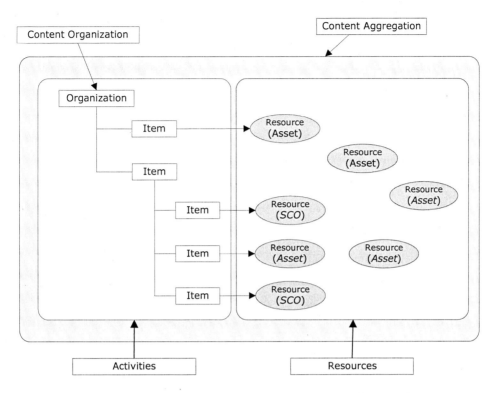

Figure 2.6: Content organization of SCORM CAM [ADL04b].

a Web client (e.g., HTML, FLASH). Assets can be combined to build new Assets. One or more Assets can also build a SCO (Sharable Content Object) that represents a single launchable learning resource using SCORM RTE to communicate with an LMS. A SCO has the responsibility to find the API of an LMS in order to communicate with this LMS, and it must be able to invoke at least the *initialize* and *terminate* methods (all other methods are optional and depend upon the nature of the content [ADL04c]). SCOs are the smallest units which can interact with an LMS to track learners' activities, whereas Assets are neither able nor allowed to interact with an LMS. To enable a maximum of flexibility and reusability, a SCO ought to be independent of its learning context. This is why SCOs are usually small units of learning instructions; however, SCORM does not determine the size of a SCO. The overall organization of the content for a certain learning experience can be interpreted as a map of activities (see Figure 2.6). Activities can be nested to present a hierarchical order, and leaf activities have an associated resource (SCO or Asset) to perform the activity. The overall construct can be seen as the SCORM

Content Aggregation that composes different units of instruction into a certain bigger
learning unit.

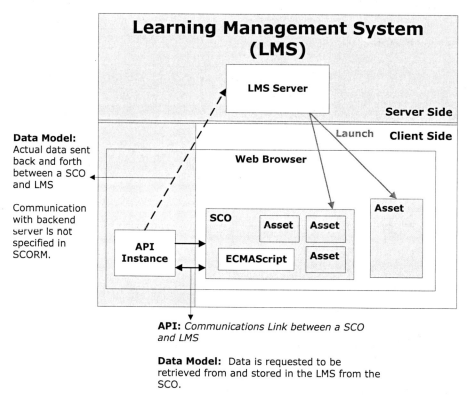

Figure 2.7: SCORM conceptual Run-Time Environment (RTE) [ADL04c].

Each entity in the content organization can be described by metadata to provide a description of the content. SCORM distinguishes between "Content Aggregation Meta-
Data", "Content Organization Meta-Data", "Activity Meta-Data", "SCO Meta-Data",
and "Asset Meta-Data". SCORM CAM defines the SCORM Content Packaging on the
fundamentals of IMS Content Packaging and, additionally, determines a set of specific
requirements and guidance. Accordingly, metadata to describe content appears inside the
Manifest document for each level of granularity. Although SCORM strongly recommends
the use of the LOM metadata standard for describing the SCORM Content Model components, other metadata specifications can also be used to do so. However, as the SCORM
specification directly references the LOM standard as well as the XML binding of LOM,
and, as LOM is widely accepted, the approach taken in this thesis will be based on LOM.

SCORM RTE [ADL04c] defines the requirements for launching content objects (i.e., any piece of content that can be launched for a learner), establishing communication between LMSs and SCOs, and managing the tracking information that can be communicated between SCOs and LMSs. The three main aspects of SCORM RTE, namely the *Launch Activity*, the *Application Programming Interface (API)*, and the *Data Model*, are shown in Figure 2.7.

LMSs can use the *Launch* process to start Web-based content in a common way. This content can be an Asset or a SCO and will be displayed on the learner's Web browser. Depending on the type of content object, the LMS has to meet certain requirements in the Launch process. The *API* provides a set of predefined functions to enable the communication between the LMS and the SCOs. Detailed information about the functions that are agreed upon by both LMS manufacturers and content authoring tool manufacturers can be found in [ADL04c]. The API Instance is a piece of executable software that communicates with the SCO by using ECMAScript (more commonly known as JavaScript). All communication (except for the Launch process) is initiated by the SCO and handled by this API instance. This means that content authors do not have to worry about communicating with the server; SCOs only have to be able to contact the API Instance and make the appropriate JavaScript calls. The way how the API Instance provided by an LMS communicates with the server-side component is not defined in SCORM and is up to the LMS implementation. It is often realized in form of Java Applets embedded into a frame of the LMS window [BNT03]; sometimes also FLASH or ActiveX-Controls are used [Kai01]. The API is pictured in Figure 2.8.

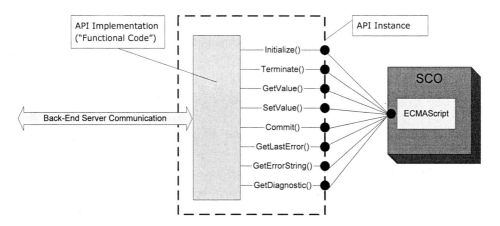

Figure 2.8: Conceptual model of the SCORM API according to [ADL04c].

The SCORM Run-Time Environment Data Model as defined by SCORM RTE establishes a way to ensure that information about SCOs can be tracked by different LMS environments. To achieve this, SCOs can use the *SetValue* function of the API Instance to request a transfer of data to the LMS. If different SCOs would use a proprietary way to represent information about the learning process, an LMS may not be able to receive, store, or process this data. The Data Model is based on the *1484.11.1 Draft Standard for Learning Technology - Data Model for Content Object Communication* [IEE04] standard published by the *IEEE LTSC Computer Managed Instruction (CMI)*. This standard defines a set of data model elements that can be used to send information from a content object (i.e., a SCO in SCORM) to an LMS. It includes information about the learner, interactions the learner had with the SCO, objective information, success status and completion status (see also Chapter 5.2.2). For example, this set of information can be used by an LMS for tracking and to make sequencing decisions. Older versions of the SCORM Run-Time Environment Data Model were based on the AICC CMI001 Guideline for Interoperability [AIC01] that was later on submitted by AICC to the IEEE for standardization. SCORM version 2004 introduces changes to the data model as defined by the *IEEE 1484.11.1 Draft Standard for Learning Technology Data Model for Content Object Communication*. However, the IEEE draft standard purely defines data model elements and their data types. Accordingly, SCORM needs to define additional requirements pertaining to the use, behavior, and relationship with the API Instance like a particular binding (dot-notation), implementation guidance, and behavioral requirements [ADL04c].

The foundation of SCORM SN [ADL04d] is the IMS Simple Sequencing Specification, which defines a method for representing the intended behavior of the sequencing and navigation in learning material. By interpreting these rules, LMSs are able to present content in a consistent way. SCORM SN defines how the IMS Simple Sequencing Specification is used and is extended in a SCORM conform platform. It defines the required behaviors and functionality that the LMSs have to implement in order to handle sequencing information in the intended way at runtime. As the IMS specification has been developed to be a part of SCORM, details are omitted here [IMS03c]. The SCORM specification is largely similar to the one explained in the parts of IMS Simple Sequencing earlier in this chapter.

In addition, SCORM SN explains how learner and system initiated navigation events can be triggered and processed, resulting in the identification of associated content for delivery. The content is then delivered by the SCORM Run-Time Environment. To trigger navigation events, a user interface device must exist, but the structure of this interface or device is outside the scope of SCORM. This device can be provided by an LMS or by content objects. The triggered events are translated by an LMS into its corresponding navigation request. An LMS processes the request, and can then choose the next learning activity for delivery. SCORM SN defines a runtime data model that SCOs can use to send navigation requests to an LMS.

2.3   Evaluation of Elearning Standards and Specifications

The huge number of standards makes the selection of a particular elearning standard a difficult task. This has been sketched only for the use of metadata, but is also the case for other standards. In the following, a brief evaluation of the standards and specifications mentioned earlier will be presented; further drawbacks will also be explained in Chapter 2.5. The SCORM reference model is already widely accepted in the elearning industry and provides a good model to explain which combination of standards works well. The possibility to share and reuse elearning content is the biggest advantage of SCORM. The standardized definition of both interfaces and data builds another big advantage. The content can store data on any LMS that is compliant to this standard. It supports also an elegant way to control the learning progress of the users. This tracking data can be used to give feedback to learners and to provide information to authors. This information can be used to improve the content.

The definition of a unique interface enables SCOs and LMSs to communicate. However, a SCO can send information merely to the LMS. The only mechanism for a SCO to check if the data has been stored is to request the same data again. In the worst case, the LMS receives the data and deletes the latter (although both parties are SCORM compliant) [BSW02]. SCOs use a very complex client code for communication. This code is often implemented by ECMAScript. It is not impossible for advanced learners to inspect the code to manipulate the tracking data.

The creation of SCOs should always consider a reusability of the content. Although SCOs are not allowed to call other SCOs directly (they always have to contact an LMS for this purpose), it is difficult to design content in an independent way since it is normally embedded into a bigger course. Above all, SCOs are not allowed to use hyperlinks to Web resources; this restricts the flexibility of the author [BSW02]. As it is common practice to use Web pages to present content, it is questionable if SCOs from different manufacturers can be integrated to build a uniform learning unit.

IMS PIFs can contain various file types. It is up to the LMS to support these files in an adequate way. In the worst case, files cannot be executed or can even contain viruses.

The Manifest documents describing the PIF can contain metadata at each level of content aggregation. As there are no recommendations how to annotate content, this can be a challenging task. Although SCORM suggests using LOM, Manifest documents can also deal with other metadata standards. DCMI provides a very simple approach, but it remains questionable if it is powerful enough for the elearning domain. On the other hand, LOM may be too complex to offer learners the possibility to search for content (see Chapter 5.1). The use of IMS Simple Sequencing within a Manifest document is appropriate and offers a mechanism to describe the content structure.

IEEE LTSA is a very general standard that provides a very helpful orientation for the development of elearning platforms. The biggest objection concerning this standard is the labeling of concepts.

The standards described in the previous chapters cover merely technical aspects. Pedagogical aspects are mostly disregarded. To cover the latter, additional standards have been defined, like IMS Learning Design[19] (formerly known as EML - Educational Modelling Language). As this thesis focuses on technical aspects, pedagogical aspects will not be explained here. Details about the latter can be found, for example, in [KT05, Mar04].

2.4   State-of-the-Art in Elearning Systems

The previous chapters have described important efforts in the area of elearning standardization. The work in this field has its main focus on the reuse (including metadata and sequencing) of content as well as on data that appears during the operation of an elearning system (e.g., tracking data and learner data). In addition, high-level architectures for the construction of elearning systems and exchange mechanisms are specified (e.g., IMS LIP; see also IMS Enterprise Web Services in Chapter 4). As most standards provide guidelines at a high level, no elearning standard constitutes how to implement a concrete elearning system. In consequence, three kinds of architectures to build elearning systems are commonly used today, which will be explained in the following Chapter 2.4.1. No matter what kind of architecture is used to implement an elearning platform, typical systems can be classified according to the kind of license used to distribute the software in commercial and non-commercial platforms. Non-commercial systems include in particular open source platforms and special university platforms. Commercial systems are offered for a certain price. A customer is afterwards allowed to use the software according to the license bought, but he or she is not allowed to change the software or copy it. Normally, the source code of these systems is not distributed, but for systems implemented

---

[19]http://www.imsglobal.org/learningdesign/index.html

in certain programming languages (for example, PHP[20]) even the code is available to customers. Open source systems, on the other hand, are characterized by a free copying and distribution at no charge. In addition, the source code is available and developers are allowed to change the code or add new features. If new features are published, they have to use the same license as the original one. In the following, some sample platforms will be sketched for both system types. Although universities can use commercial and open source systems, there are several special university platforms that do not fit into this classification. This may be the case, for example, because they are implemented in order to fulfill very specific goals and there is only a very small market for these platforms, or because they are still research systems. Examples for these platforms will be sketched in Chapter 2.4.4.

2.4.1 Typical Architectures

Elearning systems are special forms of information systems. Information systems are tools to collect and communicate information to fulfill the needs of their users, the processes in enterprises, and defined goals in enterprises [Vos00]. Information systems foster the activities in enterprises by providing information on demand. At the conceptual level the design of information systems is characterized by three layers. These layers may only exist as design abstractions, but are often identifiable when implementing information systems [ACK+04, Sta03, TS03, DLW+03]:

- **Presentation layer:** presents information to external entities. Many definitions of this layer only include the graphical user interface (see, for example, [TS03]). The characterization in [ACK+04] is taken over here, i.e., the layer also includes interfaces that process data to a given syntactical representation, thus adding layout information like in HTML. The presentation layer is not to be mixed up with the client of an information system as the client may be an external program. For example, in plain HTML, the client is a Web browser, but the presentation layer is implemented by a Web server and modules in charge of creating HTML. Sometimes client and presentation layer are one program. This is the case when a Java Applet is executed.

---

[20]PHP is a short form for "Hypertext Preprocessor". It is a general-purpose language especially suited for the development of Web applications. Details can be found at http://www.php.net

- **Application logic layer:** information systems process data rather than present them. The operations requested by clients through the presentation layer and implemented by the information systems are called application logic. They build the core business functionality provided by this system.

- **Data layer:** includes all elements that are in charge of dealing with data sources of information systems. In most cases this data resides in a database, but even a storage in a file system or in information repositories is possible. [ACK+04] calls this layer the "resource management layer" to include even external systems providing data. Again, these external systems can be information systems built of presentation, application, and data layer, and thus enabling a recursive construction of information systems.

A lot of elearning programs are implemented in the form of stand-alone applications. The three conceptual layers are implemented in a single software that often does not clearly distinguish between these layers. A second very typical architecture for current elearning systems uses the client/server model because these systems are Web-based and provide WBTs. In a general form a server is a process that provides a special functionality. This functionality can be requested by a client and the server acts and responds to this request appropriately [DLW+03, TS03, SH02]. The concept of the client/server model is not only used in Web-based systems but is also implemented in traditional distributed information systems (see Chapter 3). Which part of the layers is provided by a server and which part is implemented by a client depends on the design of a system. Owing to the layers described above, client/server (elearning) systems can be implemented in different ways as presented in Figure 2.9.

To offer an easier description, it is assumed that the client uses a Web browser to present the information to a user; and, thus, only Web-based elearning system in different implementation alternatives are presented here. Figure 2.9 (a) shows a system that uses plain HTML to present its information and user interface to a learner. More clearly, it neither uses plug-ins, client-side scripting (JavaScript, VBScript), nor Java Applets. A good example for this kind of system is the eXtreme eLearning eXperience platform (xLx, see [HLV+02, VHL01, VW04, SVW05] and Chapter 2.4.4). If some parts of the application logic are processed by the client, the architecture is implemented in such a way as shown in (b). This is, for instance, the case when a client is able to check certain input forms for correct data before sending this data to the server. This can be implemented by client-side scripting. The xLx platform is also able to use this application logic on the client side if a user enables the browser to execute these scripts. A system that uses Java Applets to present information or learning material can be assigned to case (c). The pre-

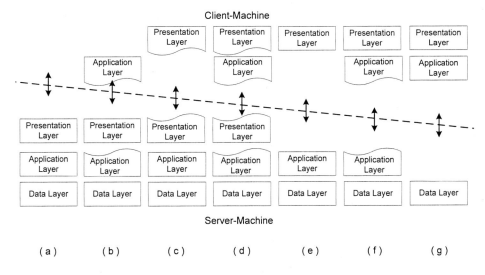

Figure 2.9: Possible implementations of client/server (elearning) systems.

sentation logic is now distributed among the client and the server because Java Applets are embedded in HTML pages. This means that the server still produces HTML with layout information, for example, where to put the Java Applet and additional pictures etc. Nonetheless, the client has to download the Applet and execute it on the client machine. If these Applets (see [Han04] for a description of educational Applets) include parts of the application logic like the execution of simulations, they belong to (d).

Figure 2.9 (e) shows an information system that implements the entire presentation logic on the client, whereas the application logic as well as the data reside on the server. As Web services communicate via data-driven XML messages (typically without any layout information, see Chapter 3.6), this is the traditional Web-service [CD02] case. If the Web-service response has to be published to a user or has to be invoked by a user, the client has to provide the presentation logic. In contrast to case (e), which describes the totally distributed environment, where the whole functionality is implemented as a Web service, case (f) describes a system that has additional application logic on the client side. For example, this can be an elearning system based on Web services that implements the user authentication on the client side. The cases (e) and (f) also fit to other kinds of distributed architectures (see Chapter 3) and build the underlying architectural concepts for a distributed elearning environment. The last case (g) describes an elearning system that implements the whole elearning application logic on the client machine, but receives its data (e.g., the learning content) from a server. It is also possible to have an additional data layer on the client side. In this case, the client is also able to work offline and is only connected to a data server to receive new content or updates.

Apart from centralized stand-alone and client/server architectures, Peer-to-Peer (P2P) architectures [Sch02b] are based on a decentralized concept. There is no central server that provides content or elearning functionalities. This concept is used if a central server is not possible or the participating partners do not want to use a central server, for instance, if institutions do not want to store content on external servers [Pan03]. In the elearning field, Edutella [NWQ+02, NWS+02] implements a platform to share elearning content. The concept is comparable to those of classical file exchange systems like Napster[21], EDonkey[22], or Kazaa[23], but implements efficient mechanisms in particular for elearning content. To achieve this, additional semantic content descriptions are modeled in RDF [BN04]. P2P file sharing in elearning can even be important for small companies in order to train employees worldwide. These companies might not want to maintain a server, but content can be exchanged in a P2P network [Hof02]. On the other hand, one disadvantage that arises in P2P networks is the availability of peers because they are not connected to the network all along; in addition, controlling the quality of issues is very difficult because there is no central instance to organize the content shared between the parties. Of course, the typical problems of copyright and bottle necks (if one peer is the connection to subnets) also emerge in educational P2P networks.

2.4.2 Commercial Systems

Commercial systems come in different architectural forms. Most common are stand-alone systems and client/server platforms. Some of them are only able to handle very specialized content, others are implemented in an open form supporting learning objects and can therefore be used for every type of content. There are quite a lot of stand-alone systems on the market, but only one stand-alone system will be sketched below. An overview of commercial LMSs that are most often implemented in form of client/server applications is given in [HK03]. On behalf of these systems, this chapter describes three commercial client/server platforms that were initially developed by academic institutions.

Stand-alone applications offered on the market have a wide area of application, but a single system often concentrates on a certain topic only. For example, a lot of applications focus on mathematics, foreign language learning, typewriting, guitar playing etc. On behalf of

---

[21]http://www.napster.com/
[22]http://www.edonkey2000.com/
[23]http://www.kazaa.com/us/index.htm

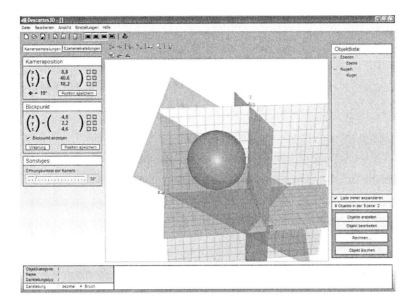

Figure 2.10: Screenshot of Descartes3D 1.2.

this kind of learning system, *Descartes3D*[24] is pictured next. It helps pupils and students to solve problems in the field of analytical geometry. Figure 2.10 shows a screenshot of the program that also supports more advanced technologies like stereoscopic glasses that can be used to get a realistic impression of the objects displayed. A typical feature of most of the stand-alone programs is the fact that they are not able to handle content from different sources. There is no import or export functionality for data, and standardization efforts are disregarded. In addition, they do not provide any interfaces to reuse functionalities. Thus, they may be helpful to learn about the topic they are dealing with, but they are not flexible at all. This results from the fact that these applications were often developed by non specialists in the field of elearning; instead, specialists in the application domain were in charge. In that form, stand-alone elearning systems are special forms of CBTs, as they fulfill the typical characteristics of the latter. However, there are some applications that are implemented as stand-alone programs and are able to process learning objects. The Learning Resource Interchange (LRN) toolkit[25] from Microsoft, for example, includes a viewer to handle learning objects. Unfortunately, Microsoft has stopped the development of this toolkit.

---

[24]http://www.descartes-media.de/

[25]http://www.microsoft.com/learning/elearning.asp

A commercial client/server-based elearning system that is widely used today is *WebCT* (*Web Course Tools*[26]). It was initially developed at the department of Computer Science at the University of British Columbia and is to make the use of complex Web-based learning environments easier. In its simplest form, it can be used to publish additional material to a course, but it can also handle complete online courses. Several different commercial versions are available today. They support the common roles as described in Chapter 2.1 and are accessible via a Web browser.

WebCT provides a configuration of the platform for learners by means of *Course Tools*. A Course Tool is a feature that can be added to a course and is afterwards displayed as an icon on the homepage (i.e., the starting point of a course) of the respective course. All courses are displayed for a user on the MyWebCT page that shows up after his or her login. Common Course Tools include email features and discussion forums to support a collaboration of learners and enable a communication with tutors and calendar tools. The "Course Content Module" is one of the most important Course Tools and provides functionalities to offer content for learners. It also enables the designer of the course to add material in an easy way by uploading HTML pages to the course and integrating the new content with existing contents. The "Selftest" Course Tool can be used afterwards to create multiple-choice questions for the content, and a feedback is provided to learners directly after having answered the questions.

Learners are able to present material to other learners by using the group functionality of WebCT. The tutor of a course can build groups of learners, and the latter are afterwards able to upload content to the system that can be accessed by other group members.

Although WebCT uses a proprietary format to store content, it is able to handle SCORM-conform content packages, which can be included to the system. It also supports an import of IMS content packages (PIF) and various content packages that are closely related to this format like packages of the Microsoft LRN Content Packaging format. In addition, it provides an interface to be integrated with common student information systems (like Datatel, PeopleSoft, and SCT), as well as an interface to be integrated with common authentication schemes (e.g., LDAP).

The platform *W3L* (*Web Life Long Learning* [BBZ04]) was developed at the University of Bochum, Germany, and the Dortmund University of Applied Science, Germany, and is now offered for sale or as an ASP solution (Application Service Providing) by the company W3L GmbH, Germany. Three main aspects pushed the development of the platform, i.e., a learner-centric approach, a suitable support to create and maintain content, and the development of print materials from the content stored inside the platform. To address

---

[26]http://www.webct.com

a learner-centric approach, the platform is able to switch between four different learning styles on demand of a user. Learners are also able to consume knowledge modules[27] in an arbitrary order, although the system suggests a certain path through the modules. At any time multiple-choice tests can be taken by a learner to check the learning progress. These tests are corrected automatically or by human tutors, who are also in charge to answer additional questions of the learners. If an answer is wrong, the platform does not provide the correct solution, but offers hints for each possible alternative of the solution to help the learner to correct the answer and thus to have a direct learning progress. These hints can be defined by an author at various levels. The W3L platform displays the correct answer only if a learner went through all levels and was not able to find the solution. The tests related to knowledge modules have to be passed in order to be able to access the final exams.

To support the learning progress, W3L has an integrated functionality to generate books or scripts from knowledge modules to be easily printed. In addition, a book for each course can be ordered in an online shop.

Authors use a special client to create content, which can be used only on Windows machines. In addition, W3L offers a plug-in for Microsoft Word to be used as authoring software. A Web-front-end to create content does not exist because the client is more flexible and easier to handle. Authors do not have to know HTML nor do they have to bother about the layout of the content and are thus able to concentrate on the development of professional aspects of the content. A special functionality does guaranty that contents by different authors have an identical look-and-feel.

A special design objective of W3L was the ability to transform content in any presentation format. This includes the generation of books, scripts, and slides to be presented in meetings. To achieve this, a Single-Source-Publishing approach was implemented on the fundamentals of XML and XSLT [Kay00]; it uses a proprietary content management system for the elearning content.

As pictured in Figure 2.11, W3L supports a collaborative learning by providing common communication functionalities. Learner activities are stored in learner profiles maintained by the learner management. W3L supports an API to connect to other systems.

From a technical perspective, W3L uses an application server that provides the main business logic and can be accessed directly by the authoring client. Learners use a Web browser to consume the content by connecting to a Web server that in turn communicates with the application server.

---

[27]Translation of the German "Wissensbaustein" that represents the learning material and can be seen as up to three screen pages to be consumed by a learner.

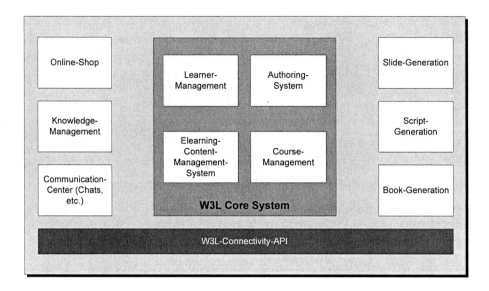

Figure 2.11: Basic building blocks of the W3L platform according to [BBZ04].

Although W3L uses a straight model to store content that was influenced by concepts of software engineering to enable the Single-Source-Publishing functionality, the system seems not to care about elearning standards at all. At the moment, the system supports neither import nor export interfaces for the use of learning objects from other platforms, although it ought to be easy to implement this functionality owing to the flexible maintenance and transformation of content.

Gradiance[28] is a platform offered by the Gradiance Corporation. At the moment, the system provides services in the fields of database systems, compilers, automata theory, and operating systems and is used particularly by universities around the world. Gradiance's goal is to offer services free of charge by sharing questions designed by instructors and teaching assistants within the community of registered people. In addition, there is a premium access to special courses that can be used via tokens included in books offered by instructors.

Gradiance uses a particular type of multiple-choice question called *root question* to present exercises to learners. The basic concept of a root question is to display the same question to all learners, but answers are selected randomly from a pool of possible solutions. The learners' answers are evaluated automatically, and "choice explanations" are presented if

---

[28]http://www.gradiance.com

the answer is wrong. Choice explanations are typically either hints or additional explanations to state why the answer is wrong. Afterwards, the learner has to answer the same question again. The evaluation process of submitted solutions in Gradiance is completely automatic. On the one hand, this reduces the workload of teaching assistants, but, on the other hand, reduces also the types of questions that can be used in the system.

To get experiences with practical work, Gradiance offers programming laboratories (called "Labs") that can be theoretically used with different programming languages. However, at the moment it supports only SQL and XQuery. The Labs offer input forms to answer questions, for example, in the form of SQL queries. Submissions are checked for syntactical and semantical errors and are executed on a MySQL database. After the submission of the solution, Gradiance offers direct feedback to learners.

2.4.3 Open Source Systems

Moodle[29] is a software package provided freely as open source software under the GNU Public License[30]. The term "Moodle" was originally an acronym for "Modular Object-oriented Dynamic Learning Environment". The software offers functionalities for producing Internet-based courses and Web sites and has a strong support for security and administration and can be seen as a fully-fledged LMS. The first version was finally released in August 2002 and was targeted to smaller classes at university level. Since then, a number of new releases and features have been published. It is now evolving towards IMS and SCORM specifications with a strong emphasis on the import of content conform to specifications of these organizations.

Moodle is suitable for full-fledged online courses and a supplement for face-to-face learning. Technically, Moodle can be installed on any platform that supports PHP and can use any common database to store data. However, it recommends to use the Apache Web server[31] and a MySQL[32] or PostgreSQL[33] database. To use and administer Moodle, people need a common Web browser.

Moodle has a modular structure allowing to customize the platform. To add a new module, it has to be stored in a subdirectory on the Web server and can then be connected to the system via a Web-front-end. Typical modules include communication facilities like chat, discussion forums, and dialogs (one-to-one asynchronous message exchange between

---

[29]http://moodle.org

[30]http://www.gnu.org/copyleft/gpl.html

[31]http://www.apache.org

[32]http://dev.mysql.com

[33]http://www.postgresql.org

instructor and learner or between learner and learner). Trainers can publish additional information for learners on the main page of a course or as documents to be downloaded. Content is presented to the learner by means of a resource module that is able to present any electronic content like Word, Powerpoint, Flash, Video, and Sound files. Files can be uploaded and managed on the server. In addition, Moodle has a built-in authoring tool to create content. The entire course can have an additional glossary module and FAQ lists to support the learning process. Moodle supports exercises in various forms, including single-choice, multiple-choice, true-false, and short-text exercises; all of them can be corrected automatically by Moodle. It also supports an upload of files for more complex solutions.

The *Open University Support System* (OpenUSS[34] [GDB04a]) is an open source project initiated by the University of Muenster, Germany. The development has begun in 2000 and focuses on the implementation of an open and expandable LMS. In consequence, it is able to meet evolving standards and new conceptual requirements.

In contrast to many other open source LMSs typically implemented using PHP, OpenUSS is developed using Java and J2EE (servlets and EJBs). It uses a component-based approach to enable an easy mechanism to include new functionalities. Owing to the use of J2EE, the development and deployment of OpenUSS components is independent of a certain container manufacturer (both for servlet and EJB container) and can use commercial or open source containers. Current implementations of OpenUSS are completely based on open source products to take the full advantage of this licensing model. Figure 2.12 shows the OpenUSS component architecture.

The OpenUSS Foundation Components include typical functionalities needed by learners or teaching assistants. The Extension Components implement the functionality that is offered for the OpenUSS users and include communication features like chat, discussion forums, and mailing lists. Learners can use quizzes to deepen their knowledge about topics introduced in class, or, on documents that can be stored within the Lecture Component. Usually, these documents are Powerpoint or PDF-Files that cover material handled in class.

Since OpenUSS is developed to serve mass lectures at universities, it supports the Application Service Provider (ASP) model and can manage any number of institutions (for example, universities, companies, or schools) within one system instance. A multi-server environment can be installed to achieve an efficient load balancing to keep the system scalable. Multiple servers can be used on different layers, particularly on the presentation and business layers of OpenUSS, but also on the data layer that can use C-JDBC (Clus-

---

[34]http://www.openuss.org

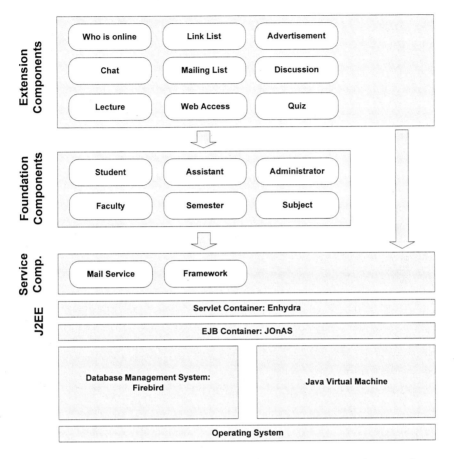

Figure 2.12: OpenUSS component architecture according to [GDB04a].

tered JDBC) to add a cluster of databases without changing the system itself. A special component monitors system functionalities and user activities [GDB04a].

2.4.4 University Systems

The University of Muenster is also working on an ongoing project involving the development of an elearning system called *eXtreme e-Learning eXperience* (*xLx* [VHL01, HLV+02, VW04, SVW05]), which is mainly used in support of the exercise portions of technically oriented university courses (e.g., database systems, database implementation, computer networks, workflow management). The xLx system is part of a "blended learning strategy" that consists of regular classroom teaching and electronic exercise work.

The xLx platform was implemented with the developers having had several technical requirements in mind. On the client side, the platform is independent of hardware, location, and operating systems used; on the server side, it is able to generate Web pages dynamically, provide security as far as personal data is concerned, and deliver 24/7 availability. The xLx system is based on open source software (except for third-party systems that can be integrated to get hands-on experience) and is implemented in three-tier client/server architecture. Web clients form the outermost layer and can access the platform via a Web browser. A Web server builds the second layer and processes client requests. A database server represents the core of the innermost layer which is also the integration layer for different third-party systems (like, e.g., an IBM DB2 database). Internet-based client access allows platform independence on the client side and enables continuous availability. The HTML pages of the xLx system can be rendered by all current browsers; and session cookies are used to identify students and to track their actions. On top of that, extended browser functionalities such as plug-ins or Java are not needed.

Learners can work on their exercises anytime and anyplace if Internet access and a standard Web browser are available. They may determine their own pace when solving exercises; however, a didactically meaningful sequencing of exercises is enforced by the system (as is a time limit per assignment). Moreover, learners may ask for additional exercises either if they have difficulties with the presented material or if they would like to work on more challenging problems. Finally, learning modules based on realistic problems and transparent access to underlying commercial systems raise hopes to have more fun and a better learning success while solving the exercises accompanying a course.

The xLx system embodies a personalized learning platform that offers hands-on experience in terms of practical exercises covering a wide range of conceptual, language specific, or algorithmic aspects of a particular field. As explained above, the xLx platform is designed as a supplement to traditional lectures, not as a replacement for them. It supports Web-based exercise solving, where exercises include "arithmetical" tasks, for example, in the context of the relational algebra, formulation of queries or programs, or practical projects based on real-world systems. The platform organizes courses in terms of closed user groups, where every member has his or her own password-protected account. The platform is divided into five parts:

1. **Learning section:** even though xLx is mostly used for blended learning, a module is included to present SCORM compliant learning objects to present additional material to learners.

2. **Test section:** in this section learners are enabled to train their skills concerning course-relevant techniques (e.g., XQuery and SQL queries, object-relational features of SQL:1999, transformation of XML documents with XSLT) by using playgrounds, which are the counterparts of Gradiance's Labs. Learners can also deepen their understanding of algorithmic techniques (e.g., database system algorithms such as algebraic query optimization, two-phase-locking protocol for transaction synchronization, redo-winners protocols for restarts after system crashes) by using animations.

3. **Submit section/Correction section:** these two sections contain the exercises that have to be solved during the term and ahead of predefined deadlines. New exercises show up in the submit section as the necessary background is covered in class. Solutions can be prepared and sometimes tested in the above-mentioned test section. Once submitted, solutions cannot be changed by learners any more, and they appear in the correction section on the work queue of a teaching assistant, by whom they are corrected and annotated. So far, the xLx platform knows six types of exercises: free-text, multiple-choice, Java-programming exercises, SQL queries, XQuery expressions, and XSLT transformations. While the first two of these exercise types are standard ingredients of elearning systems, the latter four are unique to the xLx system as they are coupled with transparently integrated underlying systems - in this case, a relational database for SQL, an XSLT processor, an XQuery engine, and a Java testing framework [SVW05]. The integration of different systems avoids technological and administrative barriers as learners do not have to install these systems at home; instead, these systems are accessed via standard Web browsers. Finally, exercises for the last four of the above types are stored along with solutions inside the xLx platform, which allows automatic prechecking of solutions and makes life easier for teaching assistants.

4. **Communication section:** as many learning platforms, xLx includes a discussion board for communication purposes and an email list as well as a news section and a download and upload area.

5. **Administration:** to maintain the courses and the platform, xLx provides broad administration functionalities like user administration, content administration, and exercise administration, to name just a few.

Although xLx is able to present SCORM compliant learning objects, the xLx exercises are not learning objects in the traditional sense. Instead, they have a proprietary format and xLx does not provide an export functionality to exchange exercises with other platforms nor does it care about standardization suggestions that are not part of SCORM and focus on an exercise exchange (e.g, the IMS Question and Test Interoperability Specification [IMS05b]). The xLx platform offers a Web service to enable a single-sign-on mechanism to be integrated with other elearning platforms.

Several university courses are offered on the Web that provide complete online courses. There are, for example, courses of the Virtual Global University[35], of VIROR[36], ULI[37], WINFOLine[38], VISUM[39], VAWi[40], and in particular offerings of the Virtual University in Hagen, Germany[41]. Obviously, these are only offerings from Germany, and many others can be found around the world. The important fact to recognize is that the institutions offering these programs use software products which are basically LMSs, communication tools, and exercise platforms, as described in the previous chapters. Some tools are proprietary solutions, others are commercial platforms or open source products.

2.5   Challenges

Chapter 2.3 has already briefly discussed advantages and disadvantages of some elearning standards and specifications at a technical level. Challenges and drawbacks that appear at a higher level have not been mentioned and will be sketched in the following.

The sample systems described in the previous subsections are implemented as full-fledged elearning platforms in a closed manner. None of them provides a reuse of functionalities, although some of them offer an interface to allow other systems to log on users for a single-sign-on. The descriptions of xLx and Gradiance have pointed out that some systems resemble one another to a large extend. However, they cannot be integrated without big programming efforts. The situation is comparable for other platforms. In the entire field of elearning, clearly defined interfaces are missing so that it is rather difficult to integrate platforms with each other, and with existing applications like ERP (Enterprise-Resource-Planning) systems. At the moment, only the IMS Enterprise Web Services

---

[35]http://www.vg-u.de
[36]VIROR - Virtuelle Hochschule Oberrhein, see http://www.viror.de
[37]ULI - Universitärer Lernverbund Informatik, see http://www.uli-campus.de
[38]Wirtschaftsinformatik Online, see http://www.winfoline.de
[39]http://visum.uni-muenster.de
[40]VAWi - Virtuelle Aus- und Weiterbildung Wirtschaftsinformatik, see http://www.vawi.de
[41]http://virtuelle-uni.fernuni-hagen.de

effort targets at the standardized integration of user data from enterprise systems into elearning systems (see Chapter 4). WebCT implements proprietary solutions to connect to student management systems, but it would be more efficient to have well-defined interfaces for almost all of the common elearning functionalities to be reused by other elearning applications.

The creation of learning objects that adhere to the SCORM specification [ADL04a] are to enable an easy exchange and reuse of elearning content. However, in the field of elearning, many "legacy" systems exist storing data in a proprietary way. Often, there is no possibility to export content as defined by the SCORM CAM specification and the IMS Content Packaging (see Chapter 2.2) to other systems because the latter are not compliant to those specifications. From an economic point of view, the situation is even worse, at least for the following two reasons:

1. The development process of content is supported by authoring tools that a legacy system provides. More powerful tools offered on the market often cannot be used. As a consequence, an efficient reuse of content is only possible inside the system if it is possible at all.

2. The exchange of elearning software to one of another manufacturer is nearly impossible because data sets stored inside the system cannot be imported to the new system. It may be possible to export user data from the proprietary data store to the new system, but it is difficult to export the content. It goes without saying that in most cases the content has to be rebuilt in the new system. From an economical point of view, this is unacceptable.

The use of physical learning objects as proposed by SCORM makes the maintenance of learning content a challenging task. The vision of SCORM is to foster the exchange of many learning objects between lots of LMSs. A small update or even a simple correction of a mistake leads to an additional physical distribution of the same learning object to all LMSs that use this content. This update is very expensive, and it would be much easier if the content was only corrected once and updates were available for all learners immediately no matter what platform they use. The physical distribution of content can take a lot of time. This is a big drawback if updates of content are critical because of mistakes in the content etc.

Several elearning platforms implement proprietary, but useful functionalities to support the learning process. The xLx platform offers playgrounds for students to get hands-on experience in certain technical areas. It offers a playground to try out SQL statements on a (commercial) relational database via a simple Web-front-end without any administration and installation effort. Gradiance offers comparable Labs. These playgrounds and Labs cannot be exchanged via the mechanisms defined by SCORM as they need a direct connection to a database engine. However, they would improve learning in many courses, particularly in the area of computer science. By opening the closed xLx and Gradiance platforms and offering their functionalities via well-defined interfaces, many learners could benefit from it. In addition, these functionalities may generate extra income for the providers of the platforms if the functionalities can be found on the Web and are integrated into any learning platform after a learner has paid for the use. Similar economical advantages apply for functionalities offered by other platforms or when learning objects are available to learners via standard interfaces outside of closed elearning platforms.

The playgrounds and Labs are not only helpful for university students but also for learners in tertiary education. These functionalities can provide the hands-on experience or simulate on-the-job experience a learner needs to prepare for the CIAD exams of Figure 1.1. If the functionalities are offered on the Web, and learners can choose any content building block they find appropriate for their needs, this would be very helpful. However, SCORM packages are not well-suited for a plug-and-play integration by learners. Typically, these packages need tutors or administrators to be included into a course program. In the case of Labs or playgrounds, they are not working at all.

The SCORM specifications are complex and still under development. Momentarily, the fourth version of SCORM is available. Even if learning objects are implemented based on those specifications, there is still some space for interpretations that may have an impact on LMS developers and content developers. This could still make an import of content difficult, and annual ADL Plugfests bring content developers and software manufactures together to bridge this gap.

To solve the problems mentioned above, elearning functionalities can be offered as standalone applications or components that adhere to well-defined technologies on the Web. These functionalities can then be used in any system that is able to access their interfaces and communicate with these components. The mechanism of offering components on a network is well known from the field of distributed systems and will be adapted for the elearning scenario in the following.

2.6 Summary

This chapter has given a brief overview of the field of elearning. Since the idea of supporting learners by computers has not emerged only recently, a short overview of important development steps and recent activities has been given. It has taken a closer look at the use of computers in teaching, learning, and education and has explained several terms used in the field of elearning today.

The development of elearning is characterized by the development of elearning standards and specifications. The standards LOM and LTSA from IEEE, the IMS specifications "Content Packaging" and "Simple Sequencing", and ADL's SCORM have been explained in detail. Several of these standards and specifications have an influence on the implementation of modern elearning platforms, and will also have an influence on the development of a distributed elearning environment as designed throughout this thesis. In particular, the SCORM specification and the IEEE LTSA standard will be used again later on. The chapter has also sketched platforms which are based on different license models. These have been, above all, commercial, open source, and university systems.

Chapter 3

Distributed Information Systems and Middleware Architectures

In many fields the reuse of building blocks is very common. When looking at the process of constructing vehicles, for example, we find that different models are based on the same chassis and various seats can be plugged into a car without changing anything. Private domain hi-fi systems stand for another good example of the reuse of building blocks. Components produced by different manufacturers can easily be plugged together to build a new system offering a more comprehensive functionality. Furthermore, TV sets and video devices can already be plugged to hi-fi systems without any technical problems.

In computing, the hardware industry has already been able to standardize system modules to an astonishingly high degree. Therefore, components can more easily be combined to build complete computer systems. However, in the beginning of the development of hardware industry, components by different manufacturers were hardly able to work together. Software engineers have also been dreaming of reusing well-accepted methods and extensively tested products and operations for decades. It must be taken into consideration that comparing the hardware industry with the software industry may not make sense because the two industries work with a different number and different kinds of parameters, as explained in detail by [Gri98], but the effects of reusing software building blocks are even stronger than in hardware industry. Well-engineered software building blocks can be duplicated nearly without any costs, which makes them very interesting from an economic point of view as well as from a quality point of view: the quality of software increases, and at the same time costs for developing software decrease [Fra99]. In 1968, MCILROY already had the vision of a software component industry that would offer groups of routines for any given job [McI68]:

> "..., yet software production in the large would be enormously helped by
> the availability of spectra of high quality routines, quite as mechanical design
> is abetted by the existence of families of structural shapes, screws or resistors."

Working on this idea for many years now, researchers and engineers have not been able
to agree on a precise definition of a *component* in computer science. The notion has
been approached in various and, in some cases, even contradictory manners (see, for
example, [Gri98, Szy97, BHB+03]). Many modern programming languages help to fulfill MCILROY's dream at least to some extend as they provide small scale programming
libraries (e.g., *java.util*), technology abstractions such as ODBC and JDBC, special purpose software components like XML parsers, large scale standardized frameworks (e.g.,
java.swing), or large scale standardized containers such as database engines. However,
these components largely depend on their providers because their documentation, component structures, interface definitions, and behavior descriptions are mostly proprietary. It
goes without saying that in software development, object-oriented technologies have con-
tributed decisively to an increase of the reuse and encapsulation of software. Nonetheless,
they clearly suffer from several drawbacks. This comprises particularly the fact that objects can often only be composed if they are written in the same programming language.
The same applies to their capability of cooperating: they must be written in the same
programming language to cooperate. Moreover, they have to be tightly coupled if they
are executed in the same process and data space. In addition, their interface descriptions
focus on the incoming interface, whereas the outgoing interface is mostly implicit. This
makes it more difficult to deploy objects independently.

Current software systems are distributed over networks and different platforms. Particularly in the future, they will have to be able to be integrated and to interact with
each other. Apparently, objects are not able to handle these upcoming challenges of
such information systems [BHB+03]. Instead, more and more components will offer their
functionality in the form of services, which can be accessed by other components. Multiple services which are logically connected can be grouped by means of an interface.
Components are to have the following characteristics [GT00]:

- **Well-defined intention:** the intention of a component ought to be well-defined,
  which is often more extensive and abstract than the intention of a single object.

- **Context freeness:** the interoperability of components ought to be independent of
  used programming languages, operating systems, network technologies, and developing tools.

- **Self-containedness:** a component ought to constitute a complete and independent unit having everything needed in itself.

- **Location independence:** services of a component consumed by a user ought to be identical no matter on which kind of machine (local or remote) the component is executed.

- **Separation of interface and implementation:** the interface definition ought to be independent of the way of how a component is implemented. To employ a component, a user can obtain detailed information about its interfaces, but a direct access to internal structures of a component is not possible. A component can also be connected to more than one interface to offer the functionalities according to the desired service [Gri98].

- **Self-descriptiveness:** a component ought to include a mechanism for a self-description of its services provided. This includes at least the signatures of the methods and attributes which are important for a simple binding.

- **Plug-and-play property:** a component ought to be able to join an existing registry provided by the infrastructure underlying the entire system. This enables an easy availability of services.

- **Integration and composition:** components ought to be able to be plugged together in order to form a new component with a wider functionality. In addition, this ought to be made possible, even at runtime, by an interaction of components by means of their interfaces. This means that a component can become a client for another component and, at the same time, a server for a third one.

- **Reusability:** a component ought to be easily reusable in its domain. Of course, this implies syntactically and semantically error-free executions.

- **Executable form:** a component ought to be provided in binary code as an executable program. In general, there is no need to publish its source code.

The most quoted definition of a software component taking all these characteristics into consideration is given by [Szy97]. It emphasizes the composition and deployment of components:

> "A component is a unit of composition with contractually specified interfaces and explicit context dependencies only. A software component can be deployed independently and is subject to composition by third parties."

Components can be divided into different classes indicating their granularity. [HS00] and
[BHB+03] describe four distinct classes of granularity. These classes can be a means of
structuring large scale systems.

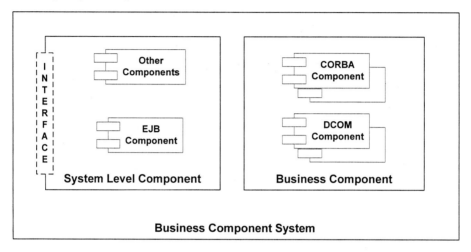

Figure 3.1: Classification of components on granularity.

The first and most fine-grained software building block can be considered the *distributed
component*. It is the usual concept of a component in industry and is typically implemented as an Enterprise JavaBean (EJB) [RSB04], a CORBA component, or a DCOM
component (see Chapter 3.3). The distributed component consists of some programming
language classes and possesses a network interface. One or several distributed components
can form a *business component* to implement a single autonomous business concept. Business components can be independently deployed. The combination of these components
to deliver a cohesive set of functionality required by a specific business need is called
business component system. If it has clearly-designed interfaces and thus is a component
on its own, it is called a *system-level component*. Figure 3.1 gives an overview of this
classification.

The remainder of this chapter will introduce different approaches of how components
can be used and located to build distributed systems. The construction of distributed
systems can be simplified by leveraging *middleware* (see, for example, [CDK02b, Emm00,
Ber96, Ber93, ACK+04]). Middleware is layered between the operating system and the
application components, as shown in Figure 3.2. Middleware provides a programming
model above the basic building blocks of processes and message passing. It offers APIs,
functionalities, and location transparency and an independence of communication protocol

details, operating systems, hardware, and sometimes even of programming languages [CDK02b]. Consequently, middleware can cope with heterogeneity and enables software developers to build distributed systems across networks by facilitating communication and coordination of distributed components at a higher level than the one an operating system offers. This is why time and money can be saved when middleware is used to develop a distributed system [Emm00].

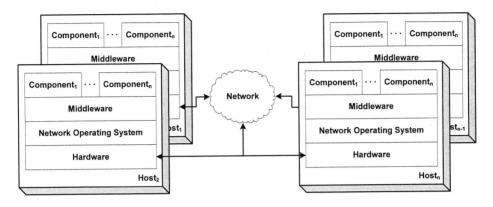

Figure 3.2: Middleware in distributed system construction [Emm00].

Based on the techniques which middleware products use for the interaction between distributed components, they can be classified into RPC-based systems, TP Monitors, object-based systems, and message-oriented systems. The interactions of RPC-based systems, which will be described in Chapter 3.1, are based on remote procedure calls, whereas TP Monitors are based on distributed transactions. TP Monitors will be introduced in Chapter 3.2. Object-based systems will be presented in Chapter 3.3; they use remote object requests as the underlying interaction paradigm. Message-based systems communicate by passing messages; they will be described in Chapter 3.4. This class of systems includes Web services, which will be dealt with in more detail than the other systems in Chapter 3.6.

For each middleware technique the use of the remote functionality will be explained basically by giving a typical example from the application domain of elearning. The search for content is a central aspect in these systems owing to the fact that the quality of the search mechanism and the quality of the result is important for the success of the entire learning process. Recalling the CIAD course of Figure 1.1, a learner has to search for appropriate content before consuming the latter. It will be shown in the respective chapters how the mechanisms described have to be used to call the search functionality on

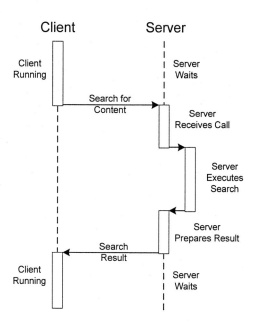

Figure 3.3: Search for content.

a remote machine. A very important aspect will be to proof if learners are able to include new remote functionalities in a suitable way on their own at runtime. As will be shown, some of the techniques require the help of a developer and a recompilation of the client code in order to use different search functionalities that are not included in the original client application. If a selection at runtime is possible, a learner can use different search mechanisms of various providers by plugging in these functionalities. Figure 3.3 explains the processing order on the client and server machine. First, the learner uses the client machine to process some activities (client running). Then the learner needs to search for new content. Search mechanisms can be implemented by several servers. Hence, this is the moment the learner has to select and include the search service to be used in the client application. Figure 3.3 does not picture the discovery and selection of the service because some techniques described in the following do not allow a dynamic selection of remote functionalities. Instead, it is assumed that the addresses and signatures of different functionalities are known by the learner. Figure 3.3 is just to show the overall steps during the search. After selecting the service, the client passes the search request to the server machine. Owing to the fact that different mechanisms will be described, the passing of the request as well as the coding and decoding of the message are implemented in different ways. The server decodes the message and executes the search procedure. The result of the search is coded again and afterwards passed to the client. The client decodes the message and presents the results to the learner.

3.1 Remote-Procedure-Call-Based Systems

The Remote Procedure Call (RPC) approach was introduced in the 1980s in the context of the Cedar programming environment [BN84] and RPC became immediately the basis for 2-tier systems [ACK+04]. The idea is to call procedures transparently that are located on remote machines. Procedures are well known, and it is thus easy for a developer to use RPC [ACK+04]. The fundamental approach is still the same in modern RPC interactions. Two actors are the essential partners that interact in the environment: one is called client, the other one is called server. A client is a program that calls remote procedures; a server is a program that implements procedures and can be called by clients. The notions of both client and server and many further concepts of RPC are still in use today. RPC uses an *interface definition language (IDL)* to describe how procedures can be called. In particular, it describes their signatures (input and output parameters). In this form a concrete IDL description is an abstract representation of the procedure. In addition to the IDL, the concept of *name and directory services* appears in most of the middleware systems in use today; and even Web services provide comparable mechanisms, which are described in more detail in the following chapters.

RPC is often implemented as a collection of libraries. For developers who want to build components of a distributed system, they have to compile and link the RPC libraries to their code. In addition, developers have to define the interfaces of their procedures in IDL. This definition is the basis for building both the client and the server. The IDL is compiled by special interface compilers that are part of any RPC or middleware implementation. As a result, the compiler creates client stubs and server stubs that handle all network programming details [ACK+04, TS02]:

- The **client stub** is a piece of code that has to be compiled and linked to the client. The stub is a placeholder or proxy for the remote procedure letting the remote call appear as a local one since the stub is a part of the client code. In fact, each signature of a procedure included in the IDL results in a client stub. If a client wants to use the remote procedure, it does not call the procedure directly, but the stub. The stub marshals and serializes the request, binds itself to the server and takes care of the whole communication process.

- The **server stub** is a placeholder for a client on the remote machine. It has a similar purpose as a client stub, but functions for the server machine. It receives an invocation from a client stub and unmarshals and deserializes the request. It passes the information to the procedure called. After processing, the server stub takes the results and sends them back to the client stub.

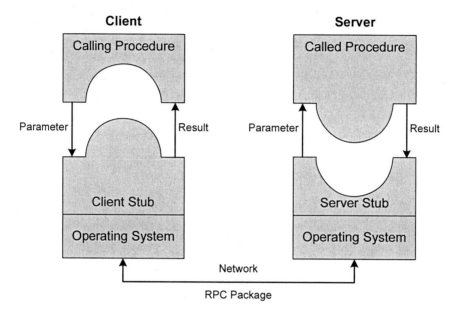

Figure 3.4: Conceptual RPC mechanism.

In addition to client and server stubs, some interface compiler can generate code templates to ease the development of client and server programs. The conceptual RPC mechanism is shown in Figure 3.4. The client calls a certain procedure by passing parameters to the client stub that in turn creates the RPC message, which is sent via the network to the server machine. The message is unmarshaled by the server stub, and the procedure is executed. The results of the execution are passed back in a corresponding way.

In RPC, binding can be static or dynamic. In case of a static binding, the handle to a server is hard-coded on the client side. Although this kind of binding is very efficient, the machines are tightly coupled. Each time the server is down, the client will not work either. If the location of a server is changed, the source codes of clients that use this particular server have to be changed to use the new server address; afterwards, the client codes have also to be recompiled. Even load balancing and the use of redundant servers face problems [ACK+04] since a hard-coded address typically points to exactly one server. Dynamic binding resolves some of these problems, but performance is not as good as in static binding. The dynamic approach uses a special name and directory service that adds another layer of indirection to the system. This service resolves server addresses based on the signatures of the procedures called. A client stub is now able to ask the name and directory service for a server that implements the requested functionality. The answer of the service is used to contact the respective server and invoke the procedure call. As a result, the client and server are not as tightly coupled as before. Advanced implementations of the directory service can track calls and perform a load balancing depending on the communication with several stubs. Directory services normally work on IDL specifications, but more sophisticated mechanisms for selection are also possible. These services are called *traders*.

RPC is also able to bridge heterogeneous systems. Because there are many systems that should be able to work together, the solution is to form an intermediate representation rather than to implement very complex stubs. This enables clients and servers to translate to and from this representation in an efficient way. To achieve this, RPC also uses IDLs to map to and from concrete programming languages. The usage of IDLs enables clients and servers to ignore differences in terms of machine architecture, programming languages, and type systems. Thus, IDLs serve as an intermediate representation for the data exchanged between clients and servers [ACK+04].

The typical communication process in RPC is synchronous. A client can only have one outstanding call, but a server can serve many clients if threads are used. However, one thread is always coupled to exactly one client. An early extension to RPC has implemented an asynchronous communication model that does not block the client until the server has processed all actions. Several extensions of RPC have resulted in many additional, different middleware systems, for example, in TP Monitors and object-based systems as well as message-based systems. Some of them will be explained in the following chapters.

The two most common RPC implementations are *SUN's RPC* [Sri95, Blo92, CDK02b] and the *Distributed Computing Environment (DCE)*. SUN's RPC is provided on most Unix systems and offers developers the choice of using calls via TCP/IP or UDP/IP. It provides an interface definition language (called RPCL meaning RPC Language), which is an enhancement of the data representation language XDR (eXternal Data Representation). It also includes the "rpcgen" interface compiler that produces C programming code (stubs and further programming code). In addition, several lower-level facilities are part of SUN's RPC like testing tools, authentication etc. The development of DCE has been supported by HP, DEC, IBM, and, later on, by the Open Software Foundation (OSF). DCE provides a specification and an implementation of RPC, which is to be used and extended by producers. However, the attempt to standardize RPC has failed because the resulting software products of producers are not compatible to each other although they are based on the same fundamental RPC implementation. However, DCE is an extensive infrastructure of RPC and still in use today. DCE provides several additional services like a sophisticated name and directory service, a time service for clock synchronization, a distributed file service to share files, and a thread as well as a security service.

The RPC mechanism is suitable for developers to use remote functionalities in their programs. However, as RPC is used at a programming-code level, users of programs are not able to combine remote procedures based on their individual needs - even not with the dynamic binding described above. Each time a new remote functionality is included into the client program, the source code has to be recompiled to make the system work. This is also the case for dynamic binding of servers, which solves problems of unreachable machines but does not provide a way to include remote procedures with an identical functionality but different signature into a running system. Recalling the search example described in Figure 3.3, this means that a learner can use a predefined search procedure without recognizing the distributed nature of the software. However, the learner is not able to include another search functionality at runtime since the client program has to be recompiled after including the stub for the new procedure. Problems can also appear if the client stub is compiled in a certain version and the server component is published with a new interface description. Thus, there is still a tight coupling of components to a client stub. Learners are also faced with problems when wanting to find search functionalities as there is no user-friendly mechanism to achieve this.

Although two implementations are commonly used as sketched above, there are several other implementations of RPC, see, for example, [DHS91, BN84, Ste90], as well as libraries for many programming languages, see, for example, [TS02, CDK02a, SMH94, Fre91, TDB97, SPD03, SPM02]. A very common form of RPC is Java RMI (remote method invocation, a Java-based RPC [Gro01]) that uses a Java Virtual Machine (JVM) at runtime, which makes it independent of platforms. However, it forces the provider of the component to write the code in Java, which makes it dependent on the programming language. An already-existing source code that is written in a programming language other than Java has to be wrapped or newly coded, which results in additional work. In general, the different RPC implementations are incompatible, which leads to problems when using different implementations at once. Most of the RPC systems can be used across architectures, operating systems, and languages, but developers must have the same RPC system on all interacting platforms [All03]. It goes without saying that these problems cannot be solved by end users of computer systems. XML-RPC is to bridge this gap by using XML for marshaling of messages and HTTP for transferring the messages.

It can be seen as a predecessor of SOAP, which will be explained in Chapter 3.6.2. Even if XML-RPC is used, the problem of recompiling codes remains.

3.2   Transaction Processing (TP) Monitors

At the end of the 1960s, IBM developed one of the first TP Monitors called Customer Information and Control System (CICS). The early systems were to allow mainframes to support efficient multiplexing for as many concurrent users as possible [ACK+04]. To achieve this, the technology had to deal with multithreading and data consistency. In consequence, a transaction concept was necessary to extend the functionality of existing systems. Much of the concept of TP Monitors was influenced by existing operating systems. TP Monitors were competing with these systems and tried to bypass some of their limitations.

RPC was originally designed to enable remote calls in a distributed environment. If there is more than one call involved in the actions a client has to execute, the basic RPC approach does not offer a mechanism to group these calls into transactions. RPC treats each one of them as an independent invocation, which leads to problems in case of recovery after failures and crashes. In the elearning context this would be the case, for example, if a learner wants to pay for content he or she had chosen to use. If the system withdraws money from the learners bank account, but crashes before the money has been deposited into the account of the provider, there is an inconsistent system state. To solve these problems, RPC has been extended to handle transactions which group several invocations into one block. This form of RPC is called Transaction RPC (TRPC) and is able to give transactional guarantees for data that is distributed across multiple, and, in some cases, heterogeneous platforms. TRPC normally guarantees an *at most once* semantic for the invocations of a transaction. Other models have also been implemented like *at least once* or *exactly once* [WV02].

The transactional guarantees are achieved by using a transaction management module that is implemented as a component in modern TP Monitors. This component is the reason for the name *TP Monitor*. Its main purpose is to coordinate interactions between clients and servers. The grouping of invocations into transactions is achieved by using *Begin of Transaction* (BOT) and *End of Transaction* (EOT) statements as calls for the corresponding stubs.

Apart from the features already mentioned above which help to deal with RPC and the transaction manager, which implements logging, locking, recovery mechanisms etc., TP Monitors typically offer further services. A monitor system is in charge of scheduling

threads, assigning priorities etc. and thus gives performance and flexibility to the TP
Monitor. Special components and tools give further functionalities to the system to
support special scenarios or systems. Figure 3.5 gives a rough overview of the architecture
of a TP Monitor, which is described in detail in [ACK+04]. Apart from the services and
transaction manager, a TP Monitor has an interface component that provides an API
to clients or for direct access. Wrappers, on the other hand, hide the heterogeneity of
different resources to make communication easier. The program flow component loads
and executes procedures, and routers map operations to invocations.

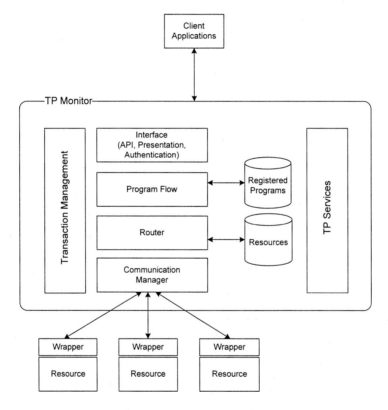

Figure 3.5: High-level view of a TP Monitor according to [ACK+04].

Although TP Monitors handle problems that appear during the execution of remote functionalities, it is just another layer of indirection at the programming-code level and helps
particularly developers to build distributed systems more easily. The problems of discovery of the resources as well as the recompilation of client programs after including
additional remote functionalities are not solved from an end-user's perspective. Recalling

the search functionality example, the overall proceeding to include new search function-alities into a system for learners is basically still the same as described in Chapter 3.1 (RPC). Making things worse, even BOT and EOT calls have now to be handled by the client programming code and forwarded via the client stub to the TP Monitor.

The additional layer of indirection raises the question which instance provides the TP Monitor service. Particularly in an open, distributed elearning system where providers and learners are not known in advance, this problem is difficult to solve since there is no central instance that can be seen as a trusted third party.

3.3 Object-Based Middleware Systems

When the object-oriented programming paradigm gained increasing acceptance in the 1980s and 1990s, the emergence of object brokers was a consequent enhancement of the RPC mechanism described above. Objects hide most of their details about their structure, their implementation, the programming language used to realize them, the operating system on which they are running, as well as hardware details and location information. Again, the goal of object brokers is to hide much of the complexity behind remote invo-cations by making them look like local calls from a developer's perspective. In contrast to RPC, where a client invokes a procedure, in this case, the client invokes a method of an object. This means that objects may perform different actions owing to inheritance and polymorphism depending on the classes contained, although the same method has been called. Consequently, the middleware must bind a client to a specific object running on the remote server and has to direct the interactions between these parties. This is achieved by object brokers, and many of the latter have been enhanced by further func-tionalities described below in more detail [ACK+04]. In the following subsections, two programming-language-independent approaches will be described. Sun's Enterprise Jav-aBeans (EJB) [RSB04] will not be explained as they depend on the Java programming language.

3.3.1 Common Object Request Broker Architecture (CORBA)

The *Object Management Group (OMG)* is a non-profit organization, founded in 1989. It has approximately 800 members and released the first specification of CORBA in the early 1990s. CORBA itself is not a distributed system or product, but a specifica-tion of a producer-independent architecture (see, for example, [OMG04, TS02, CDK02a, ACK+04]). CORBA's goal is to specify a distributed system to overcome many of the interoperability problems by integrating network applications. Applications using CORBA are able to communicate with each other no matter what kind of programming language they use or what kind of hardware and software, as well as networks, they are running on. Applications are built of so-called CORBA objects, which implement the interfaces described by the OMG Interface Definition Language (IDL), an ISO International Standard[1]. The core of any CORBA-distributed system forms the *Object Request Broker* (ORB), which is responsible for enabling communication between objects and their clients while hiding issues related to distribution and heterogeneity [TS02]. It offers the basic communication services and enables a discovery and activation of remote objects. The ORB is usually implemented in form of libraries that are used in client and server applications, but it can also be implemented as an operating system service. Although CORBA uses an object model, it is similar to the client/server model with respect to the communication mechanisms and thus is not a component architecture in the common sense, but a middleware which can act as a foundation for one [Gri98]. Apart from the ORB, the CORBA specification distinguishes between CORBA facilities, which are logically divided into horizontal and vertical facilities. Horizontal facilities cover general-high-level services that are independent of the application domain like user interfaces and information management, whereas vertical services consist of specific application domain services like banking, ecommerce etc. Figure 3.6 shows the high-level CORBA architecture. In addition to the above-mentioned partitions, the CORBA architecture defines CORBA services[2] which are accessible through a standardized API and provide functionalities commonly needed by most objects. This includes, for example, naming services, transaction services, trading services, and security services. They will not be discussed here in detail.

To be used by an application, an object has to declare its interface first. Using this declaration a client is able to recognize the methods the object provides. As already mentioned, this definition is specified in OMG's IDL, which supports many object-oriented concepts like inheritance and polymorphism, but is not a programming language itself. It provides a precise syntax for expressing methods and their parameters to invoke the objects. CORBA interface definitions can only be given by means of IDL. These definitions have to be mapped to special programming language requirements to use the object. Every ORB carries one or more IDL compilers, one for each language supported. The IDL compilers are able to generate stubs and skeletons (a skeleton is a server stub) for the respective programming languages. The stub is a proxy object that marshals an invocation request and sends it to the server. The corresponding response of the server is marshaled

---

[1]Number 14750

[2]See http://www.omg.org/technology/documents/corbaservices_spec_catalog.htm for an overview of the CORBA services.

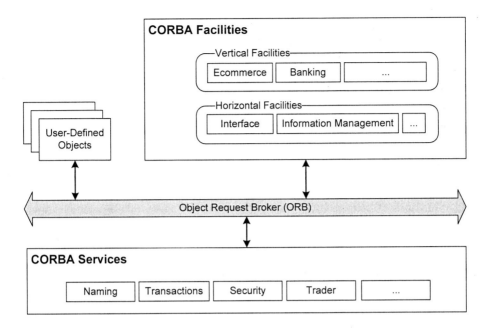

Figure 3.6: High-level view of the CORBA architecture according to [ACK+04].

and passed to the client application. In the static case, a client application has one stub for each object it invokes. These stubs make calls of (remote) objects look like local ones. The stub's source code has to be linked to the client code and includes the declarations of the methods provided by the object implementation to obtain the executable client application. The skeleton on the server side is linked to the server program and shields the server object from all issues concerning distribution. Thus, it provides static interfaces to call methods of an object implementation. This makes the requests from remote clients look like calls from local objects [ACK+04]. As shown in Figure 3.7, CORBA provides an object adapter, which takes care of forwarding incoming requests to the appropriate object and activating the latter, which is running in the address space of the server. The skeleton receives the method invocation and unmarshals the request, which is then passed to the method called.

The most crucial things implementors must know to develop applications are the IDLs of objects they want to use. Of course, it has to be kept in mind that IDLs only provide a syntactical description, not a semantical one.

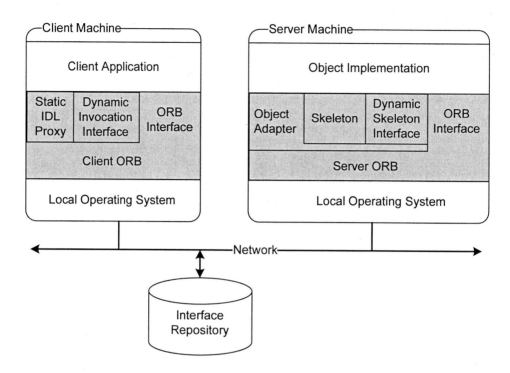

Figure 3.7: The general organization of a CORBA system according to [TS02].

So far, the mechanism described requires a client to be statically bound to an interface. To enable a dynamic usage of objects, an application has to find out at runtime how an interface looks like. CORBA offers an interface repository, which keeps all definitions of interfaces known to the ORB. In many systems, the interface repository is implemented by means of a separate process offering a standard interface to store, delete, and retrieve interface definitions, which can be accessed by applications. Whenever an interface definition is compiled, the IDL compiler assigns a repository identifier to that interface which is by default derived from the name of the interface and its methods. This means that there is no guarantee for uniqueness. On the client side, CORBA offers a Dynamic Invocation Interface (DII), which provides standard operations to query the repository and construct invocations in order to build requests at runtime from the newly discovered interfaces [TS02]. A client can locate a server object by requesting an object via the CORBA naming service, which allows a retrieval based on the name of the service. In addition, the CORBA trader service can be used to search for objects based on criteria. This service can be compared to what is known as telephone white and yellow pages.

On the server side, CORBA supports a Dynamic Skeleton Interface (DSI), which makes creating server interfaces on the fly during runtime possible.

The static binding of an object in CORBA has to be coded in the program-code of a client before compiling the application. Recalling the search functionality example, a learner is hence only able to use predefined objects for which a proxy has been included in the client application. As described above, CORBA also provides a dynamic discovery and binding of objects by means of the Interface Repository and Dynamic Invocation Interface. The CORBA Naming Service can be used to discover objects based on their names; it returns references of CORBA objects to which clients can connect. In addition, the CORBA Trading Service enables an advanced lookup, registration, and discovery of services based on service types and properties, but is mainly based on the interface definition, which makes searching for a learner very difficult. Properties are characterized by (name; type; value) triples, and it is assumed that the names of the properties are known to the searcher [RLT97]. Both mechanisms do not support a learner who wants to include objects during runtime very well. Searches are executed at a syntactical, not at a semantical level. This means that a learner would have to use the CORBA Trading Service to find a search service, contact the CORBA Naming Service to retrieve the object reference, and invoke the operation by using DII.

Additional problems arise from different ORB implementations of different manufacturers. Although the CORBA specification is available, the manufacturers implement their products in an incompatible way to bind customers to their product [Coe01]. This makes the use of CORBA difficult across ORBs of different manufacturers. However, now CORBA specifies the General-Inter-ORB Protocol (GIOP) to achieve interoperability among different implementations of ORBs. CORBA compliant systems are to speak at least GIOP over TCP/IP, called Internet Inter-ORB Protocol (IIOP), but the systems can support further protocols.

One of the most important reasons why there is not, and probably will not be, a market for off-the-shelf reusable CORBA components are these different ORB implementations. Although the latter may adhere to the standard, they can achieve source level compatibility at the most, but not an interchangeability of binary components. Manufacturers have to offer source codes for their component implementations or compile and test their components not only for each target platform, but for each target ORB implementation. Although there is an inter-ORB protocol, different implementations of different manufacturers provide proprietary extensions to the object model, the language bindings, and the inter-ORB protocol [Mic96].

Another problem that arises when using CORBA is the complexity of software that has to be installed on a client machine. Even a thin client wanting to use CORBA will have to support an ORB, which may lead to higher costs of such devices owing to more complex hardware (memory, faster processors, etc.). In addition, CORBA does not use a single port on a machine like TCP/IP, but a huge number of different ports (approximately 100) that have to be administrated and that cause problems with firewalls [HG03].

3.3.2 Distributed Component Object Model (DCOM)

DCOM is not the work of a standardization committee, but a development of Microsoft Corporation. It is described, for example, in [TS02] and [GT00]. Although it is widely used, there is no official specification, but a draft of a specification for the *Component Object Model (COM)* from 1995 [Mic95]. In addition, a COM runtime module is provided that implements the basic services necessary to build further components in any programming language that can cope with the binary structure used. DCOM is the distributed counterpart to COM [Mic96]. In other words, it is a technology very similar to COM, but multiple machines may be involved. DCOM is shipped with the Microsoft Windows operating systems and works on millions of machines every day. There are also a couple of DCOM implementations for other operating systems [Mon97].

The development of *compound documents* marks the beginning of Microsoft's component architecture. These documents comprise building blocks of different formats like images, text, spreadsheets etc. Each part is directly associated with an application and can thus be directly edited in the compound document. The first technology to build compound documents was *Object Linking and Embedding (OLE)*, which was built on *Dynamic Data Exchange (DDE)* and used a message passing mechanism. It has been replaced by a more flexible version also called OLE (or OLE version 2), which is based on COM. The latter is a general mechanism for components to interact with each other. Although there was a coordination of the developments of the new OLE and COM in that times, COM provides much more functionalities than needed to implement OLE version 2. The overall organization of OLE and COM is shown in Figure 3.8. The latter also pictures ActiveX, which comprises everything covered by OLE and COM, but with some new features in addition.

Components in (D)COM are mostly executable programs (EXE files) or executable codes contained in a *dynamic link library (DLL)*. Remote DLLs are loaded into the same address space as the client and are called "In-Process-Servers". Communication is realized through function calls. "Out-of-Process-Servers" are typically executable programs that run in another process on the same machine as the client and communicate via interprocess communication, or they are running on a remote machine and can be accessed via DCOM protocols. If a DLL-based component is accessed remotely, a *surrogate* (program) is used to make it available over the network.

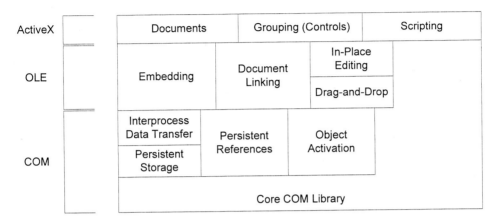

Figure 3.8: The general organization of ActiveX, OLE, and COM according to [TS02].

COM itself is also a library that is linked to a process [TS02]. COM components are only able to interact if they are running on the same machine (even in different processes). DCOM extends the environment to interact across different machines. The basic mechanisms to interact are the same as for COM. Thus, it is almost transparent to a developer if the component is accessed locally or remotely.

Microsoft's interface definition language (MIDL) is the counterpart to the OMG IDL of CORBA. The MIDL can be used to generate the binary interfaces of DCOM objects. Binary interfaces are programming language independent and are essentially tables that store pointers to the implementations of the methods that are part of the interface (this is known in C++ as *vtable*). In contrast to CORBA, a special mapping of IDL specifications for each programming language supported is not necessary as the interfaces have a binary format [TS02].

Active Directory [ALN00] is a service available since Windows 2000 Professional. It is a directory service that stores among other things information about components. The directory itself is placed on a central Domain Server that can be queried by all clients of the domain and is not a proper part of DCOM. This is why all clients can read the latest information of the components available [Off00].

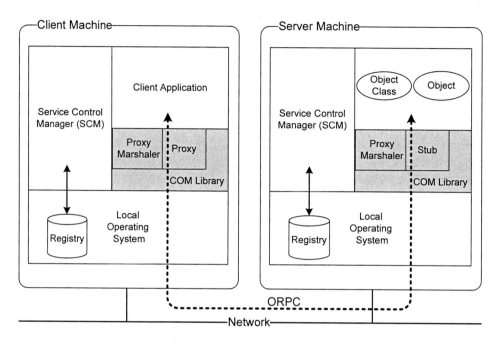

Figure 3.9: The overall architecture of DCOM according to [TS02].

DCOM adds to COM in particular the ability to support communication between objects over a network. To achieve this, supplementary services are added like security, scalability, and location transparency. The fundamental communication mechanism is the *Object Remote Procedure Call (ORPC)*, which is an object-oriented extension of the traditional RPC and designed to communicate with DCOM objects [CHY+97]. It uses the standard network protocols like TCP/IP and HTTP. Like a classic middleware, DCOM is layered between two components to handle the communication process, see Figure 3.9. This is achieved by means of an RPC channel that cannot be accessed by the client directly. Like in CORBA, a proxy is used on the client side (called stub in CORBA) that marshals the request and passes it to the server. On the server side, a stub (called skeleton in CORBA) receives the request, unmarshals the message, and passes the information to the object. Thus, DCOM replaces the local communication of COM with a communication across a network. Proxy and stub make the request look like a local one for both client and server [Mic96]. To invoke a DCOM object on a remote server, a client passes the (globally) unique identifier of the corresponding class of the component to its local *Service Control Manager (SCM)*. The SCM is itself a DCOM object that searches its registry to look up the host of the corresponding component. The identifier is then passed to the SCM of the server machine, which looks up the file of the identifier in its local registry. The SCM starts a new process and instantiates the new object. The binding information is returned to the client.

The dynamic invocation of objects is similar to the DII of CORBA and uses a special interface called IDispatch. DCOM is consequently not very suitable for a learner to add functionalities at runtime.

It is worth mentioning that DCOM does not form a complete distributed system. It always assumes the existence of external services. For example, the naming service is offered by the Active Directory service of Windows 2000 Professional. As a naming service is in general a part of a distributed system, portability to other platforms is difficult. It is obvious that, for example, Linux systems cannot use this naming service.

3.4 Message-Oriented Middleware

The techniques described in the previous subsections are mainly based on synchronous method invocations in their original versions, although more advanced implementations may also support asynchronous calls. The communication patterns of the basic systems are always similar to each other: a client invokes a method which is offered by a server. Afterwards, the client blocks processing until the server has processed the method and has returned an answer. The server can be selected statically or dynamically; this depends on the technique used. Message-oriented Middleware (MOM), which will be described in this subsection, provides more flexibility and asynchronous communication. First approaches to an asynchronous interaction have been implemented in enhanced forms of RPC and TP Monitors with queuing systems (e.g., Tuxedo[3]); MOM can be seen as a descendant of this special form of TP Monitor. The biggest problem that arises with the systems already explained (RPC, object brokers, etc.) is the fact that they have to be very robust against failures. If a server is not up and running when the messages arrive, the latter will be lost. MOM stores the messages in queues, and a server requests the next message if it is able to process it. Of course, MOM has to be very robust against failures, but not the individual server. Messages can carry an expiration date at which they are discarded if they are still in the queue [ACK+04].

Another difference to RPC and object brokers is the fact that the distinction between a server and a client is only conceptual. MOM is not able to recognize which part of the entire system acts as server and which one as client. This is an important difference to

---

[3]http://www.beasys.com

object-based middleware as well as to RPC and TP Monitors. For MOM, the partners just exchange messages and the semantics of these messages are also transparent for MOM.

The core of MOM consists of a queuing system providing an API that can be used to send, receive, or wait for messages. A client that sends a message to a queue does not block, but can continue processing. A message typically contains a name and may be bound to a special recipient. However, it is also possible that servers implementing the same functionality listen for messages arriving in the same queue. This enables the implementation of a load balancing or priority handling by MOM. A recipient that is ready to process a message invokes a method in MOM to retrieve the first message of the queue.

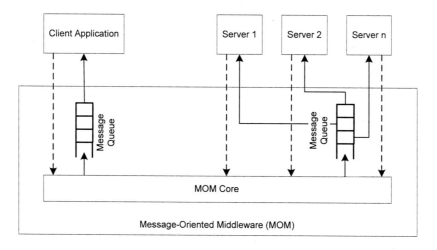

Figure 3.10: The overall architecture of MOM according to [ACK+04].

Some MOM systems provide a transactional queuing that is to ensure that a message sent to the queue is transmitted once and only once to the recipient, even if the MOM temporarily goes down. It also provides the concept of atomic units. A unit combines several messages; and its execution is fulfilled with the property all-or-nothing.

Several commercial MOM platforms exist, e.g., IBM WebSphereMQ (formerly known as MQ Series), Microsoft's MSMQ, and WebMethods Enterprise by Web Methods, to name just a few. CORBA also provides a messaging service. Most of the MOMs are compliant to the Java Message Service (JMS) API, which can be used by developers. A message in MOM is a structured data set that depends on the system used. In consequence, clients and servers that interact via MOM depend on one particular system. In the case of elearning functionalities (e.g., the search functionality), the respective component has to be able to handle messages for all kinds of systems learners might want to use; or, vice versa, a learner's client has to support several systems of different providers. In addition, the central character of the queuing system raises the question again where to offer the middleware and who is a trusted instance to offer this service. However, for the search service, the communication is easier now. If the client software is able to generate flexible messages and if a trusted MOM provider can be found for learners and providers of functionalities, learners are able to include different services by changing the format of the messages sent to the different systems.

3.5   Limitations of Conventional Middleware Approaches

The past subsections have described different techniques to build distributed systems and tried to show problems that appear if these techniques will be used to build a distributed elearning system that should be - at least in parts - maintained and configured by a learner. The small use case of integrating and calling a search component by a learner has illustrated how the remote functionality has to be included and invoked. Although the functionality of this search component is not very complex, it is sometimes impossible for a learner to integrate new functionalities at runtime. This subsection is to sum up the problems and point out additional problems showing up from a technical perspective. Web services as will be described in Chapter 3.6 are motivated at the respective scenarios to show how problems can be solved.

The overall finding is that conventional approaches bear a couple of problems that make them not easy to implement and even to use. Particularly in the field of elearning, where learners should be able to select distributed components at runtime, conventional approaches suffer from an easy handling and compatibility problems [Bir03].

The level of integrating functionalities is important for the choice of the technique since it is not possible to use approaches that have to be integrated at a programming language level or component level where learners have to compile systems after adding new components. This is the case for RPC-based systems, for TP Monitors, and even sometimes for CORBA and DCOM if dynamic models are not used. The level of integration of Web services is higher than the one in the conventional approaches already described. Web service are characterized as real services that shield all of their details concerning implementation and platforms they are based on.

Another big problem with conventional approaches is the fact that there is no obvious place to put the middleware since the basic intention is to place the middleware between the applications that have to interact [ACK+04]. Obviously, in case of a distributed elearning system, it is difficult to place a middleware since learners ought to be able to select the functionalities depending on their own preferences. Offering this flexibility to learners, the providers are not known at the time of implementing the client applications.

An installation of middleware systems on the client side would be a very challenging task for a learner without advanced information technology knowledge owing to the complex nature of these systems, e.g., because of security and transaction handling. In an elearning offering, as it is assumed in this thesis, there is neither a central instance nor an administrator to install and supervise a middleware system. This may be different in campus wide systems, but is not the case in an open system. Web services as will be described in the next chapter are installed on the providers' machines. The only thing a user of a service needs is a Web service client to use the services via common Internet protocols like HTTP. If the client is offered as a portal on the Web, a learner needs just a Web browser, which makes installing and maintaining easy.

Many technologies described above are not compatible with each other. That makes it necessary that all peers in the environment must use the same form of RPC, the same object model (CORBA, DCOM, etc.), or a unique form of messages. In consequence, the operating system is implicitly forced to the connected clients as most of them are not platform-independent, in particular in the case of DCOM. DCOM is used primarily on Windows machines [KB03], although there are some implementations for other operating systems. Apparently, the participants of a distributed elearning environment do not have agreed upon a special object model and not upon an operating system. Above, they are not able to agree on a certain message format. However, even if all users have agreed on using a CORBA system, problems may occur owing to the fact that CORBA implementations of different suppliers may be incompatible [Coe01], although GIOP ought to solve this problem. The situation is more difficult in open scenarios that should work across company boarders or for learners that work at home and should offer a plug-and-play integration of components. These problems can be solved because Web services are independent of platforms, of operating systems, and of programming languages and are not based on a protocol of a special company because the entire communication is based on XML and common Internet standards. Messages are transmitted using a standardized format and the Internet. With the open standards a plug-and-play integration of services at runtime can be achieved, as will be shown in the next chapters. It is also possible to integrate the existing techniques by means of Web services, see Figure 3.11.

EJB and Java RMI have been mentioned in the previous subsections. As programming-language dependent approaches they force the developer of components to use Java. Web services, on the other hand, can be written in any programming language.

In the communication processes of systems that are not based on Web services, frontiers of companies become a big problem as platforms may be shielded by firewalls. An open elearning platform also serves company employees to do training on the job. The usage of protocols like CORBA to communicate with elearning providers outside the company boarders may cause errors because of problems resulting from closed ports etc. because firewalls are widely used today. As described above, CORBA uses about 100 ports. Using DCOM through firewalls causes trouble because it dynamically allocates one port per process (configurable through the registry), and requires in addition the ports for UDP and TCP to be opened. To use DCOM via port 80 and enable a use with firewalls, Tunneling TCP/IP as the underlying transport protocol can be used. However, this is not very reliable, does not work through all firewalls, and introduces additional limitations (e.g., lack of callback support) [Was02]. By opening further ports, security guidelines may be disregarded. A direct connection of two peers is not possible either, if the company uses a proxy. The proxy problems can be solved, but the performance will deteriorate. Web services do not need additional ports as their communication is based on transport protocols which are already in use (in particular HTTP). [Jon02a] remarks that the advantage of using an open HTTP port disappears in the moment the first virus is propagated through a request or response of a Web service call or through additional files transported with these messages. Other authors like [KKS+03] also mention similar security problems.

In conclusion, RPC and TP Monitors can only be used by developers to realize distributed systems. DCOM and CORBA can be used in local area networks with little heterogeneity and a central administration. Traditional MOM implementations face compatibility problems and are suitable within local area networks. Web services as a special form of message-oriented technology are the best option in open environments across the Internet, where a lot of heterogeneity exists (see Chapter 3.6).

3.6 Web Services

Sometimes Web services are referred to as a "revolution" in computing. However, as will be shown in this subsection, the concepts of Web services are not new and, therefore, can better be called an evolution rather than a revolution [Ley03]. In fact, there are several similarities to the techniques already described, in particular to RPC, CORBA, and the basic idea of software components. Web services represent an important approach to realize a *service-oriented architecture* (SOA), an abstract architectural concept. People

often think of Web services and SOA as though they were one, but Web services are
only one possibility to build a service-oriented architecture [WCL05]. The W3C standardization organization[4] defines a service-oriented architecture as "a set of components
which can be invoked, and whose interface descriptions can be published and discovered"
[BH03a]. This definition is very broad and also encompasses, for example, DCOM and
CORBA components. In consequence, the remainder of this thesis does not use the term
SOA to emphasize the special technology used to implement a service-oriented elearning
environment.

[Ley03] describes a Web service as a *virtual component* because it can be implemented in
many different ways, for example, by a real component or by any other piece of executable
code (see Figure 3.11). However, this description of a Web service is very imprecise, and
many other definitions existing in the literature vary considerably. This is why Chapter
3.6.1 gives a precise definition of the phrase *Web service* and how it is understood in this
thesis.

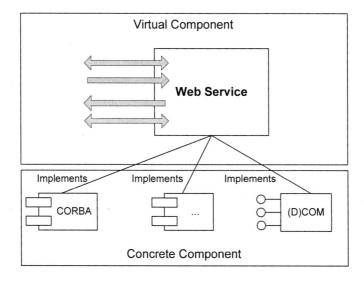

Figure 3.11: A Web service as a virtual component according to [Ley03].

So far, Web services play an important part in the business-to-business (B2B) area because
they enable an integration of applications more rapidly, easily, and with less costs than
in the models described before. Even though the early use of Web services has been
peer-wise and ad hoc, the concept still addresses the complete problem of program-to-

[4]http://www.w3c.org

program communication, which includes describing, publishing, and finding interfaces [Kre01b]. In the meantime, the use of services has grown, and more dynamic models for accessing and binding services have evolved [KKS+03]. Nowadays, Web services are obtaining a growing importance even in the business-to-consumer (B2C) area, a major field for elearning applications.

3.6.1 Definition and Characteristics

The scientific literature offers numerous definitions for Web services. They range from very generic and all-inclusive ones to very specific and restrictive definitions [ACK+04]. Not even do different working-groups of the W3C standardization organization use the same definition for Web services. This chapter will present some of the current definitions and will have a closer look at them to show how widely spread they are. At the end of this chapter, a unified definition will be presented to make the view of Web services clear on which this thesis is based.

Very general definitions describe Web services as applications that can be accessed by other applications over the Web. The following one, found in [CT03], can be regarded as a good example:

> "A Web Service is a piece of business logic, located somewhere on the Internet, that is accessible through standard-based Internet protocols such as SMTP or HTTP."

This very open definition implies that everything that uses standard Internet protocols is a Web service. This also includes, e.g., CGI scripts. The definition says that a Web service must be "a piece of business logic", but a definition for the latter is not given. Hence, the differentiation from normal Web sites is very imprecise as they can also be accessed via HTTP. Other definitions concentrate on a special characteristic of Web services. [Kre01b] gives such a definition, reducing a Web service to its interface:

> "A Web service is an interface that describes a collection of operations that are network-accessible through standardized XML messaging ... The interface hides the details of the implementation details of the service..."

This definition emphasizes the interface, but does not focus on the application itself. However, as the interface on its own does not provide any service functionality from which a consumer could benefit, this definition is too specific on the one hand and incomplete on the other hand. In contrast to the first definition, which does not explain at all how communication and interaction is brought about, the second one puts at least an emphasis on encapsulation and on XML messaging. Because of the missing functionality and the imprecise description of what network-accessible means, the definition has to be improved. The definition given by the *W3C Web Services Architecture Working Group* in [ABF+04] describes Web services as:

> "a software system identified by a URI, whose public interfaces and bind-
> ings are defined and described using XML. Its definition can be discovered
> by other software systems. These systems may then interact with the Web
> service in a manner prescribed by its definition, using XML-based messages
> conveyed by Internet protocols."

This definition describes an entire software system as a Web service. Additionally, it includes standardized mechanisms and protocols to be used to define, describe, and discover the service and thus explains how Web services can be accessed. Furthermore, it mentions the unique address (URI, Unified Resource Locater [BFM98]) of the service and abstracts from underlying protocols to manage the transport of the messages. [ACK+04] concludes from this definition that Web services are components that can be integrated into a more complex distributed application, which is consistent with the perception of classic software components. This interpretation only makes sense when understanding reusing functionality as a black box which can be plugged to software systems to extend their functionality. In addition, several ideas based on these two concepts are comparable, for example, using a repository and regarding components and Web services as self-describing. However, one of the major differences between the concepts is that components are normally designed to be downloaded or bought by a software developer, but Web services are intended to be used only remotely. Another difference is the way of how the applications communicate with each other. Web services are message-based; software components can use an event-based pattern, remote method calls, or messages to communicate [KB03].

In contrast to the definition of the W3C mentioned above, another narrower definition by the same W3C working group is given in [BHM+04]. This one includes explicitly named XML standards (SOAP and WSDL), but does not cover the discovery of the services. It does not even include the unique address of the service:

> "A Web service is a software system designed to support interoperable
> machine-to-machine interaction over a network. It has an interface described
> in a machine-processable format (specifically WSDL). Other systems interact

with the Web service in a manner prescribed by its description using SOAP
messages, typically conveyed using HTTP with an XML serialization in conjunction with other Web-related standards."

As the second definition of the W3C has a scope that is too narrow because it includes
particular standards, this thesis also uses the first W3C definition given in [ABF+04].
However, as WSDL, SOAP, and UDDI are commonly used in the implementation of
Web services today, they will be used in the following as well. They will not be used
in the definition of Web services to be open for additional developments in future. In
conclusion, a Web service as used and understood throughout this thesis is defined as
follows [ABF+04]:

"A Web service is a software system identified by a URI, whose public
interfaces and bindings are defined and described using XML. Its definition
can be discovered by other software systems. These systems may then interact
with the Web service in a manner prescribed by its definition, using XML-
based messages conveyed by Internet protocols."

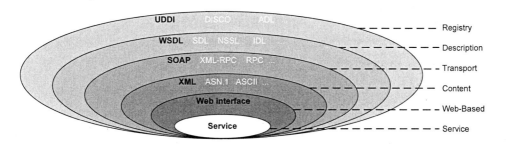

Figure 3.12: Step-wise definition of a Web service according to [Jec04].

[Jec04] provides an overview of how the different techniques and services are related. Figure 3.12 shows the model in which a software system offers a service, as defined in the
classical sense. This service is extended by an additional interface to offer its functionalities via the World Wide Web. The typical hardware infrastructure and the Internet
protocols like TCP/IP and HTTP alone are indispensable to invoke the service. Based
on these fundamental layers, several additional ones increase the interoperability of the
service. Consequently, it is easier for the consumer to replace services by other ones if
necessary.

XML adds to the Web-accessible service a layer of standardization in form of a meta format. Both the request of the service and the response of the respective execution are described by using XML. XML does not define the appearance of specific communication messages, but enables the service provider to define the appearance of messages. XML is, certainly, not the only way of defining the format of messages. Earlier used methods like ASN.1 (Abstract Syntax Notation One [ASN02]) or EDI (Electronic Data Interchange [EDI05]) can achieve a similar effect, but are not as widely used as XML.

As a result of the definitions of the messages in an XML format, XML should obviously also be used in the communication process. One approach for this is the already-described remote procedure call (RPC), which can use XML messages for communication as a special characteristic. In this form, the RPC is called XML-RPC [5]. A further development resulting from the XML-RPC is the Simple Object Access Protocol (SOAP [GHM+03]), which also uses XML-encoded messages for non-proprietary messages. Now, after the consequent usage of XML in these two layers, the definition constitutes services offered on the Web and use standardized mechanisms for communication with coordinated content in a coordinated format.

However, service consumers are not able to call up a service because they do not know how the messages for the communication process have to look like. To solve this problem, the Web Service Description Language (WSDL [CCM+01]), developed by Microsoft and IBM, provides a mechanism to describe Web services by means of their offerings, handling, parameters etc. WSDL is comparable to the already-mentioned IDL of CORBA and to other XML languages like the Network Accessible Service Specification Language (NASSL [CWD00]) or the Service Definition Language (SDL, formerly known as Service Contract Language (SCL) from Microsoft), which are not as widely used as WSDL or obsolete today. WSDL consolidates concepts found in NASSL, SCL, and SDL.

So far, consumers of Web services are only able to use services they know because there is no registry which helps them to find services. To offer an additional search mechanism on the Web, the Universal Service Description, Discovery and Integration (UDDI [CHR04]) is implementing a corresponding registry service, an outcome of the former protocols DISCO (Discovery of Web Services) and ADS (Advertisement and Discovery of Services [NCW00]).

Not all of the above-mentioned protocols and descriptions must be realized in a technical implementation of a Web service architecture. However, as SOAP, WSDL, and UDDI are the common protocols today, the Web services developed throughout this work use these protocols to enable a maximum flexibility and exchangeability.

---

[5]http://www.xml-rpc.org/spec

Two main characteristics of Web services [FFE+03] directly result from their definition. Web services are based on standard Internet protocols which have been existing and successfully operating for a long time. These protocols include HTTP and TCP/IP, to name just a few. In addition, Web services are XML-based and platform-independent. Unlike other messages used in DCOM or IIOP, these messages are neither strongly typed, nor come in binary format; instead, they are coded in an extensible and generic format controlled by a standardization organization. Conventional middleware platforms determine the type system by the underlying platform (e.g., CORBA). The use of XML also enables a cross-platform communication no matter what kind of programming languages and operating systems are used. Like the majority of distributed systems, Web services are message-based and support both asynchronous and synchronous communication. In contrast to the bulk of distributed systems, Web services make use of two interaction patterns to send and receive messages. The first one is to invoke an RPC on the server by passing the necessary information in the request; the second one is a simple document exchange like passing orders in ecommerce applications. No matter what type of interaction pattern and what type of communication is used, Web services are stateless, having no actual channel between the client and the server. Although there may be a session management through URLs, cookies, etc., all state information must be passed to the Web service in each request. Exceptions to this occur if an unusual transport protocol is used. In consequence, this means that there is usually no information stored in memory of the server machine between requests. This has impacts on the implementation of services and clients, but has the advantage that services can be exchanged at runtime without losing any information.

The combination of passing documents that are based on XML standards within an asynchronous communication model and the possibility of an easy binding to the service at runtime makes Web services loosely coupled. The passing of entire documents (including, for example, all information about a learner) in contrast to single data sets (e.g., the name of the learner) implies that Web services are often implemented in a coarse grained style.

Recalling the example of the search for content in a distributed learning environment, Figure 3.13 pictures the overall architecture to use Web services for this purpose. As it has been sketched above and it will be explained in more detail in the following chapters, the architecture is typically centered around the basic concepts of SOAP, WSDL, and UDDI as well as of the basic roles of a client and a provider. If a client application is aware of the search functionality of a Web service provider, for example, service provider 2, the service is called by sending a SOAP message via HTTP and TCP/IP to the server of provider 2. Provider 2 extracts the necessary information from the message and executes the search functionality. The response of the server is also sent as a SOAP message to

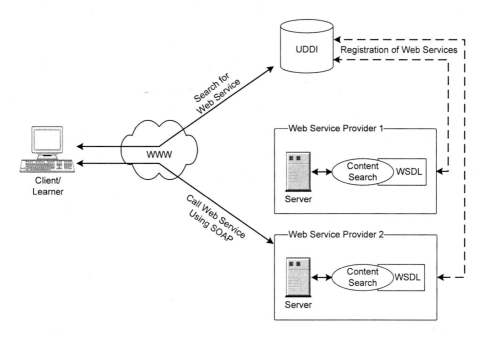

Figure 3.13: Web services roles.

the client machine. The structure of the SOAP message is described in the WSDL file
and the client is able to interpret this description to form an adequate message.

In a more dynamic and loosely coupled scenario, the client does not include a static
pointer to a predefined service. Instead, the user of the client application first has to
look up available content search services by calling the UDDI directory. This directory
stores information about the various services that have to be registered by the respective
providers, i.e., two content search services of two different providers in the example of
Figure 3.13. By choosing one of the services, the learner obtains a reference to the WSDL
document of the services that is needed to call the service from the client application.
The service and the transmission of the response message is invoked again by means of
SOAP. The entire procedure will be explained in the following in more detail and from a
more technical perspective.

3.6.2 Technical Aspects

The purpose of Web services is to provide a software functionality to be accessed remotely. Three roles of a Web service scenario can be deduced directly from the definition of a Web service because the interactions in the field of Web services include publishing, discovery, and the use of services. The first role is the service provider, who is the *owner* of the service. On the one hand, this is the *implementor* of the service. On the other hand, this is the platform that hosts the service. The interpretation of the term depends on the perspective of the description. Owner or implementor are terms from the business area, whereas *host* reflects a more technical view. The second role involved is the requestor of the service. This is the business which requires a certain functionality, or, in technical terms, the application that is looking for and invoking or initiating an interaction with a service. In the following, this application is called client or consumer application. The third role involved is the service registry. It offers a searchable directory where service providers publish their descriptions to be found afterwards by service requestors. The three steps of publishing, finding, and binding as shown in Figure 3.14 are described in more detail in the following. The interplay of the actions has already been mentioned briefly in Chapter 3.6.1.

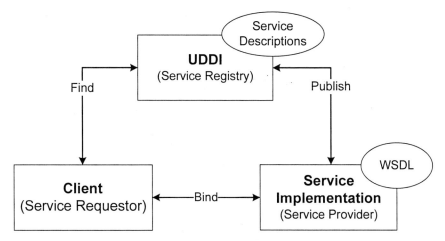

Figure 3.14: The Web services triangle.

- **Publishing:** in order to be accessible, a Web service must carry a description of its interfaces. For example, WSDL is used for this purpose. The publication of a Web service includes the production of the service description and its publishing as well as storing the service implementation on a network accessible server. Publication can be done directly by sending the descriptions to partners or by registering the service to a public directory. For example, this can be the UDDI registry, which stores additional information about Web services.

- **Discovery:** often, service requestors do not know the addresses of certain services providing the desired functionalities. Besides, they do not know how to invoke the services even if they know their URIs. To use a service, a requestor has to acquire the service description first. Depending on the manner of how the description was published, a requestor can get the description from a local archive or cache (e.g., in direct publishing) or from a special registry. If a registry is used, a requestor has to retrieve the description using a look-up mechanism to query the registry. Such a look-up mechanism is provided by UDDI, which stores pointers to WSDL documents. The information they retrieve from the directory suffices to bind the client to a service and use it [Ley03].

- **Binding:** after acquiring the service description, a requestor needs to process the WSDL document to be able to find the necessary binding information in order to use the service. This information contains data to locate, contact, and invoke the service.

Each of the activities is assisted by at least one of the XML standards, namely WSDL, SOAP, and UDDI, which will be described in detail in the following. The IMS has already specified guidelines for the use of general Web-service technologies in the field of elearning [IMS05a]. These guidelines include particularly WSDL 1.1, although version 2.0 is nearly ready for standardization. WSDL 2.0 is less complex and less powerful than WSDL 1.1 [WCL05] and has changes in its naming concept. Currently, WSDL 1.1 is widely adopted in industry and is strongly supported by development tools. It remains questionable if WSDL 2.0 replaces WSDL 1.1 completely in future [WCL05]. Owing to these reasons, WSDL 1.1 will also be used to realize LearnServe service descriptions. The IMS also specifies the use of SOAP 1.1. However, this is only a *W3C Note*. As the current SOAP 1.2 recommendation clarifies protocol bindings and the XML encoding, SOAP 1.2 will be used in the following.

WSDL: Web Service Description Language

As already mentioned above, WSDL [CCM+01] pursues a similar goal like IDLs in conventional middleware do and enables the separation of the implementation and the description of a service. Nevertheless, WSDL has to cover more information than conventional IDLs because IDLs are always linked to a concrete platform. The mechanisms to access a service using a conventional approach are always the same, and there is no need to describe the corresponding techniques in a conventional IDL. Merely the name and the signature (input and output parameters) of a service are indispensable key features. In contrast, WSDL has to cover also protocols to be used to invoke a service. This results from the fact that SOAP supports bindings to different transport protocols. Apart from the protocols, the requestor of a service needs to know the address of a service. In traditional middleware systems, the requestor does not have to bother about the address since the middleware coordinates the communication and activations. The lack of a common middleware in the field of Web services makes it necessary to define the location of a service explicitly [ACK+04]. WSDL specifications are divided into an abstract and a concrete part (see

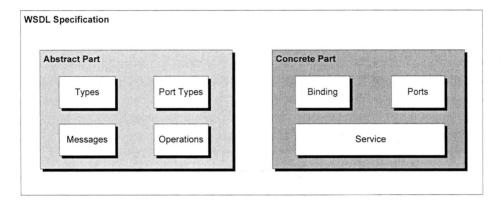

Figure 3.15: WSDL: abstract and concrete part.

Figure 3.15), and each part can be stored in a different file. If this is the case, the abstract part has to be imported into the document of the concrete definitions. The abstract part is conceptually comparable to the definitions of conventional IDLs, whereas the concrete part includes information about XML encoding, protocol binding, and a definition of a concrete service. The abstract part consists of the following elements:

- **Types:** to interpret the data being exchanged between a service and a requestor, WSDL demands a type system. By default, it uses the same one as XML Schema, but it can use a different one if necessary.

- **Messages**: messages are used in the field of Web services for communication. The message definition in WSDL represents the data that is exchanged in an individual logical transmission in an abstract way. WSDL defines a message as a typed document that consists of several parts, each of them having a name and a data type. The data type can be specified if it differs from the standard types.

- **Operations:** WSDL knows four basic operations: one-way, request-response, solicit-response, and notification. Synchronous interactions use request-response and solicit-response, where two messages are passed. Asynchronous interactions use only one message and use one-way and notification patterns.

- **Port types:** port types form groups of several operations that belong logically to each other into a port type.

So far, the definitions still lack a concrete binding, an encoding, and a specific service. Such information belongs to the concrete part of the WSDL interface definition.

- **Binding:** for a given port type, the binding specifies the message encoding and protocol binding for all messages and operations of it. For example, this includes input and output parameters in an RPC style operation or the documents for a document style operation. Moreover, it could also specify that the SOAP and HTTP protocols are used because WSDL allows different protocols than these.

- **Ports:** a port (also called EndPoint) defines the combination of the binding and a network address. Specified by a URI, the port type can be accessed at this address.

- **Services:** a service is a logical group of ports belonging together.

SOAP: Simple Object Access Protocol

The SOAP specification [GHM+03] defines how messages can be structured and typed to be exchanged between peers. It is a lightweight protocol intended for exchanging structured information in a decentralized, distributed environment. SOAP messages are used in the field of Web services as a fundamental technique for interactions. SOAP uses XML to build the messages and is a stateless and one-way protocol that does not care about the semantics of the information the messages carry. To employ SOAP for more complex interaction patterns, e.g., synchronous communication, it has to be connected to an underlying middleware or protocol that is able to provide these additional properties [ACK+04].

SOAP messages are used in the form of an *envelope*, which carries the information sent between the peers. The envelope is subdivided into two parts, an optional *header* and a mandatory *body*, as shown in Figure 3.16. Both header and body can contain subparts in the form of header and body blocks. The body encloses the information a sender wants to transmit to a receiver. Additional information for processing or further actions is kept

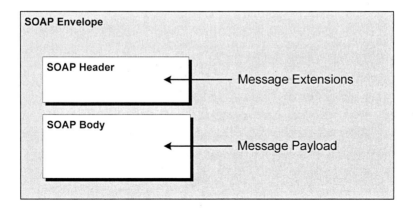

Figure 3.16: The SOAP message syntax.

in the header. A SOAP message has a sender and an ultimate receiver. SOAP even knows intermediaries, called *nodes*, which are able to receive a message, process it (e.g., removing blocks, performing actions) and send it to another receiver. The intermediary is responsible for analyzing and processing incoming messages. Information for nodes is specified in the header of the SOAP message. This information may include a role which defines certain instructions for a node to process the message.

No further structure is required in the header or body block. However, patterns that are commonly used to construct header and body blocks depending on the interaction and encoding style have to be taken into consideration. Interaction styles include the *RPC style* and the *document style*. The document style is to send documents from one peer to another. Both peers have agreed on the structure of that document, which is transported in the SOAP message. In the RPC style interaction, the partners have to agree about the signature of the method called. One message carrying the name and the input parameters in the body is used to invoke the method. A second message carries the return values in the body to the requestor. All additional information, e.g., transaction information, goes into the headers of the messages. The encoding rules specify how entities and data structures are transformed to XML. For this purpose, SOAP defines a special encoding called *SOAP encoding* that specifies how simple data types (integer, string, etc.) and complex data types (arrays, structures, etc.) can be serialized into XML. However, as this encoding is not mandatory, peers are able to agree upon a different encoding.

So far, the ultimate receiver has not been addressed. SOAP itself does not contain the address of that peer, but uses the methods of transport protocols to be chosen for communication between the peers. Although HTTP and SMTP are currently used, SOAP does not prescribe transport protocols. The specification of the protocol is called binding and defines how a message is wrapped within a transport protocol and how it is treated using the primitives of this transport protocol [ACK+04]. For example, for HTTP the SOAP message is included into the HTTP request, and the URL of the ultimate receiver describes the final destination of the message. The HTTP request is sent in form of a HTTP-post message to the server that answers (if necessary) sending a SOAP message wrapped into a HTTP response. In fact, the use of SOAP and HTTP is nowadays very common on the Web.

Additions to the SOAP specification make the handling of binary files, e.g., images or movies, in SOAP messages easier. Although these files can also be included in the SOAP body, the overhead for encoding the data to an acceptable XML representation is high. This is why the SOAP attachment specification represents an abstract model for SOAP attachments. Details are omitted and can be found in [NR04].

UDDI: Universal Description Discovery and Integration
To be employed, Web services have to be found by users. Two basic scenarios that vary on the time of demand can be distinguished in the discovery process of Web services. At development-time implementors are interested to find services to be used with and integrated in a certain application that ought to use a special service. On the other hand, at runtime, clients should be able to search for functionalities offered by services that implement a certain interface and find references for a dynamic binding of these services. To describe and discover Web services and enable these possibilities, UDDI [CHR04] specifies a framework that consists of data structures and APIs for publishing and searching for service descriptions in a registry. UDDI APIs can be accessed as a Web service because they are specified in WSDL with SOAP bindings, too. UDDI registries can be publicly accessible or offered as private registries only available for a closed community (e.g., in an Intranet). Public registries are sometimes implemented as Universal Business Registry (UBR [Ste04]), representing a storage for publicly available services. UBRs are hosted by a few companies (e.g., IBM and Microsoft) and are observed by the OASIS organization. UBRs fulfill the rules defined by UDDI and must keep their data synchronized with other UBRs.

Information kept in the UDDI registry is subdivided into different categories that are often compared to those of the telephone directory [ACK+04]. White pages contain information about details of the company offering the service. Besides, white pages include descriptions of services to provide the ability to search for services a special organization is offering. Yellow pages carry classifications of both companies and Web services according to taxonomies. They enable a search for services based on categories they belong to. The taxonomies can be either standardized or user defined. Green pages cover technical information about Web services and specify how they can be invoked. These descriptions are just referenced and typically stored outside of UDDI. Table 3.1 gives a rough overview of the information offered by each category[6].

Table 3.1: UDDI categories.

Information in UDDI registry		
White Pages	**Yellow Pages**	**Green Pages**
- business name	- services and products index	- ebusiness rules
- contact information	- industry codes	- service description
- human readable description	- geographic index	- application invocation
- identifiers (DUNS, tax ID, etc.)		- data binding

UDDI uses a set of complex data structures to store information. These data structures are subdivided into four main entities and are shown in Figure 3.17.

- **businessEntity:** describes the organization that offers the Web service. It includes name, address and further contact information.

- **businessServices:** cover a group of related Web services provided by a special organization that is stored in the businessEntity. A businessService always belongs to exactly one businessEntry and provides one kind of service (e.g., tracking service), which is offered with different technical characteristics.

- **bindingTemplate:** covers technical information to invoke a special Web service like the address and further detailed information describing service properties (like the references to tModels).

- **tModels:** the key information about a service is the reference to a tModel (short form for technical model), which can be used in a UDDI environment both as a technical fingerprint of a service and as a namespace identifier. A tModel can represent anything that can be written in any language (even in natural language). However, as they describe Web services, tModels in general reference WSDL documents. This service description is stored in a document outside the registry to which the tModel points. A tModel published within the registry is assigned a unique key that can be referenced by other UDDI entries. The underlying idea is the possibility that several

---

[6]DUNS, the Dun and Bradstreet Number, is a worldwide unique identifier for companies.

Web services with a comparable functionality can reference the same tModel. This enables a dynamic binding of the client, see Chapter 3.6.4, because the client must merely implement a standard interface for the group of services of this tModel. Additionally, the tModel is able to carry further classification information to be defined in the tModel.

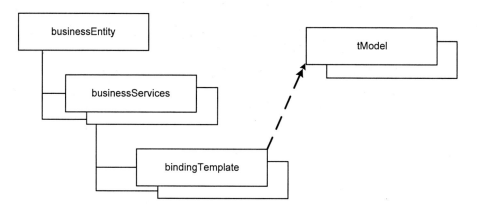

Figure 3.17: The main UDDI data structures.

Another data structure is the publisherAssertion that stores information about business connections. Users can access the UDDI registry entries by using the UDDI APIs. Communication with the UDDI registry is typically realized by applying XML documents in combination with SOAP. To achieve this, UDDI specifies the format of the documents to be used in request/response interactions. Three types of users can be distinguished: service providers publishing services, requestors searching for services, and other registries that want to exchange information. UDDI offers six sets of APIs for these users:

- **UDDI Inquiry:** this API includes operations to query the data using criteria and operations to provide information about entries stored in the registry. Two kinds of queries can be distinguished. On the one hand, Browser-queries enable a high-level search. On the other hand, Drill-Down-queries allow a more detailed return of results if an identifier for a certain service is already known.

- **UDDI Publication:** service providers use this API to register, update, and delete information in the registry. Each new entry is assigned a unique key.

- **UDDI Security:** the security API is employed to authenticate and authorize users.

- **UDDI Custody and ownershipTransfer:** these APIs enable a modification of registry entries and the exchange of data between different UDDI nodes.

- **UDDI Subscription:** this API monitors changes in the registry.

- **UDDI Replication:** the replication mechanism is used to synchronize UDDI nodes.

Most interestingly, the UDDI Inquiry API is kept very simple and does not provide the power a query language like the one SQL provides. It defines about 25 queries and 15 response documents. In particular, it does not allow joins [KKS+03]. Several proposals exist to extend the search abilities of UDDI, but they are not part of the standard itself. One of these extensions is also part of this work and is described in Chapter 5.1. Another problem is the fact that information about services is keyed in by human beings. That is why attributes are sometimes misunderstood, which leads to poor query results [ACK+04].

The main advantage of UDDI is its ability of coping with changes in other standards as it does not overlap in particular with WSDL. WSDL definitions are registered in tModels and point to the corresponding WSDL document using the UDDI bindingTemplate. Any changes in WSDL do not influence UDDI. In order to tie UDDI and WSDL together, the UDDI-initiative has published a best practices guide [CER01] which explains how WSDL ought to be used in combination with UDDI.

3.6.3   General Requirements

From a consumer perspective a Web service can be seen as a black box that published its interfaces, but the internal architecture and implementation are hidden and do not matter to the consumer. However, the conceptual model of a Web service implementation and the server of the Web service provider always involve some core software components no matter what kind of functionality the Web service offers. Figure 3.18 shows the process of consuming a Web service. Each step of this process and the responsibilities of the components involved are explained next (see [FFE+03]).

To invoke a service, a consumer application must be connected to the network and must be able to send SOAP messages via the transport protocol as defined by the service provider. The consumer marshals a service invocation into a SOAP message and sends it to the address of the Web service. Typically, this is done via HTTP, but services can use other protocols as already mentioned before. First, a request is received by a *Listener*. Often the

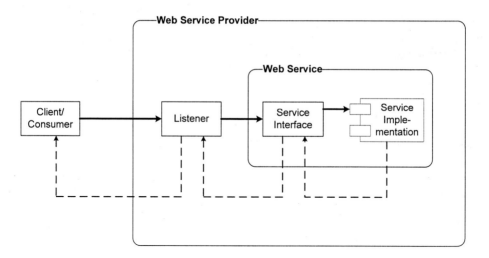

Figure 3.18: A client consuming a Web service according to [FFE+03].

Listener is a Web server like the Apache HTTP Server[7] and is responsible for listening and accepting incoming messages. When the message arrives, the Listener figures out which service has been called. If the SOAP message uses HTTP, the Listener reads the HTTP header within the message to gain the information about the service requested. It removes the HTTP information from the message that is afterwards forwarded as an XML message (i.e., the initial SOAP message) to the *Service Interface.*

The Service Interface consists of two parts, a SOAP implementation and the WSDL description, which is mentioned at this point for the sake of completeness. The SOAP implementation offers the payload of the message in form of XML or even in form of variables depending on the implementation of the provider.

The *Service Implementation* is a set of classes or functions that implement the business logic of the service. These can be, for example, components that have initially not been written to be consumed as a Web service like pictured in Figure 3.11, or a code that has been written specifically for this Web service. In either case the Service Interface determines which function or method must be called to invoke the service. In addition, it has to pass the deserialized parameters within this invocation.

The response of the Service Implementation (shown as dotted lines) takes the way vice versa. First, it is passed to the Service Interface, which is now responsible for wrapping

---

[7]http://www.apache.org

the response into a SOAP message. The SOAP message is sent to the Listener (or Web server) that adds HTTP headers and sends the response back to the client.

3.6.4 Selection of Web Services

Building a system on the idea of a collection of Web services basically needs to combine a variety of services in order to enable and provide the functionality of a comparable centralized application. The reason for this is the fact that a Web service normally has a clearly defined, limited functionality. This kind of Web service is called *atomic*, a composition of several Web services is called *complex*.

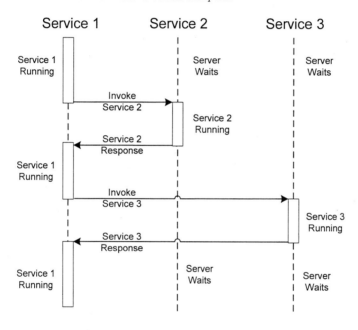

Figure 3.19: Static Web service composition and selection.

The simplest scenario for a Web service selection and composition is shown in Figure 3.19. Three servers provide different services, i.e., the complex Service 1 offers the functionality provided by Service 1 itself and the functionalities provided by the atomic Service 2 and the atomic Service 3. At development time of Service 1, the implementor included the functionalities of Services 2 and 3 because these services were the predefined services that had to be included in the overall processing. The addresses of the services are hard-coded in the source code of Service 1 and no additional discovery of services is needed at runtime.

At runtime, there is only a binding to the integrated services, which are called afterwards and which return their responses after processing to Service 1. Coordination and the dataflow is implemented in Service 1 by means of conventional programming languages.

From a technical perspective, complex Web services composed of atomic ones call each other by using the URI of a follow-up service at the moment that service is needed. A flexible exchange is in this model not possible because the URIs of the services are hard-coded. If one of the included Web services is not reachable or available at the moment of the call, the entire process is disturbed and fails in the worst case, which depends on the implementation of Service 1. Since this is unacceptable in all those cases an included service is not unique, a more dynamic form of service selection would solve the problem. In this case, services are not called directly; instead, a technical description of the required service is requested first. The underlying service platform needs to select the appropriate services by using the information available in the UDDI directory. Accordingly, the use of tModels gives the opportunity to select a service at runtime if several services use the same tModel [KKS+03, ACK+04].

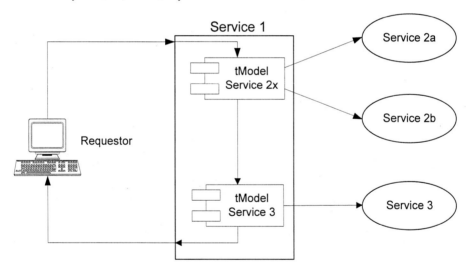

Figure 3.20: Dynamic call using tModels according to [KKS+03].

Figure 3.20 shows a sample dynamic service call of Service 1. The requestor calls Service 1, which here consists of two activities to simplify matters: the Service 2 and the Service 3 thereafter. Both activities themselves are implemented as Web services. UDDI uses the same tModel for services with the same semantics; as a result, Services 2a and 2b are assigned to the same tModel "Service 2x". Web service 1 just calls tModel "Service

2x", and the service platform calls the assigned Web services. Upon completion, the requestor selects one of the assigned Services 2x and has afterwards to use Service 3. This is realized by calling tModel "Service 3" from Web Service 1. Since there is only one Service 3 registered, only that one can be used (and is thus a problem if it is not reachable).

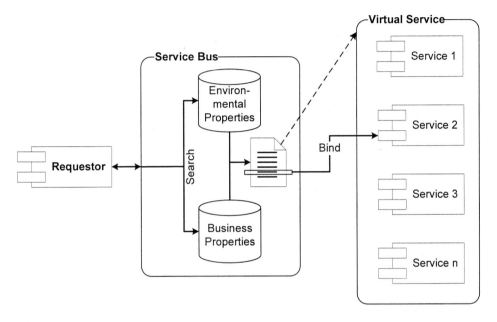

Figure 3.21: Dynamic selection with a service bus according to [Ley03].

A similar idea of a dynamic selection of services is given by [Ley03], who uses a *service bus* to choose services for a given requestor. As shown in Figure 3.21, the underlying idea is that a requestor sends the necessary information about the desired functionality to the service bus. This includes both the business goals and the policies of the requestor. This information is used to derive a set of matching services offered by various providers. For the requestor, all services are equivalent, i.e., the set of qualified services represents a *virtual service* described originally by the requestor. The service bus selects a service for the requestor. This choice can depend, for example, on the workload and response time of the individual provider. The service bus binds to the service, passes the request to the provider, and invokes the service. The response is delivered to the original requestor.

The dynamic selection of services has several advantages over a static one. Indeed, the availability of complex services no longer depends on the availability of each single service in a chain of services if more than one service for a required functionality exists. A dynamic choice enables the system to call the accessible services and call only these, no matter which service might have crashed. In addition, the system can call more than one service of the group of identical services. The result of the fastest execution is taken to continue the execution of the process. Of course, this generates unnecessary network traffic and workload on the servers.

Although a flexible approach has been shown to exchange Web services at runtime, up to now only linear models have been used to combine services. In many circumstances, it might be helpful to have a choice between different services to be included. An XML language to support these definitions will be presented in the next subsection. From a developer's perspective, these choices are still static since all possible execution paths have to be defined at development time of the entire process. However, the possibility of selecting services according to the tModel approach or the use of a service bus are still feasible.

3.6.5 Web Services Orchestration

The combination of SOAP, WSDL, and UDDI for Web services provides a mechanism to offer and use functionalities of a system via a standardized, system-independent interface. The invocations are independent of each other and stateless. To build processes that use several Web services across many partners and run for a broader period, the existing framework has to be extended [BCC+02, BDF+02]. In particular, languages for the composition of (atomic) Web services to bigger (complex) Web services are missing in this Web services stack as well as languages to coordinate the flow of the activities and transactions.

Two basic models have to be created when Web services are composed. On the one hand, this is the control flow model that describes the order of the invocation of the (atomic) Web services. On the other hand, a data flow model has to be created to show how data is passed between the partners. Several languages exist in the area of business-process and workflow modeling that could also be used in the area of Web services. Statecharts [BDF+01], Petri nets [Rei01], and the π-calculus [MPW92] process algebra which has inspired modern languages such as XLANG and BPEL4WS (see below) are important in this field. Several other languages like Activity Hierarchies (see, e.g., Little-JIL [CSM+00]), Rule-based Orchestration (see, e.g., [KLR+95]) or Event-Driven-Process Chains (EPC [Sch98]) exist.

IBM has introduced the Web Service Flow Language (WSFL [Ley01]) for a composition of complex services. The entire process is modeled as a directed graph in which each activity is implemented as a Web service. Control flows are illustrated as arrows and can use additional rules, data flows are represented by dashed arrows. Each activity is represented by a node of the graph. The graph is transformed into an XML representation. One representation is the *flow model* that describes activities, additional information like the condition to start the process, the order of the activities, and the data flow. The flow model can be used by a workflow engine to execute the process and can be seen as a usage pattern of a collection of Web services. The second one, called *global model*, describes the interaction pattern of a collection of Web services, thus modeling the overall partner interactions. The interactions are represented as links between endpoints of the Web services' interfaces. Each link corresponds to the interaction of a Web service with an operation of another Web service's interface. Composed Web services can be published as a new Web service again. Hence, they can be used as a component in new compositions again. This is known as recursive composition [Ley01]. A second language for Web service composition has been introduced by Microsoft and called XLANG [Tha01]. It extends a WSDL service description by elements that illustrate the role of a Web service in a business process. The interaction patterns are described by *port maps*, which map messages of an outgoing Web service to an incoming port of another Web service. Special language constructs in XLANG allow a handling of messages based on conditions.

In addition to WSFL and XLANG, a couple of other languages for the composition of services exist [KSK+03, Aal03] like HP's WSCL (Web Services Conversation Language [BBB+01]), BPML (Business Process Markup Language [Ark02]), BPSS (Business Process Schema Specification [LCC+01]) and XL [FGK02], to name just a few. However, one language has managed to become the convergence point for all other analogous proposals [ACK+04]. This is the Business Process Execution Language for Web Services (BPEL4WS or BPEL for short, see [ACD+03]), which may solve the problems of the competing standards without a clearly added value in the area of Web service composition. [Aal03] calls this problem the Web Services Acronym Hell (WSAH). BPEL has in many ways the same characteristics as XLANG and WSFL because Microsoft and IBM have been the driving forces in the creation of the language. BPEL allows to specify business processes and how they relate to Web services. Processes defined in BPEL are fully executable, and they are portable between BPEL conform environments [LR04]. BPEL supports the specification of composition schemas and coordination protocols in the field of Web services. Thus, BPEL can be used to model the external behavior and the internal implementation of processes. The external behavior is modeled as an abstract process in which the message parameters and control flow can be unspecified, the internal representation is called executable process [ACK+04].

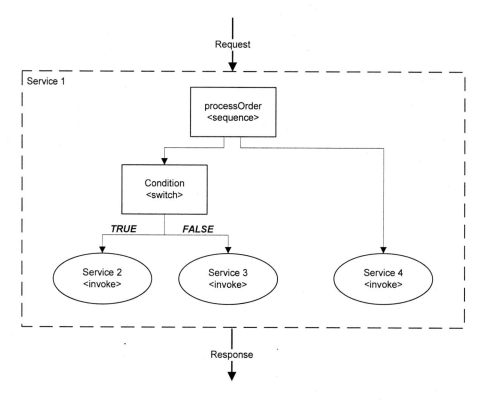

Figure 3.22: Orchestration of Web services with BPEL.

BPEL process specifications are XML documents that use predefined language constructs to model control flows. The language provides several types of primitive activities: to allow interactions with the applications being composed (invoke, reply, and receive activities), wait for some time (wait activity), copy data from one place to another (assign activity), indicate error conditions (throw activity), terminate the entire composition instance (terminate activity), or to do nothing (empty activity). Data is available in global containers.

The primitive activities mentioned above can be used in more complex flows using structured activities. These are the constructs to define ordered sequences of steps (sequence activity), constructs to choose from different alternatives using the "case-statement" approach (switch activity), constructs to define loops (while activity), constructs to follow one of several alternative execution paths (pick activity), and finally constructs to indicate that a collection of activities should be executed in parallel (flow activity).

BPEL4WS supports long running processes as well as interactions with users. Complex services are offered as Web services again and are also described by WSDL. Figure 3.22 pictures a small example for a Web service orchestration with BPEL4WS. Again, service 1 is a complex service that has to include two other services. The main sequence shows that, in the beginning, service 2 or service 3 is executed according to a certain condition. Thereafter, service 4 is executed to finalize the functionality of service 1.

3.6.6   Other Standardization Efforts

The basic Web services stack centered around the SOAP, WSDL, and UDDI specifications is enhanced by additional standards and specifications. According to the horizontal and vertical services provided by the CORBA architecture, these approaches can also be classified according to the same schema. Horizontal approaches are built on top of already-existing standards, whereas vertical ones add additional features to already-existing standards (see Figure 3.23). The situation in the entire Web services area (and within the XML language development as well) is comparable to the one mentioned in Chapter 3.6.4, where the variety of languages has been called the Web Services Acronym Hell (WSAH [Aal03]). As standards and specifications appear and disappear permanently, only some major directions will be sketched here. A couple of standards like OWL-S and WSRP will be used for the realization of the service-oriented system and will be explained when they are used.

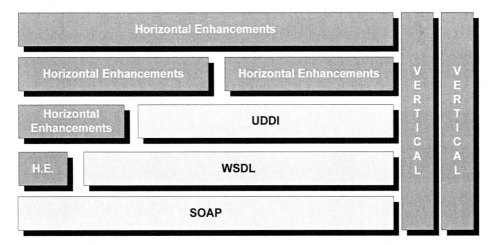

Figure 3.23: Vertical and horizontal enhancements of Web services.

Several horizontal enhancements to the basic stack have already been mentioned in Chapter 3.6.5 about Web services orchestration. These are WSFL, XLANG, and BPEL4WS. Other horizontal specifications address the discovery of Web services. Apart from UDDI, there are other possibilities to describe and discover services. WS-Inspection (Web services Inspection Language [Bri02]) is an addition to UDDI, not a competitor. A document of this standard is a collection of references and is intended to describe the services at the place of execution (and not in a separate registry). To find WS-Inspection documents, the standard suggests to save the file with the name "inspection.wsil" in the root directory of the Web server, or to give a reference in the META-tag of a HTML-page. UDDI, as well as WS-Inspection, enables a search for Web services based on classifications by keywords. These classifications are not standardized, which makes them only usable for human beings. Thus, software agents are not able to understand the semantics of search results. OWL-S (formerly known as DAML-S, see Chapter 5.1.2) is a standardization to provide a way for a semantic description of Web services. Again, the underlying idea is not to provide a competitor to already-existing standards, but to offer a complementary approach.

Vertical enhancements are specifications and standards like Web Service Security, approaches to realize transactions in the field of Web services [CCC+02], and specifications addressing the quality of service aspect. The Web Service Security Standardization [Oas04] essentially improves the SOAP standard. It adds enhancements that provide added quality of protection through message integrity and confidentiality. It allows, for example, the use of XML Encryption and Signature within SOAP messages and is explained in Chapter 4.2.3.2.

3.7   Summary

The chapter has introduced the general idea of reusing software components. Several approaches are well known in the field of distributed systems. They are basically an evolution of RPC, which has been explained in Chapter 3.1. Afterwards, TP Monitors, object-based middleware, and message-oriented middleware have been explained. Each technology has been inspected for a use in a distributed elearning system. A short analysis of the shortcomings of the traditional approaches has led to Web services.

Web services are a special form of message-based systems and are often implemented on the foundation of WSDL, SOAP, and UDDI. Each of the latter specifications has been explained in detail. In addition, the chapter has sketched the selection and orchestration of Web services as well as further horizontal and vertical standards and specifications.

Chapter 4

A Service-Oriented View of Elearning

In Chapter 1, it has been argued that in future elearning manufacturers have to offer solutions that sell access to learning content and services. Common centralized elearning platforms do not provide the necessary interfaces to offer this access. From a developer's view it follows that functionalities have to be implemented in a service-oriented way, and Chapter 3 has explained that Web services can offer a technique suitable for this approach. However, until now it has not been explained what is meant by a "reasonable" elearning service. Conceptually, it is possible that a service offers very small-grained or very coarse-grained functionalities.

This chapter is to describe a service-oriented view of elearning. It will start with the description of its underlying basic ideas in Chapter 4.1 by dividing a hypothetical elearning platform into several separated building blocks following the rules of a top-down method. These building blocks define reasonable service offerings for a reuse in elearning. The conceptual services resulting from the top-down division will be mapped to the IEEE LTSA standard to prove if the service concept is still compatible to the LTSA requirements. Chapter 4.2 will further model the interactions and processes of those services. It will concentrate on the most important aspects of a distributed elearning system.

The data necessary for the distributed organization will be sketched in Chapter 4.2.2, but will not be modeled in detail here because data will be stored and maintained on servers of service providers. As a consequence, the realization of data models depends on the design decision of the provider and can vary with each manufacturer, even if services might offer an equivalent functionality. The modeling of data will be shown in Chapter 5 with the realization of possible elearning services. Chapter 4.6 will further show related work in the field of distributed elearning systems and will explain their differences to the LearnServe approach.

4.1   Basic Ideas

The definition of reasonable services in general can be done either by executing a *bottom-up* or a *top-down* approach [BFH+03]. The reasons to build services can be manifold and are not discussed here. A bottom-up approach starts from the underlying techniques and builds separated services. These services are later on combined to build more comprehensive functionalities. In consequence, the services that are available determine the processes that can be built. This approach faces two difficulties for the elearning field:

1. Services are or have been designed without targeting on the development of a global elearning platform. This may be suitable for applications with simple interfaces like search engines, but is not appropriate for complex business applications.

2. Currently most services needed to build a service-oriented elearning environment are not available.

The other way round, processes define which services are needed. The top-down approach is based on the definition of an entire target environment at a high level. It can be based, for example, on high-level functionalities or high-level process descriptions. Taking either of the latter as a starting point and executing a stepwise subdivision of functionalities in reasonable stand-alone applications leads to an identification of services [Che02]. The top-down approach creates conceptual cleaner service definitions [BFH+03] within a certain application domain. The latter approach is also used in the following to define elearning services on the foundation of a hypothetical elearning platform as shown in Figure 4.1.

The hypothetical platform covers the common functionalities of centralized elearning platforms. From a high-level learner perspective, a platform provides learning functionalities, communication (and collaboration) functionalities, and management (or administrative) functionalities. From a provider's perspective, who wants to design, implement, and offer elearning Web services, the elearning functionalities of the hypothetical platform can be distinguished according to another criterion. This perspective focuses on the environments in which the functionalities may be (re)used. They can basically be classified into four groups:

1. **Enterprise services** are used for a classical integration approach of LMSs with business applications. This can include, for example, user data.

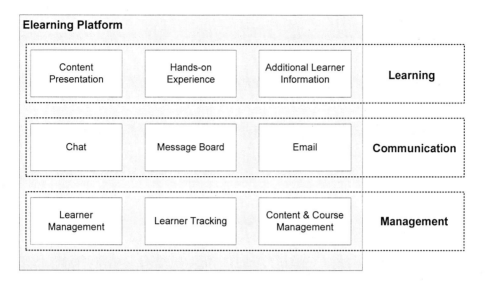

Figure 4.1: Basic building blocks of a hypothetical elearning platform from a learner's perspective.

2. **Non-elearning-specific services** provide functionalities that were initially not constructed to be used in special elearning platforms, but may be helpful for the learning experience for an individual learner or a group of learners.

3. **Communication services** are part of almost all learning platforms. They can be provided by external manufacturers and have just to be included into the system. The services that are part of this class are not special ones for teaching and learning; they are used in cooperative work, too. However, in cooperative work there are no hierarchies within the users as it is common for teaching with students and teachers [BES03].

4. **Elearning services** offer the specific learning functionalities of a learning platform and include technical and user-facing services. As will be shown later, it makes sense to subdivide this class into two groups.

4.1.1 Top-Down Division at a High Level

Starting from a centralized elearning system and performing a top-down approach to subdivide a hypothetical elearning platform into its main parts figures out at least the four kinds of services mentioned above. These services have a connection to the elearning field at different application levels. Corresponding to these types of services the top-down approach to define Web services for the distributed elearning environment consists of at least four steps. For each of these steps a short conceptual overview will be presented next. In addition, examples for Web services that can be used and implemented at each level will be provided to deepen the understanding of the concepts. Of course, these examples will not be exhaustive because the variety of services that can be used in elearning but have initially not been implemented for elearning is very huge. These services are in particular part of the clusters "non-elearning-specific services" and "communication services".

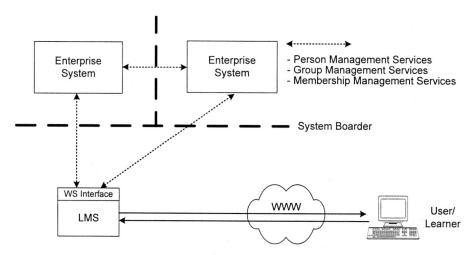

Figure 4.2: Conceptual model of IMS Enterprise Services.

Enterprise services with a general character are defined by the IMS Enterprise Services Specification [IMS04b]. It defines how systems manage the exchange of information that describes people, groups, and memberships within the context of learning. Figure 4.2 highlights the scope of the IMS Enterprise Services Specification as dotted lines. It defines the *Person Management Services* to manage information about individuals who are undertaking some form of study. The person record of the specification is designed to be a data model for all of the personal information to be exchanged about an individual. The *Group Management Services* describe information about a collection of objects related to learning activities or individuals. The group is a generic container that is used to define any set of related activities (e.g., a tutor group, a class, a curriculum, etc.). There are no restrictions defined on how a group and a sub-group structure can be used with respect to containing other groups, people, etc. The *Membership Management Services* manage information about the membership structure that are used to define the members of groups. A member can be a person or another group, and a group or person can be a member of any number of groups. All management services include functionalities like *add*, *delete*, *update*, and *read* of the respective data. The IMS Enterprise Services Specification focuses on the exchange of data between different information systems, particularly between an LMS and an enterprise system, but also between enterprise systems.

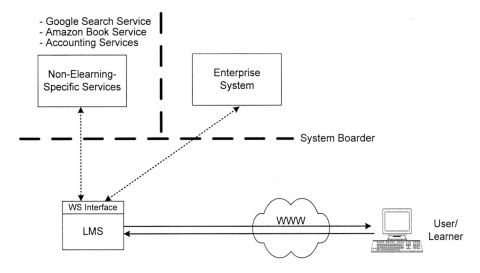

Figure 4.3: Use of "non-elearning-specific" Web services.

As already mentioned, the enhancement of an LMS by adding a Web service interface provides more potentials than a simple integration of data. The use of functionalities that have initially not been intended to be used by elearning systems ("non-elearning-specific Web services") offers potentials to include functionalities from several application domains. The important issue to be recognized about the use of Web services at this stage is the fact that they offer only an *expansion* of functionalities that can be used by learners and other users. The LMS still provides the entire functionality of a learning platform and is still implemented as a centralized system. As shown in Figure 4.3, the platform can, for example, consume the Amazon Web services[1]. This would provide access to search and order mechanisms for books which learners may need to deepen their knowledge without leaving the platform. The CIAD sample course of Figure 1.1 references Oracle Press books to be used for preparing exams. By using Amazon's shopping services it would be possible to order these books directly from the LMS. In addition, a course designer

---

[1]http://www.amazon.com/webservices

can use the services to provide literature links for a learner. A couple of Web services providing access to search engines would offer the learner the possibility to receive extra information on topics covered by the learning material. Search Web services are offered, for instance, by Google [2] and Yahoo[3].

As elearning cannot be considered to be free of charge, an appropriate accounting has to be added to an elearning platform (see Chapter 6.2.1). This, again, can be achieved by using Web services. For example, Payment Resources International provides a Credit Card Processing Web Service for its customers[4] to authorize, credit, and void credit card transactions. An LMS provider can, for example, use this service to credit a learner of the CIAD course online and allow a direct access to content afterwards. Apart from payment services, Web services can also be used to improve the knowledge of learners, and are consequently turned into learning services. For example, a stock quote Web service can be used by bank trainees to get the latest quotes for a company[5]; or a currency exchange service[6] can be used to calculate exchange values. Another Web service[7] provides access to the King James Bible and can support the learning process of theology students. If translations have to be made by users of the platform, a translation service[8] can be invoked.

Communication mechanisms are part of almost all learning platforms because they provide collaboration possibilities for learners and teachers. However, as they are not part of LTSA, they are not a mandatory building block of an LMS that is compatible to this standard. Several of these communication functionalities are provided on the Web as services and can be included to be used in an LMS, as shown in Figure 4.4. Communication services provided on the Web include sending Fax[9], SMS[10], Email[11], and the use of message boards. Each of these functionalities can be interpreted as a service since they implement a self-contained application. At this step of distribution, the LMS still implements the most important functionalities of an elearning platform like the maintenance of users, tracking of data, and the storage and presentation of learning objects.

Up to now, the use of general, non-elearning-specific Web services in elearning platforms

---

[2]http://www.google.com/apis/

[3]http://developer.yahoo.net/

[4]http://webservices.primerchants.com/creditcard.asmx

[5]http://www.webservicex.net/stockquote.asmx

[6]http://www.xmethods.net/sd/CurrencyExchangeService.wsdl

[7]http://www.webservicex.net/BibleWebservice.asmx

[8]http://www.webservicex.net/WS/WSDetails.aspx?WSID=63&CATID=12

[9]e.g.: http://www.webservicex.net/WS/WSDetails.aspx?CATID=4&WSID=7

[10]e.g.: http://www.webservicex.net/WS/WSDetails.aspx?WSID=60&CATID=4

[11]e.g.: http://webservices.matlus.com/scripts/emailwebservice.dll/wsdl/IEmailService. The WSDL document for this Web service is shown in Appendix A.1.

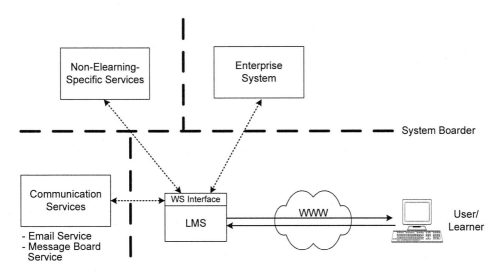

Figure 4.4: Separation of communication Web services.

has been described. However, by analyzing the structure of activities and processes supported by a learning platform during the learning process, several additional Web services can be identified. By subdividing and implementing these functionalities as Web services a huge amount of reuse is possible even for elearning functionalities. Figure 4.5 pictures the conceptual subdivision of a Web-services-based elearning system.

The concept distinguishes between basic elearning services and core elearning services. Basic elearning services include services that can easily be separated from the learning platform, e.g., search mechanisms for learning content, playgrounds as provided by the xLx system, and Labs provided by Gradiance. Core elearning services include the presentation of content to the learner, exercise Web services, tracking, and "learner services" that are to manage learner data. As will be shown in the following, these functionalities can be provided by Web services that have to communicate with each other, with the learner, and, moreover, may be combined with other Web services to offer complex functionalities. Using basic and core elearning Web services implies the fact that the central LMS does not exist any longer, and content is stored in a decentralized way. A platform is now responsible for integrating the necessary services, and learners use this platform to access the elearning functionalities that are included as a collection of different Web services running on remote machines. Depending on the integration of services, learners do not have to be aware of the fact that their "learning system" is a collection of Web

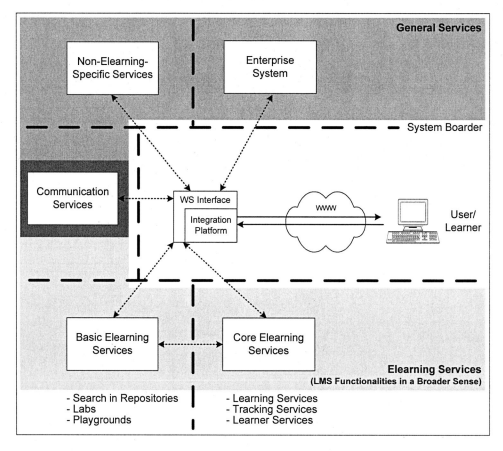

Figure 4.5: High-level model of elearning as a Web service.

services instead of a centralized platform[12]. Possibly, learners are also able to include functionalities and, thus, have a very flexible platform.

In contrast to the other classes of services mentioned above, basic and core Web service provider cannot be mapped easily to self-contained stand-alone applications. The definition of the latter is explained in the following on the foundation of the IEEE LTSA standard.

---

[12]Of course, the integration platform can conceptually be an LMS using learning services from other manufacturers. However, the further descriptions assume the use of a separate integration platform.

4.1.2   Learning Service Analysis

In Layer 3 (called "System Components"), the LTSA specification [IEE03] describes the conceptual building blocks of an elearning system in detail. As described above, merely this layer is normative in LTSA. It identifies generic features and specifies general components of a learning system. It does not cover functionalities that have been classified into enterprise services, non-elearning-specific services, and communication services. Although commercial systems might not implement the component boundaries exactly owing to implementation or commercial efficiency, the components are still conceptually separate [IEE03]. The basic meaning of this architecture is a description of general learning processes. It does not describe the authoring of learning content. However, it defines critical activities that have to be handled during the learning process. The core and the basic elearning services match exactly to LTSA and will be mapped to the standard in order to identify reasonable Web service providers. First, this subsection presents more details of the LTSA Layer 3 and maps the hypothetical elearning system to this definitions. Having this concept in mind, the same approach will be executed for a service-oriented elearning system.

Layer 3 of LTSA describes four processes, two stores, and thirteen data-flows [IEE03], which will be described in more detail in the following. Processes are defined as "an active system component that transforms its inputs into outputs" [IEE03] and are shown as ellipses in Figure 4.6. The names of the processes are chosen in the LTSA standard in a confusing way, as one process is called *Learner Entity* which does not really give the impression to describe a process. Stores are "inactive system components used as an information repository" [IEE03] to save data and control information and can be interpreted as databases or files in a file system. They are pictured in Figure 4.6 as rectangles. Flows shown as arrows in Figure 4.6 embody the "transfer of information from one system or subsystem to another" and can include data as well as control information [IEE03]. Solid lines represent data flows, whereas dashed lines represent control flows. The letters in brackets correspond to the letters of Figure 2.3.

The overall organization of LTSA Layer 3, earlier shown in Figure 4.6, corresponds to the global organization of a learning platform, shown in Figure 2.2, but describes a platform in a more technical way and focuses on information instead of roles. Roles are not explicitly defined in LTSA, but the learner is implicitly part of the *Learner Entity*, the author and trainer are implicitly part of the *Coach* processes [Vos04]. Furthermore, the authoring process is not described in detail.

The *Learner Entity* is the conceptual process that represents an abstraction of a human learner. Technically, it is often implemented in conjunction with the *Multimedia* flow as an

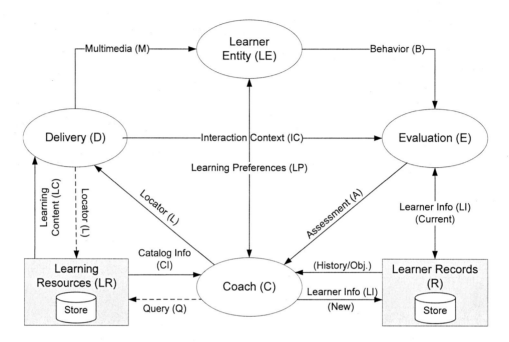

Figure 4.6: LTSA system components according to [IEE03].

environment used by the learner to work on the learning content. The *Delivery* process is in charge of transforming the learning content retrieved from the *Learning Resource* into a presentation, which may be transferred to the *Learner Entity* via the *Multimedia* flow. Neither the form of the learning content nor the way of storage is defined by LTSA. However, the content can be addressed by a *Locator* to retrieve the desired material. The data flow *Learning Content* helps to create, coach, suggest, deliver, etc. learning experience and thus can be used by different actors of the entire system.

Learning activities are tracked by the *Behavior* flow that sends information about learners' activities to the *Evaluation* process. For example, this can include keyboard clicks, mouse clicks etc. and may produce measurements of the learner entity in the *Evaluation* process. A measurement also includes the analysis of multiple-choice exercises. To enable the evaluation, the *Interaction Context* may deliver data to provide context to the learner's behavior. The *Evaluation* process can retrieve or store data about the learner in the *Learner Records*. This data can represent past, present, or future learner information such as activities, grades, or logs. The granularity of this data is not defined by LTSA and can be defined by the implementor of the functionality. For example, the data stored can be as detailed as the data at the level of mouse clicks or as coarse grained as the data at the level of entire courses.

The *Coach* process is an abstraction of the author as well as of the trainer of the system. In addition, it can be an automatic system component that does not have to interact with human users. A *Coach* may obtain information about learners from the *Learner Records*. Typically, this information includes historical data or preferences of a learner, but can also include information about future objectives of learners. On the other hand, a *Coach* may also store information about a learner in the *Learner Records*. Additional information about the current status of a learner can be retrieved from the *Coach* by the *Assessment* flow from the *Evaluation* process.

The *Coach* incorporates information of several sources to search (*Query*) and select (*Locator*) learning content to be delivered to a learner or to create new courses. This content is in turn presented by the *Multimedia* flow to the learner and improves the learning experience. In LTSA the *Query* flow is considered as control flow because it does not represent data to be stored in the data store but a query to get information from the data store (e.g., an SQL "select" query). The result set of the *Query* is returned as *Catalog Info* and can be interpreted as the learning object metadata (see Chapter 2.2).

In addition to the already-mentioned flows, the *Learning Preferences* represent the interaction between the *Learner Entity* and the *Coach*. For example, this interaction can be interpreted as negotiation.

The high-level abstraction of LTSA can be mapped to various implementation options to build elearning platforms. The way of mapping the conceptual components to software components depend on the implemented architecture. A conceptual component can be realized by one software building block, but can be also spread across several software components. Figure 4.7 shows the mapping of the conceptual components to the layers of the hypothetical (Web-based) learning platform of Figure 4.1. The implemented architecture of this platform has a common form for Web-based platforms and comprises a data, application, and presentation layer, as introduced in Chapter 2.4.1. This architecture is also used in the implementations of xLx and W3L. Basically, all functionalities of the management and the learning layers of Figure 4.1 are implemented by the application layer and the corresponding flows. In addition, it maps the two humans, *learner* and *author*, to the architecture. LTSA data stores are mapped to the data layer of the learning platform. The courseware database corresponds to the *LTSA Learning Resources*, the *LTSA Learner Records* to the student records. The application layer of the learning platform includes the main functionalities of the LTSA processes *Delivery*, *Evaluation*, and *Coach*, although the Coach is at the same time an author. The presentation layer

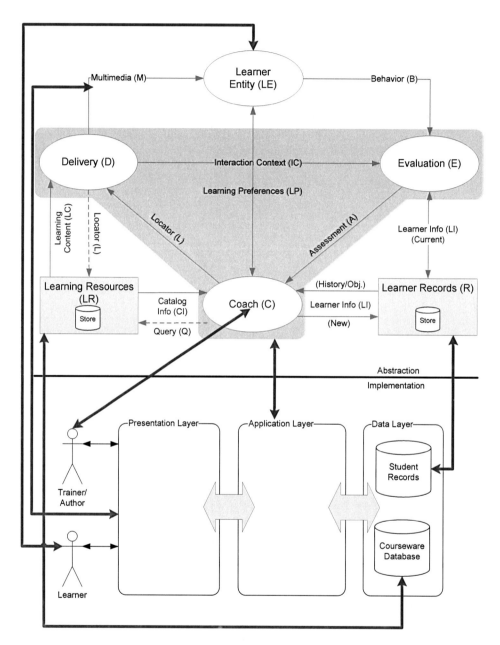

Figure 4.7: Mapping of LTSA to a hypothetical Web-based learning platform.

is mapped to the *LTSA Multimedia* flow and is technically seen a Web server that adds HTML code to the content. This enables a correct displaying by a Web browser on the learner's client machine. The other flows are part of one of the three layers depending on the way of implementation. For the sake of clarity, their mapping is not part of Figure 4.7.

To be used for elearning Web services, the LTSA specification has to be enhanced because the flows of LTSA do not support certain communications that are necessary in the service-oriented architecture. Figure 4.8 shows the core and basic elearning building blocks of the top-down division of a common elearning platform at a high level again. This figure is a section of Figure 4.5. The basic assumption of LTSA that all data is logically stored on one server does no longer exist, and additional data flows must be realized to ensure that services can be used in a correct manner. The central *LTSA Coach* process has to be changed to a more decentralized model since the selection of learning services ought to be flexible and possible for a learner. LTSA does not support a direct query functionality for a learner to search for appropriate content. Two additional flows are necessary to support this search mechanism that are similar to the search functionalities of the *Coach*. A control flow *Learner Query* is needed to offer learners the functionality to search for content services or other learning services like playgrounds to be integrated into the platform. The result of the search is a data flow *Learner Catalog Info* that contains the metadata of the corresponding learning content. To achieve a higher flexibility, it is also useful to implement the search mechanism in an extra repository to separate metadata and content. A search for metadata on the remote servers of content providers is currently not feasible (see Chapters 4.2.3.4 and 5.1.2). This argumentation results in two conceptual service providers. This is, on the one hand, a content provider, and, on the other hand, a repository provider. As a data store in LTSA can be mapped to several software components, this separation is implicitly covered by the *LTSA Learning Resources*. For this reason, the model does not have to be enhanced.

The LTSA data store *Learner Records* cannot be queried by the *Delivery* process. As both entities are decoupled in a decentralized elearning platform, the *Delivery* component needs to receive information about the learner for advanced functionalities, described in detail in Chapter 5.3. In particular, this is important to figure out if a learner has the required prerequisites to access a certain learning content. This information can be obtained from the *LTSA Learners Records* by a direct data flow *Learner Info* between the *Delivery* process and the *Learner Records*. The maintenance of learner records builds the third conceptual Web service provider called provisioning server. A further decomposition of its functionalities into several separated servers is not reasonable because learner data should not be maintained by several providers.

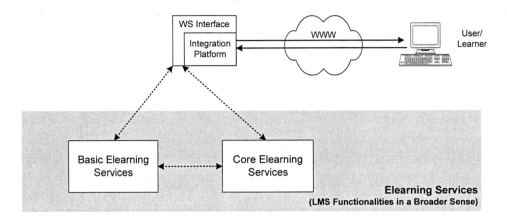

Figure 4.8: The basic and core elearning services to be mapped to LTSA.

The mapping of the enhanced LTSA to the Web services scenario is shown in Figure 4.9. The functionalities of an LMS that were classified as core elearning Web services are offered by the content provider and the provisioning server. Basic elearning services are also offered by content providers as they can be seen as manufacturers of playgrounds and Labs. The look-up mechanism for content that was classified as basic elearning service is implemented by a separated content repository. In addition, the client software is in charge of integrating the services. The new flows are shown in green color and, again, not all mappings of services to flows are shown in the figure to provide at least a minimum of clearness.

The central functionality of a learning platform is the presentation of learning content. As this is realized by a Web service, there is no central storage for courseware or learning materials anymore, which could correspond solely to the *LTSA Learning Resource*. Instead, content is provided by many providers that keep their content on separated servers. Thus, each provider has an own mapping of the entire content presentation to the LTSA components. Owing to the distributed nature of the content services, they have to implement at least a storage functionality and a delivery functionality in conjunction with the flows *Learning Content* from the *Learning Resources* to the *Delivery* process and with the corresponding *Locator*. It is also important that the content service implements a part of the *Multimedia* flow since the presentation aspect of learning content is important and cannot be taken over by the client application completely. Instead, the client application needs a minimum amount of instructions to present the content. The *Coach* process may be in charge of selecting content for learners. As these content services can select the con-

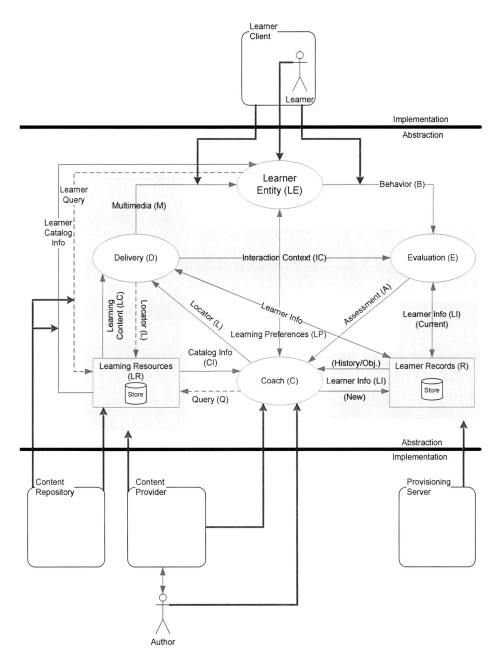

Figure 4.9: Mapping of LTSA to a hypothetical Web-services-based elearning platform.

tent automatically, as will be shown in Chapter 5.3, the content services are also mapped to the *Coach* process. In addition, the *Coach* process is mapped to a human author, who has to create content that is stored and maintained within the content services.

In a broader sense, content services also include exercises. To evaluate the learners' solutions, the *evaluation* has to be coupled to the content Web services as well. A separation of these functionalities and an implementation as individual Web services is possible but not really helpful because the evaluation is directly coupled to the Web service implementation of the exercise. In consequence, an internal functionality of the content service implementation to evaluate the solutions is sufficient.

The results of the exercises sometimes have to be stored in the *Learner Records*. The new flow *Learner Info* between the *Delivery* process and the *Learner Records* can be used to achieve this. Conceptually, it is the same flow that connects the *Learner Records* with the *Evaluation* process. Technically, it is also the same functionality that is offered by a tracking service and called by the *Delivery* process. The tracking services also implement query functionalities that can be used by the human author and are provided by the provisioning server.

The *LTSA Learner Entity* is mapped to a human learner who employs a client application to use Web services. As mentioned before, the client application has to implement a part of the *Multimedia* flow since the content has to be displayed for the learner. The client application can also include the *Behavior* flow that can keep track of the user's behavior to send information to the provisioning server. However, most of this information is handled by the content services. Nonetheless, very special functionalities still have to be considered like the login/logout and authentication of a learner in order to be able to learn.

As there is no longer a central content provider, learners need to be able to search for content in an adequate way. Since the UDDI directory and other search mechanisms suffer from an efficient support for this task, as will be explained in Chapter 4.2.3.4, a content repository is necessary to offer the search functionalities via Web services. A new control flow *Learner Query* is to send the search request to the repository, and a new data flow *Learner Catalog Info* is to return the result sets of the search. As both flows are implemented as Web services, they can conceptually be used for the *LTSA Catalog Info* respective *LTSA Query* as well. The search is performed on the metadata of the courseware, and thus a part of the *LTSA Learning Resources* is mapped to the repository.

Figure 4.10 gives an overview of the basic functionalities implemented as Web services and the parties involved in their execution process. The size of a circle is to be interpreted as the involvement of its provider in the execution. The client is mentioned for the sake of

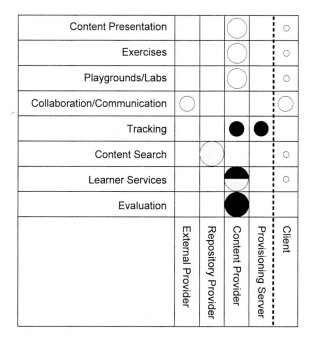

Figure 4.10: Mapping of service providers and functionalities.

completeness as is does not offer any Web services. It consumes services and is to provide the user interface. The white circles are user-facing Web services. Messages passed from the provider to the client have to include presentation information in order to display the content in a correct manner. The black circles describe technical services a learner will not get in touch with directly. Gray circled services are used by the learner directly, and the client provides a generic interface. Tracking services are offered by the provisioning server, but content providers have to initiate the interactions and decide which data to track when. The tracking depends largely on the evaluation implemented by content providers but not offered via a Web service interface. Content search mechanisms are offered only by the repository and can be used by clients. The learner services can have a user interaction (like login, logout) or implement technical services (e.g., verifying access rights).

4.2   The Logical View

The overall architecture and general functionalities that have to be offered by particular service providers can be generated from a mapping of the LTSA components to services, as explained in the previous subsections. This is conceptually shown for the identified providers from Chapter 4.1 in Figure 4.11. From the functionalities that have to be provided by the services in order to be able to rebuild the hypothetical Web-based learning platform pictured in Figure 4.7, several function calls can be generated.

A learner accesses the system by using a client or consumer application that implements the user interface for the services included. The client can also realize additional functionalities. The entire maintenance of the user data, particularly tracking and authentication, is performed by the provisioning server. The repository stores the metadata of the content and provides a search front-end for learners and authors. The content developed by authors is offered by content providers and can include exercise services. Thus, content provided for a learner may be a complex service implemented by several distributed servers. Message board services and further services sketch the use of functionalities that have not been classified as core or basic elearning services before. Services that ought to be publicly available are registered in the UDDI directory and can hence be discovered. Content and exercises need special descriptions and are thus not necessarily registered in the UDDI directory but in the repository. The architecture shown in Figure 4.11 builds the foundation for the LearnServe system.

A detailed modeling of the interactions between several services, and between services and a consumer application for the most common activities based on the LTSA flows is given next. In addition, a couple of non-LTSA flows are introduced, like the login and logout of learners. The models show the message flows between the peers of the service-oriented elearning architecture and picture the external architecture of the environment. The internal organizations of the services are only roughly sketched here and will be described in detail in Chapter 5.

4.2.1   Service-Oriented Elearning Processes

The process models that will be described in the following distinguish between a consumer and a provider of services. The consumer can be implemented in various forms, for example, as Web portal that integrates the services and can be used by a learner via a Web browser, or as stand-alone application that is installed on the learner's machine and calls the Web services on demand. For special kinds of services, it is also possible that

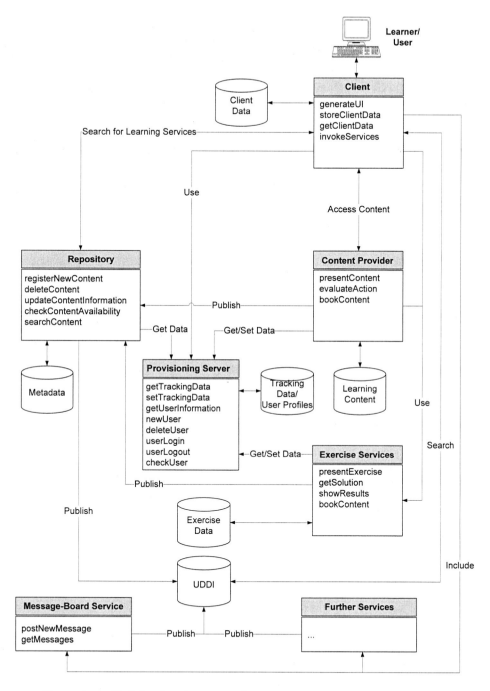

Figure 4.11: High-level architecture of the service-oriented elearning system.

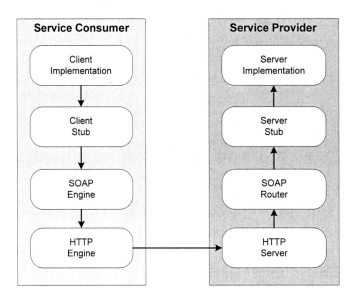

Figure 4.12: Steps to call a Web service via SOAP according to [ACK+04].

a Web service itself becomes a consumer of another Web service to integrate additional functionalities, as described in Chapter 3.6.4. For the general modeling of the activities that proceed in a service-based elearning system, the form of the consumer's implementation is not important because a consumer can be seen as an abstraction for all client applications. The consumer's activities will be symbolized by a light-gray box, whereas the provider's activities will be symbolized by a dark-gray box.

As explained above, the common form of Web services is based on a communication model that uses SOAP via HTTP on the Web. Figure 4.12 shows a simple approach of the activities that have to be processed by a consumer and a provider to use a Web service via SOAP and HTTP [ACK+04]. The model is very similar to the one used by RPC, as explained in Chapter 3.1. The basic steps of this communication and implementation are always identical for the services that will be described in the following. In consequence, the overall processing of SOAP will be explained only once and will not be mentioned in the other process models of this chapter again. Instead, an abstract activity, called "SOAP", will be introduced that covers the concepts and is used in the following models for the sake of clearness.

In Figure 4.12, the client implementation is any piece of software that runs on the consumer system and wants to use a remote Web service implemented by a provider. To achieve this, the client makes a call that looks like a local call, but in reality it is a call of a proxy procedure implemented by the stub on the consumer. The stub forwards the invocation to the SOAP engine on the consumer machine that generates a SOAP message, which is thereafter sent to an HTTP engine that is in charge of sending the message to the remote machine. Often the HTTP engine is a Web server, but it can also be implemented in other forms.

The remote machine executes a similar processing in reversed order. The HTTP server receives the message of the consumer machine and forwards it to the SOAP router. The latter analyzes the SOAP message and forwards the content to the server stub that calls the corresponding procedure of the server implementation. The return values of the execution of the Web service are passed back to the consumer in a similar manner by the server. Thus, for the modeling of these steps the same abstract SOAP activity is used again. Figure 4.13 shows the invocation of a Web service with the abstract syntax in a Petri net form, as it will be used in the remainder of this chapter. The SOAP activity now includes everything necessary to wrap, send, and unwrap the message and implements the entire stack shown in Figure 4.12 except the business logics of the consumer and provider. In consequence, it is placed in the middle of the consumer and the provider side because it includes process steps that are part of the consumer and of the provider. Figure 4.13 shows a consumer implementation that sends a SOAP invocation to a Web service provider. The response of the server would have been modeled exactly in the same way, but with the arrows pointing into the opposite direction.

Figure 4.13: Abstraction of the SOAP implementation.

From a service-oriented high-level perspective, six overall processes appear in a distributed elearning system. On the one hand, this is the learning process itself, i.e., the learners try to broaden their knowledge and have to perform several subsidiary activities to achieve this. On the other hand, there are registration activities to offer content for the learners as well as accreditation (or certification) activities of content reviewers to certify the quality of content [ESW05]. In addition, tutoring has to be offered to help the learners to

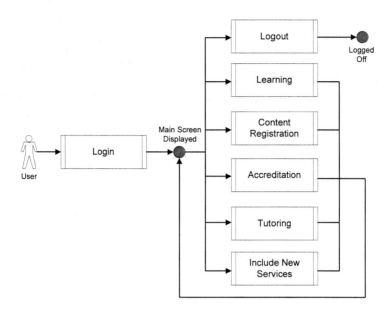

Figure 4.14: High-level process model displaying the basic functionalities.

handle the content. This can include answering questions, maintaining a message board, or giving feedback to exercises and is executed by means of communication services. Furthermore, login and logout activities have to be performed to identify the user and, in case the user is a learner, to ensure that data about the learning process is stored correctly within the learner data. It also ensures that a learner gains access to services that need an authentication. In contrast to a centralized elearning platform, there is no need for centrally performed administration tasks. Instead, each of the Web services is maintained by an administrator of the service provider and thus will not be explained here. The high-level process model for the tasks just mentioned is shown in Figure 4.14. Each of the activities can be seen as invocations of one or several Web services. The details of the interactions are explained in the following. It starts with a high-level modeling of the learning process. This process in turn is made of several sub-activities explained afterwards. Some Web services are used in several of the high-level activities shown in Figure 4.14: for example, the search service for content is used in the learning as well as in the accreditation process.

4.2.1.1 High-Level Learning Process

Figure 4.15 shows the high-level learning process as a Petri net. It displays the order of activities by means of black arrows and conceptual communications with providers by means of blue-dashed arrows. The latter ones are to show the manifold interactions among several providers that have to be executed during the entire learning process.

In Figure 4.15, the learner is already logged into the system and starts learning by searching for new content. This is performed by using a Web-services-based repository that can use advanced search mechanisms by including learner information and ontologies during the search. After the learner found appropriate content, the content has to be booked, i.e., the learner has to buy a license to use the content. Several interactions like the creation of the license by the content provider and the triggering of bank transactions have to be considered within the booking activity. After the learner bought the license, the content can be consumed. Above all, this includes the presentation of content or exercises for the learner and interactions that determine the learning path through the content. Each time a learner interacts with the content provider tracking data can be stored into tracking records maintained on the provisioning server. The frequency of the tracking interactions depends on the implementation of the content provider. Afterwards, new content can be presented. When the presentation of content is finished, the learner may want to give direct feedback to the author of the content. Here, for example, emailing can help out. After the processing of the feedback or in case the learner does not want to give feedback, the learner's profile is updated. Again, this depends on the implementation of a service provider because profiling is not defined in SCORM. In this case, it is up to the provisioning server to generate new profile information. Then the entire process can start again with the search for content, or the learner returns to the main screen of the client.

4.2.1.2 User Maintenance and Authentication

To use an elearning system users have to login first. The login has to be performed for several reasons. First, tuition cannot be seen as a process that is executed without charge. Instead, learners have to pay fees to use content etc. (see Chapter 4.2.1.4). Even in the service-oriented elearning approach, Web services ought to be accessible only with an authentication for learners that consume them. Second, the maintenance of learner profiles is important because of several reasons. On the one hand, this is the storage of already successfully finished learning content and exercises that may be a prerequisite to access other content or exams. On the other hand, the information about a learner can determine services and content that can be used by the respective person. Typically roles

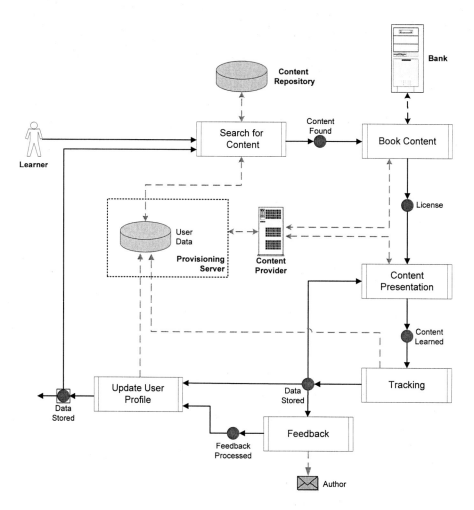

Figure 4.15: High-level learning process.

of users are differentiated based on records stored in their profiles.

To use the service-oriented elearning environment, a profile for a new user has to be created first. The data that is used for this profile depends on the implementation of the provisioning server. The interface can be generated from the WSDL document of this service. Figure 4.16 shows this activity as a Petri net. After the basic personal data has been keyed in on the consumer side, a SOAP message is generated and sent to the provisioning server that maintains user data. The provisioning server creates a new profile for the user and stores the data in the learner records. If the creation of the profile is successful, a message is created to inform the user about this success. Otherwise an error message is generated. The message is sent to the consumer and displayed for the user. In case of an error the process has to be repeated. An update of user data is comparable to the creation of a new profile, but only changes special information. For this reason, a detailed modeling is omitted here.

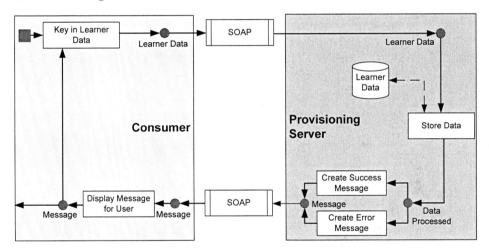

Figure 4.16: Creating a new user profile.

The existing user profile can be used for the authentication of a user. To achieve this, users have to key in their login data. This comprises typically a username and a password. The data is transmitted to the provisioning server and compared to the corresponding information of the learner record. If the data is identical, the login sequence is executed on the provisioning server and a success message is generated for the user. Otherwise, an error message is generated. The message is displayed for the user on the consumer side. In case of an error the user can repeat the login process; otherwise he or she is logged in. The activities of the login sequence are described in more detail in Chapter 5. These

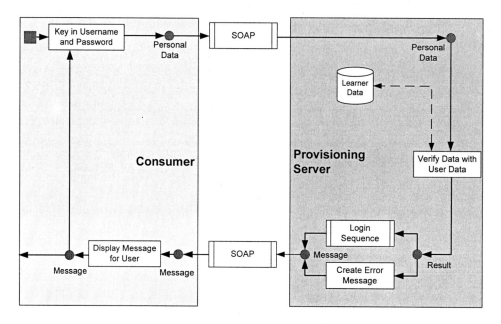

Figure 4.17: Login to service-oriented system.

activities include, in particular, the creation of a session for the user by the provisioning server and an enhancement of the SOAP header used in every message thereafter. This session in combination with the enhancement of the SOAP header can be used by other Web services to implement a Cross-Domain-Single-Sign-On (CDSSO, see Chapter 5.2.1). The CDSSO ensures that a user merely has to login once at the consumer application to use services that are offered on the Web if he or she is allowed to use these services, for example, proven by a valid license.

Based on the central maintenance of the user session by the provisioning server the logout process for all Web services and the consumer is quite simple. The user merely invokes the logout sequence, and a SOAP message is generated to inform the provisioning server about the logout of the user. Upon arrival of the message at the provisioning server, the user session on the provider side is terminated. The CDSSO mechanism ensures that other Web services in the environment cannot be used anymore. The result of the service execution is sent to the consumer and displayed for the user. The logout process is pictured in Figure 4.18.

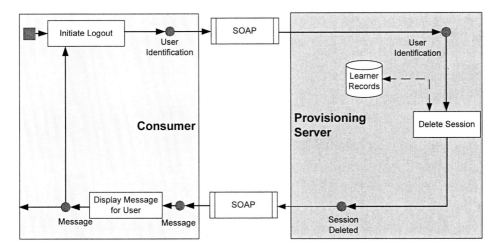

Figure 4.18: Logout from service-oriented system.

4.2.1.3 Basic Repository Processes

The registration of new content in the repository is a task mainly carried out by authors. Content in this sense includes also courses. For both types of content authoring tools create *Manifest* documents as defined in the SCORM specification to describe important information including metadata, content structure, and references to content building blocks. It has a well-defined structure and is already an XML document itself that can easily be transferred via a SOAP message, as shown in Figure 4.19. The information necessary to be stored by the provider has to be extracted from the Manifest document. Afterwards, the existing data has to be searched to figure out if the content already exists. If not, a new data set has to be created in the database of the repository with all information necessary to support the search for content.

If the content is already in the repository, the activity is not a registration of new content, but an update of existing content. Depending on the version defined in the Manifest document, the existing metadata has to be updated or a new version of the same content has to be created. Updates of metadata have to be made to correct mistakes in the descriptions or to give a more detailed characterization of content because the latter was not accessed as frequently as assumed by the authors. A new version is particularly reasonable if changes in the content are material and learners would run into trouble if they have already used this kind of content. Conceptually, a registration of a new version of content executes the same activities like a registration of new content. After saving the

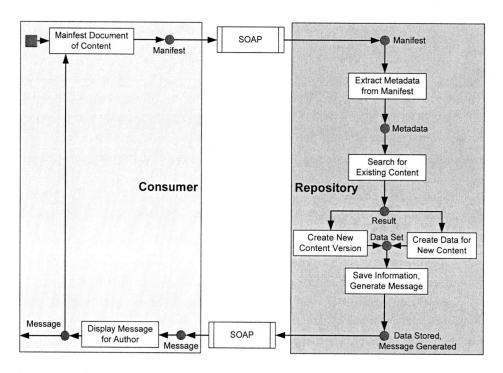

Figure 4.19: Registration and updating of content information in a service-oriented repository.

new or updated information in the database of the repository, a message for the author is sent to the consumer indicating whether the process was successful. The message is then displayed for the author.

References and metadata of content that is not up-to-date anymore has to be deleted from the repository. To delete this information, an (authorized) author calls the erase functionality of the repository with the corresponding identification of the content. After processing the call, the repository sends a message to the consumer indicating whether the deletion was successful. This message has to be displayed for the author.

The search for content is the most important service provided by a repository provider. Content includes learning material that covers very specific topics, and courses that are combinations of basic content building blocks. The repository does not keep the content itself, but the metadata about the content. The service can be used by several users of the system, for example, learners to find content, authors to find existing content to be used in their own courses, or reviewers who want to accredit content. The overall process

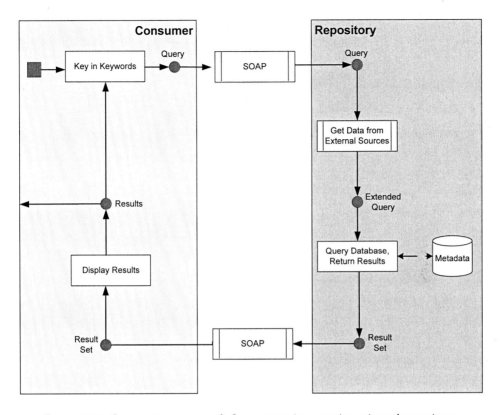

Figure 4.20: Interactions to search for content in a service-oriented repository.

of using the search functionality of a service-oriented repository is shown in Figure 4.20. After keying in keywords to execute a search through the data of the repository, the consumer sends a SOAP message with these keywords to the provider. Advanced search mechanisms can include additional external information to get better results if possible. This information can, for instance, be requested from user profiles if there is an appropriate interface offered by the provisioning server of the searcher. This is again carried out by a Web service invocation. The entire set of information is used to query the database containing content metadata. The resulting output is sent back to the consumer and displayed to the user. The user can select content to learn or perform another activity, or he or she can start another search with a different search string to achieve a better result set.

4.2.1.4   Booking of Content

The booking of content can be interpreted as an assignment of a learner to content. In traditional elearning systems an assignment of content is executed by a tutor. In the service-oriented environment this activity is initiated by learners themselves. After searching for content, a learner selects a certain service to be used for his or her education. In general, this can be a service to present content, to use exercises, or to get hands-on experience like provided by the xLx playgrounds etc. The learner must receive the information how to gain a license from the metadata during the search for content (LOM *rights* metadata section). An identification of the selected service and the payment information of the learner are transferred via a SOAP call to the content provider. The SOAP message invokes the booking service. The provider executes the payment and generates afterwards a license that allows to access the content service later on. Depending on the implementation of the access rights strategy, the generated license can be, for example, a token or an XML document [BBS04, Sch02c]. The payment activity can include bank transfers, credit card payments, or even the physical transfer of invoices. For the transactions that can be processed electronically, Web services like the above-mentioned Credit Card Processing Service can be used. The type of payment does not matter for the further description of the service functionality of an elearning platform as long as the provider of the booking service ensures a correct processing of the payments.

After the payment has been received, a message is generated for the learner that depends on whether the payment was successful. If there was an error in the payment process, an error message is presented to the learner after transmitting it to the consumer platform. If the license for the user was generated successfully, it must be stored in order to be available for learning sessions in future. Therefore, a SOAP message has to be generated to connect to the provisioning server. It must be suitable for the latter and must keep information about the license, the service this license belongs to, and about the user who bought the license. The last information is already part of each SOAP message that is passed in the entire system to ensure the CDSSO, as will be explained in detail in Chapter 5. Licenses for users are stored with the learner records on the provisioning server for two reasons:

1. The user data is maintained on this server and licenses are always owned by a certain learner. Consequently, it is reasonable to store both data sets on one server.

2. The provisioning server is used to verify if learners have access rights to certain Web services. These checks are conceptually very similar to those which control if licenses are available for certain services. Thus, the storage on the same server reduces the network traffic since both checks can be carried out at once.

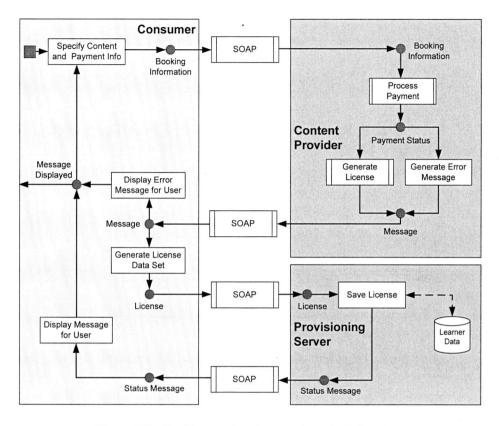

Figure 4.21: Booking services in a service-oriented system.

After the license is stored on the provisioning server, a message is sent to the consumer and displayed for the learner.

4.2.1.5 Content Presentation

The presentation of content is one of the core elearning services and also includes the presentation of exercises and playgrounds. As will be shown in Chapter 5, exercises can be seen as special (interactive) content services. Figure 4.22 shows the overall process of displaying content for a learner in a service-oriented architecture. After searching for an appropriate content (not shown in the figure), the consumer calls the Web service to present content. The latter call can also be executed after an interaction with the content displayed for a learner to get another content granule. The SOAP message to invoke the content presentation includes in particular the identification of the content to be displayed as well as the identification of the learner (included in the CDSSO information). In most cases, the call of content is only a follow-up call of the next block of content to be presented for the learner. In this case, the learner's access rights to the requested content are already checked by the provider, and thus there is no need to connect the provisioning server again.

In the other case, a learner calls a certain learning content for the first time. In consequence, the content provider has to contact the provisioning server by sending a SOAP message with the user identification and an identification of the content in question. The provisioning server has to check particularly two things within the learner records:

1. **License**: if a license is necessary to use the learning content called by the learner, it is inevitable that the learner has already bought a valid license.

2. **Prerequisites**: some learning material depends on knowledge that has to be obtained prior to the execution of the material in question. Data about content already learned by the learners is stored in the learner records on the provisioning server.

The data sets for the learner are passed to the content provider who in turn verifies the data and generates an error message if the verification is not successful, e.g., if the learner does not possess a valid license. The error message is passed to the consumer and displayed for the learner, who can then decide to use other learning material.

If the verification is successful the content has to be extracted from the database containing the courseware. The selection of this content can be influenced by several facts, like the profile and preferences of the learner or the learner's hardware (if known). Owing to the fact of clarity, the querying of learner information is not shown in the picture, but will be explained in Chapter 5.3. It can be seen as a processing step within the complex activity "Get Content" and can connect to the provisioning server again in order to obtain information about the learner. Afterwards, the content selected has to be enriched by presentation and navigation information (called layout in Figure 4.22) because the presentation of content cannot solely depend on the implementation of the consumer platform. Instead, precise information has to be added in order to display the content in a pedagogical correct way. The layout provided for the learner can be influenced by the personal preferences of the learner again.

Before content and presentation information is transferred to the consumer, the provider can process any tracking activity that is defined for the content. This can be, for example, the information that the content is requested by a learner.

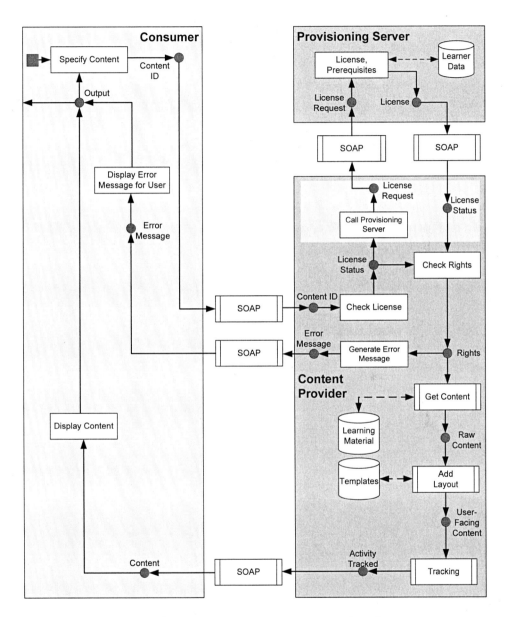

Figure 4.22: Content presentation in a service-oriented system.

If the content presented to the learner was an exercise, submissions of the learner are stored on the server of the exercise provider. The manual corrections of the material, particularly the achieved points for submissions, have to be stored on the provisioning server with the tracking data of the respective data set. This information can be transferred by including a tracking service and transmitting the data. Details will be described in Chapter 5.2.2.

4.2.1.6   Feedback and Communication Services

The feedback process shown in Figure 4.23 can be based on existing email Web services which are offered on the Web. One WSDL document for a simple service of sending emails is shown in Appendix A, Listing A.1. The learner just keys in the necessary information like the address block and the text of the email and calls the service by submitting the information. The Web service generates the mail and sends a response back to the consumer. The response is displayed afterwards. The same service can also be used for communications with other learners or tutors. Details for other communication services are not described in detail because they are very similar to the model presented here. In particular chat rooms, message boards, and file sharing services implement simple set and get functionalities for the exchange of messages.

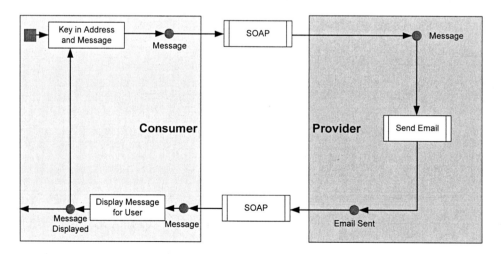

Figure 4.23: Giving feedback using an email Web service.

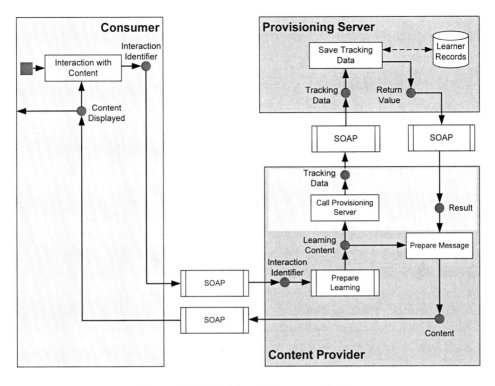

Figure 4.24: Tracking of learner activities.

4.2.1.7   Learner Tracking

The tracking data sets of learners describe the observable behavior of a learner and are covered by the evaluation process in LTSA. Data is sent by the behavior data flow and includes, for example, keyboard clicks, mouse clicks etc. These examples are very fine granulated, and other authors only write tracking records after much bigger events, for example, the completion of a learning object [VJO02]. The granularity of the data is not defined by LTSA and depends on the implementation of the system [IEE03]. Even SCORM does not define the granularity of tracking interactions and leaves it up to the provider of the content which data to store at which point of time [ADL04c]. Thus, it is a design decision. SCORM does define that the content is to find the API of the LMS and has to contact the LMS in order to store tracking data; typically this is carried out via ECMAScript. In the service-oriented environment the clients are not known in advance and their technical resources are not known. Accordingly, a provider of content can assume neither that the client is able to execute ECMAScript nor that the client is able to find the API of the server that maintains the learner records. It is thus feasible to shift the tracking interactions to the server of the content provider.

Figure 4.24 shows the process model for the tracking of learner activities. Tracking is pursued by the provider of content after a learner has initiated an interaction with the server of the provider. The "prepare learning" activity covers the entire tasks that have to be fulfilled by the provider of learning content like the enrichment of raw content with presentation instructions (see Figure 4.22). The tracking process as pictured here in detail is shown in Figure 4.22 as complex activity "Tracking". If the provider does not want to track the current user activity (depending on a design decision of the content author or implementor of the service), a SOAP message that includes the content is created and sent to the consumer. Otherwise, if the provider wants to track the current activity, a SOAP message is generated. It is sent to the provisioning server and carries all necessary information to store the tracking data set included in this SOAP message. In particular, this is an identification of the learner (achieved by CDSSO extensions), and information about which kind of tracking data is included, and the value of the data itself. The rules for this communication and the data elements that can be exchanged between the provider and the provisioning server are predefined by SCORM and will be explained and adapted for the Web-service case in Chapter 5. The provisioning server returns an acknowledgment to the content provider which in turn sends the content prepared in the "prepare content" activity to the consumer.

4.2.1.8   Content Accreditation

Content accreditation and content reviewing are not covered by LTSA. However, in the distributed organization of an elearning environment comments of reviewers are very important for learners. Decisions for the selections of content can be based on the quality statements of reviewers.

The review process is very similar to the high-level learning process. The difference is that no tracking actions have to be performed by the content provider. The review itself is a feedback activity of the reviewer that is in this case executed by a Web service call that does not generate an Email for the author, but stores the review in the database of the content provider. Afterwards, the review should be published in the repository to be accessible for learners. Reviews or accreditation information can be added to the metadata in the "Annotations" section. Figure 4.25 shows the overall process.

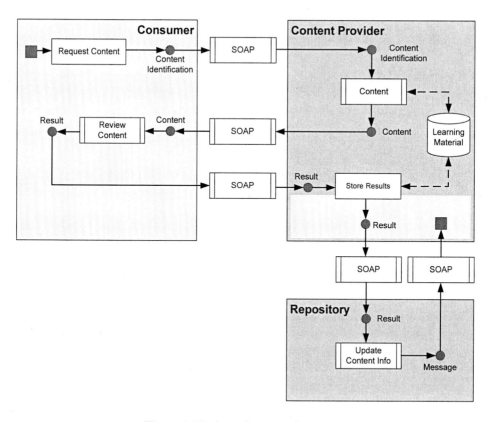

Figure 4.25: Accreditation of content.

4.2.1.9 Selection of Further Services

As already described in Chapter 3.6.2, UDDI or special repositories can be used to search
for and include services at runtime. This enables learners to configure the platform based
on their own needs and wishes. In principle, services that can be included at runtime
can be all kinds of services to be found in the UDDI directory or in any other repository
containing data about Web services.

To include new services to be found via UDDI, a learner keys in keywords to search for a
certain functionality. The keywords are submitted via SOAP to the UDDI Inquiry API.
The latter executes the query and returns all services providing the desired functionality
together with technical information. This response is wrapped into a SOAP message and
transferred to the consumer platform. The platform displays the results for the user. If

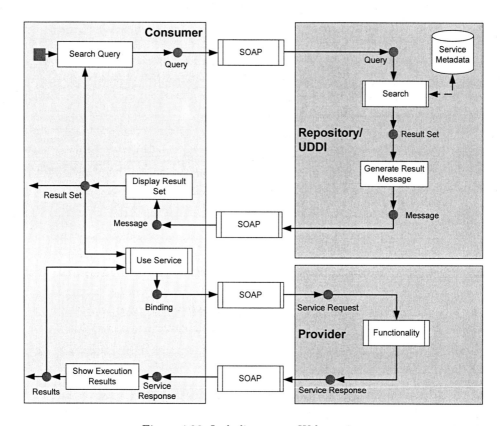

Figure 4.26: Including a new Web service.

there is no hit suitable for the user, the search can be repeated with different keywords or some other activity can be performed. The overall process is presented in Figure 4.26.

Recalling the CIAD example, a learner likes to deepen his or her knowledge by getting hands-on experience on SQL. Assuming that xLx playgrounds and Gradiance Labs are offered as Web services and can also be found via UDDI, the result set would include these services. The learner selects the xLx SQL playground from the list presented, and the consumer platform downloads the WSDL document of this service to receive all information necessary to use the service. A user interface is generated, the SQL statement is keyed[13] in by the learner and the message submitted. The service executes the functionality and returns the results to the consumer platform.

---

[13]The "use service" activity contains technical activities like the analysis of the WSDL document as well as learner activities like the definition of the SQL statement.

4.2.2   Elearning Data

The top-down division of the hypothetical elearning platform has resulted in a couple of distinct components that implement parts of the entire functionality. The LMS as commonly implemented in centralized elearning platforms does not exist any longer. Instead, at least content services, repository services, and provisioning services can be distinguished according to LTSA. Additional providers offer communication services or non-elearning-specific functionalities. All providers have to maintain and store data; this can even be the case for the client or consumer platform. According to the LTSA standard, the core of an elearning platform has at least two data stores that can be used by different system components no matter what kind of architecture is chosen. These are, on the one hand, the *Learning Resources (LR)* and, on the other hand, the *Learner Records (R)*.

The organization of the data in just two conceptual data stores is not appropriate in the service-oriented organization of an elearning platform. This has already been sketched in Figure 4.9, where service providers have been mapped to elements of LTSA, and in Figure 4.11, where service providers communicate with their own databases. The separated data stores have also been pictured in the process models of Chapter 4.2.1. As the modeling of data is service-provider specific and data is maintained remotely, a detailed modeling of data will be performed with the description of the internal structure of each LearnServe provider in Chapter 5.

From a high-level perspective, the *LTSA Learning Resources (LR)* are stored on servers of content providers in the service-oriented environment. These *Learning Resources* include building blocks of content that are used in the content presentation services or higher level course maps that bundle presentation services to course programs. As will be shown below, the course maps can also be separated from the presentation services and offered by mediators which compile courses comprising content from different manufacturers. Some data about content that is part of the *Learning Resources* of LTSA has to be stored on the server of the repository provider to enable a search for content. This includes at least the metadata of the content.

The tracking and profiling functionalities offered by the provisioning server have to access learner records. Although many components can make use of data sets stored inside this data store, it is located on a single server since it keeps data related to one user that ought not to be distributed or subdivided into several parts.

4.2.3   Specific Requirements

The top-down division, the modeling of the elearning processes, and the distributed organization of the entire environment expatiates additional requirements to be met in order
to implement a elearning system based on Web services. Most of them stem from the
fact that the basic Web service stack based on XML, SOAP, WSDL, and UDDI does not
support enhanced technical services implemented in other distributed architectures like
CORBA (see Chapter 3.6.6). In particular, the horizontal facilities provided by CORBA
(see Chapter 3.3) are not covered by these standards. The solutions of these problems
are implemented on top of the basic Web service stack and result in more complex implementations of additional functionalities on both the client and the provider side. The
underlying architecture described in Chapter 3.6.3 is still in place in these services.

Presentation information is very critical for elearning systems because content is designed
in a certain way to support the learning process. However, the traditional form of Web
services is data-oriented, which means that it is up to the consumer or client how to
interpret and display information for a user. In addition, security and authentication
problems have to be solved in a distributed environment. These aspects will be dealt
with in the following.

4.2.3.1   Cross-Domain-Single-Sign-On

As already sketched in Chapter 4.2.1.2, the basic architecture for a distributed elearning
system has to be enhanced by a well-defined mechanism to check user access rights and
provide a Cross-Domain-Single-Sign-On (CDSSO) for users of Web services. This concerns, on the one hand, the interfaces of a provisioning server and, on the other hand,
the messages used for the communication between all protected system components. The
central server to offer this mechanism is provided by the provisioning server and will be
explained in Chapter 5.2. This chapter will also cover the extensions other Web services
have to implement to use the CDSSO. The basic idea of the CDSSO is the assumption
that each SOAP message that is sent in the entire system carries a unique identification
token and the URI of the provisioning server used by the learner in the optional part of
the SOAP header. Above, the provisioning server stores this unique identification token
for each learning session as long as the user is logged in. Each connected Web service
receiving a SOAP request is then able to extract the unique identification and contact the
provisioning server to verify this identification token.

4.2.3.2   Security

Security concerns are not covered by SOAP to be as flexible as possible. However, in a service-oriented elearning system several SOAP messages are passed between consumers and providers which may contain data that has to be protected against a tapping of the line or against other adversaries. In particular, data that has to be protected includes all payment information like credit card numbers, authentication information like usernames, identification tokens for the CDSSO, and passwords as well as tracking and profiling data about a learner. Security aspects are explained roughly in the following. For the further modeling and the implementation aspects covered in Chapter 5 they are not mentioned anymore for the sake of clarity, but are of course important for a reliable system.

As already explained in Chapter 3.6.2, the use of SOAP via HTTP is very common. As there is the de facto standard *Secure Socket Layer* for the use of *secure HTTP* (HTTPS for short), it makes also sense to use these concepts with SOAP via HTTP. Conceptually, the Secure Socket Layer (SSL) protocol [TS03] is used between the third (TCP) and fourth (HTTP) layer of the ISO/OSI reference model [TS03] and secures the message while it is transported on the Internet starting from the fourth layer of the ISO/OSI reference model. SSL is divided into two main parts. The first one establishes a connection between the client and the server. This includes also the authentication of the server so that the client can assume that the server is authentic. Thereafter, both parties agree on a session key that is used to encrypt the following communication. A detailed description of the connection process can be found in [TS03].

SSL can use various encryption algorithms like Triple DES [Meh99] in combination with SHA-1 [NIS02], or RC4 [Riv92b] in combination with MD5 [Riv92a]. As a HTTP message can be of any size, it has to be divided into several blocks for the transport on the Internet via TCP. For each block a checksum is calculated via SHA-1 or MD5 to recognize manipulations of the message. The checksum is added to the block. Thereafter, both the block and the checksum are encrypted with the Triple DES or RC4 algorithm and transferred to the TCP layer. The entire payload is thus encrypted.

Although the use of SSL ensures a secure transportation of a SOAP message, the entire message is encrypted and routed by means of the TCP header, not by means of the SOAP header. This results from the fact that the SOAP header is also encrypted and cannot be read by intermediaries. As the processing of SOAP messages is also designed to allow intermediaries to process parts of the message if necessary (these parts are defined in the header of the SOAP message, see Chapter 3.6.2), SSL is not able to secure these messages. Instead, messages still have to be processable for intermediaries, at least to some extend. The Web Service Security (WSS) Standardization [Oas04] addresses this problem. It enhances SOAP by adding encryption and digital signatures and only secures the security-relevant information in the body of a SOAP message. The header can still be read by the intermediaries. The standard is based on the concepts of XML Digital Signature [W3C01] and XML Encryption [W3C02].

XML Digital Signature ensures that certain parts of a SOAP message have really been created by the sender of the message and that the sender is really the peer it pretends to be. It is based on Public Key Encryption approaches like RSA (RSA algorithm is named after Ron Rivest, Adi Shamir, and Len Adleman [RSA78]). They are based on the assumption that users have a set of keys, one private key only known by themselves, and a key publicly available for everybody. The function of the digital signature is to encrypt a message with the private key of the sender. The receiver can only decrypt this message with the public of the sender. Two things are ensured by this approach:

1. The receiver of the message can be sure that it has really been created by the sender because only the sender is able to encrypt the message with the private key corresponding to the public key known by the receiver.

2. The message has not been changed by intermediaries. If somebody changed the message, the decryption would not work correctly.

The sender can digitally sign only parts of a SOAP message that are specified in the security header of the message. For these parts a checksum is calculated that is afterwards added to the message and signed digitally. The receiver of the message decrypts the encrypted checksum and calculates it again based on the data received. If the checksums are identical, the receiver can be sure that these parts of the message were sent by the original sender and that they were not changed by intermediaries.

Intermediaries as well as other adversaries are still able to read all the information contained in the SOAP message. XML Encryption also uses the public key approaches to encrypt parts of a SOAP message to protect them. This time the public key of the receiver is used to encrypt the information by the sender, and only the receiver is able to decrypt the data with her or his private key. The elements of the SOAP message that have been encrypted are listed in the SOAP header as well as the algorithms used. In principle, each element can be encrypted by a different algorithm.

It is worth mentioning that WSS does not specify how to exchange the keys between the partners. This can be coped with by employing approaches like the key-exchange defined by Diffie and Hellmann. Details can be found, for example, in [TS03].

Figure 4.27 pictures the use of security standards for a service-oriented system, where

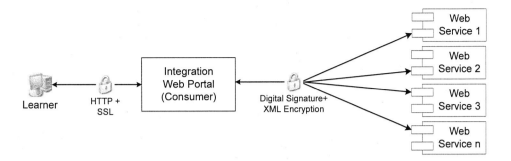

Figure 4.27: Security overview for a service-oriented system.

the consumer as integration platform for the Web services is implemented as Web portal. This concept is not only usable in the elearning case, but is more general and can be used for several application scenarios. The learner or user employs a common Web browser to access the Web portal. Security is implemented via HTTP and SSL (HTTPS) as it is common on the Web. The back-end security for the Web services communication with the portal uses XML Digital Signature and XML Encryption.

4.2.3.3   Presentation

Web services have originally been intended to allow business applications to communicate and cooperate over the Internet. To pursue this, the traditional form of a Web service is data-oriented and uses raw-data objects in its SOAP messages. The consumer system sends a data object to the provider to invoke the service. Afterwards, it receives a data object from the provider. This data object is encoded in an XML format that is typically service-type-specific regarding structure and semantics. Thus, this approach requires consumer applications to provide specific presentation logic for each service and is not well suited to a dynamic integration of elearning content as a plug-and-play solution since presentation of content is an important aspect of the learning process.

In order to enable a plug-and-play integration of Web services, the OASIS WSRP (Web Services for Remote Portlets [KLT03]) standard defines user-facing, interactive Web services which conform to a well-defined, common interface description defined in WSDL. WSRP is a Web services protocol for aggregating content and interactive Web applications from remote sources [AB04]. The common interfaces of WSRP are implemented by a *producer* that interacts with the implementation of business functionalities called *portlets*. Portlets can only be accessed through the producer. WSRP services can be

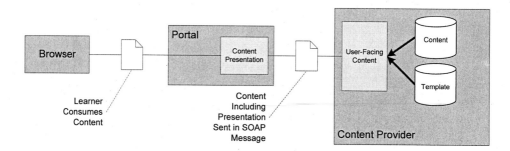

Figure 4.28: Presentation-oriented Web services.

implemented in any programming language as long as they implement the common interface. The difference to data-oriented services is the fact that the SOAP response of the provider includes presentation information in form of markup fragments (see Figure 4.28) and that they have one common interface. This enables a dynamic plug-and-play integration of the services on the consumer side. The latter has to extract the markup fragments and include them into the presentation sent to the end user. In Figure 4.29, this end user is a common Web browser, and the consumer is part of a Web portal.

As a standard remote control protocol, WSRP replaces proprietary, product-specific solutions for the aggregation of remote content and interactive applications. This means that consumers as well as providers can integrate the content as long as they adhere to the standard. The WSRP standard defines different interfaces as well as security, markup, and user-information handling and is based on the common Web service standards (see Figure 4.30). The markup comprises different markup fragment rules to be considered to generate the response message for the consumer. They include markup languages like HTML, XHTML, and XHTML basic because they use tags like *body, frame, frameset, head, html,* and *title,* which can cause errors by either including the markup into the portal or parsing the SOAP message. Clearly, the markup is not limited to these languages and can also contain information for presentations on mobile devices like WML (Wireless Markup Language).

The standard also pays special attention to links included in presentation fragments since they may reference yet another Web service. When an end user activates such a URL by clicking on a link or by submitting a form, this has to result directly in a new Web service invocation. This is why URLs must be encoded so that the consumer intercepts them and reroutes them to the correct Web service including the proper context. Owing to this interception, the consumer is actually able to perform additional operations before

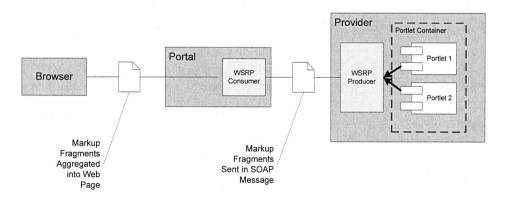

Figure 4.29: Overall architecture of a WSRP-based system with a Web portal integration according to [Cas05].

invoking the Web service. To communicate via presentation-oriented Web services, the consumer and provider must meet the following requirements: the provider has to implement the interfaces described in the standard, and the consumer must be able to include the presentation-oriented messages into the user presentation. In addition, the interaction between the consumer and the provider is based on some rules which are defined in the standard.

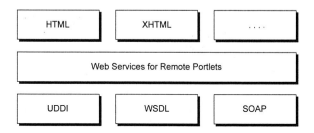

Figure 4.30: WSRP and existing Web technologies according to [Cas05].

In WSRP the provider of a service (in the elearning case, e.g., the content provider) has to implement at least the *Service Description Interface* and the *Markup Interface*. The Service Description Interface enables a consumer to receive information about the services offered by the provider. To realize this, the *getServiceDescription* method returns metadata about the provider (e.g., whether a registration for a portlet is required) and the services offered by this provider. In the case of elearning services it is more likely that information about services is obtained by a learner from an elearning repository. This repository might use the WSRP Service Description Interface to obtain information on the provider.

The second and most important interface is the Markup Interface. It is used to generate markup, i.e., presentation information, and to process interaction requests. The consumer invokes the *getMarkup* operation of this interface to get the markup for the content to be displayed. Interactions of the consumer and the provider initiated by the end user are blocked by the *performBlockingInteraction* before a new markup request is sent. This is necessary, for example, if learners submit forms that contain solutions of exercises that have been presented to them. The blocking interaction is to transfer the data to the content provider to store it. Afterwards, the consumer receives a confirmation that the data is stored and that the state of the learning session has changed. The consumer is then able to request the next content page by using the getMarkup service again. Examples for these interactions and a more detailed description of the *getMarkup* and *performBlockingInteraction* operations are presented in Chapter 5. As the WSRP standard is used in the following as defined by OASIS, no further details will be given on the detailed interface definitions here. Descriptions of additional WSRP operations of mentioned interfaces and information about the optional *Registration Interface* and the optional *Portlet Management Interface* can be found in [KLT03].

4.2.3.4   Search for Content

To search for commercial Web services, UDDI directories are in common use today (see Chapter 3.6.2). As elearning content should be provided as a Web service in this thesis, it seems obvious to use UDDI also for the discovery of this kind of Web service, although the subdivision based on LTSA resulted in a separated repository. UDDI is a global directory service made up of several connected servers, which use a replication mechanism to offer the same amount of knowledge on each node. Providers of Web services register their services at one of the UDDI nodes by providing meta information about the services, but the services themselves, i.e., their implementations, are stored on servers of the providers rather than inside the UDDI directory. This meta information for each service includes, for example, the author, the service category, and technical specifications and is stored in data structures inside the UDDI directory. Furthermore, UDDI defines a query language to ensure that a service can effectively be found in response to a request; a request is answered by delivering information on how to use and call the service at the server of the provider. The communication rules for client and Web service are described in a WSDL file, which is not part of the UDDI directory; instead, it is referenced by the information a client obtains from the UDDI directory upon his request. The WSDL document includes technical information about the service and primarily cannot be used to search for certain elearning content. UDDI itself can be accessed via a Web service interface.

UDDI uses an XML-based language to represent service descriptions. Since this language is not as flexible as it could be, a well-structured description of functional and non-functional characteristics of the service is not possible [TBG01]. Instead, it has to be stored as an unstructured string. For an elearning Web service providing content, this means that typical metadata (e.g., price and category of the content) has to be stored as a string without any further structuring or annotation. Although a more detailed structuring is possible in documents outside of UDDI referenced by tModels, this information cannot be handled inside UDDI [DOH+01]. Apart from its restricted flexibility, UDDI does not provide a type-system in the description of Web services. In particular, this would have been important to describe non-functional characteristics like the price of the content (or service). In addition, the support of generalizations and specializations would have been important to offer information about a service at different levels of abstraction, which is particularly useful to classify content.

The query language of UDDI is unable to handle restrictions of certain characteristics of a Web service. For example, a learner would not be able to formulate a condition to search for content services that are cheaper than a special price. Problems also arise when interpreting descriptions as they can be ambiguous. UDDI does not support a formal and machine-readable representation of service characteristics. Thus, the semantics of a search condition might not match the semantics of the service characteristics. Due to these ambiguous data, an automatic use of the results of the search in the UDDI directory is difficult. On the other hand, wrong hits would be part of the result due to homonyms. Of course, UDDI is not able to present results of related content services because of the missing semantics.

The use of general search engines such as Google[14] or Altavista[15], or specialized Web-services search engines like Woogle[16] enable a search on many resources on the Web. However, the quality of the results is bad because these engines are not intended to specifically search for elearning content or Web services. The results will contain a lot of irrelevant hits in the form of Web sites or documents that were not created to be used as elearning content. Moreover, the information about learning material provided by metadata like LOM will not be handled and indexed in an adequate way as the index mechanisms of general search engines have a broader range of application. However, as

---

[14]http://www.google.com

[15]http://www.altavista.com

[16]http://www.cs.washington.edu/woogle

some of these engines provide a Web services interface, they could be used in a Web-services-based elearning platform to search for content, but a more appropriate approach would result in a better search quality.

To achieve acceptable search results, a repository for the service-based architecture must be implemented that is accessible via a Web-service interface and that implements an intelligent search mechanism. UDDI or current search engines on their own are not sufficient to serve the needs of learners in a service-oriented elearning environment. The architecture and realization of the LearnServe Repository will be explained in Chapter 5.1.

4.3   The Physical View

The physical view of a service-oriented elearning system will be described in the following. As the physical realization of Web services is almost transparent to consumers it will be modeled at a general level. Specific realizations for LearnServe will be explained in Chapter 5.

4.3.1   LearnServe Architecture

The IEEE LTSA standard does address neither implementation nor platform details; however, the implementation of a service-oriented elearning environment implies several physical components that have to be included by the services. This is in line with the ideas pointed out about the general requirements of a Web service implementation in Chapter 3.6.3. In comparison with the explanation of Chapter 3.6.3, there is no concentration on a single service and its detailed processing steps here. Instead, the functionalities of the Listener and the Service Interface are covered by the building block "Server Function-alities" in Figure 4.31, for which no details will be addressed here. It is assumed that the "Server Functionalities" and the SOAP Engine are able to handle all requests and responses in an adequate way. In the following a general overview of the main build-ing blocks of a service-oriented elearning environment, the components of each service provider at an abstract level as well as general protocols will be given. This overview builds the foundation for the realization of the LearnServe system presented in Chapter 5. A selection of the precise components that are used to implement the services is given with the implementation since it is a design decision of the service provider as the Web service appears as a black box in the external architecture.

Figure 4.31 shows the general physical architecture of a service-oriented elearning plat-

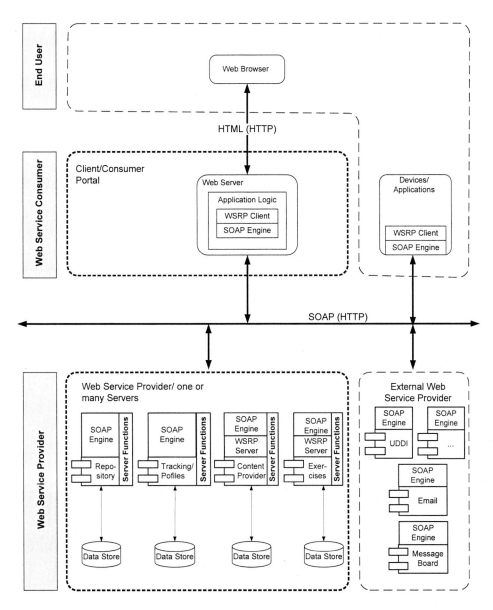

Figure 4.31: General physical architecture of a service-oriented elearning environment.

form. It is subdivided into three layers. The first layer is an abstraction of the service implementations. To provide the basic elearning functionalities, four service providers offer content, exercises, tracking and profiling, and repository services. Each of these servers has a SOAP Engine to send and receive SOAP messages. The payload of these messages is generated by the servers using a certain application logic (shown as an adapter with the name of the service). In addition, each server has a data store, e.g., a database, to save service-specific information. Depending on the implementation and the application components the service is based on, there may have to be additional server functionalities, e.g., a Web server that implements the Listener (see Chapter 3.6.3). The presentation-oriented services have to offer a WSRP server to add the presentation information to the raw content. At least, this functionality has to be included by exercise and content providers since the didactically meaningful presentation is an important part of the content.

External Web services include all services that were implemented for a huge variety of applications, like email services or the UDDI services. In fact, UDDI is a very important service that belongs to this class because it offers a directory to discover additional services by a user. UDDI is also implemented in form of a Web service.

All services communicate via SOAP messages over HTTP. The communication can take place between services on the first layer (for example, the tracking service implemented by the provisioning server receives data from content services) or with applications on the second layer (for example, content to be displayed). This second layer implements the Web service consumer. The consumer can be implemented as a Web portal that must be able to send and receive SOAP messages and interpret WSRP instructions within the payload of the messages. To pursue this, the portal comprises a SOAP engine for the communication with the remote Web services. SOAP messages that comprise WSRP presentation information or other WSRP instructions have to be extracted and handled by a WSRP client. A Web server provides the user interface by generating HTML Web pages. In addition, the portal can implement further application logics if necessary. The Web portal can be accessed via a common Web browser using HTTP by an end user as sketched on the third level at the top of Figure 4.31. This is the most likely way to consume the services and is possible for common computers having a connection to the Internet and powerful mobile devices having an online connection and being able to display HTML pages. It is also possible to consume the Web services directly without a consumer Web portal, e.g., by an existing application or any other Web service client. In this case, there is no distinction between the second and the third layer; the end user layer is identical with the consumer layer.

The implementation of each part mentioned, in particular on the provider and consumer layer, is up to design decisions of the manufacturers of these components. This concerns the selection of software, hardware, internal realization, and programming languages used to offer services. However, it is currently common practice to publish interface descriptions by means of WSDL files (not shown in Figure 4.31). Because of this flexibility, Chapter 5 will explain only one possible implementation for elearning Web services used in the LearnServe environment, which is based on the architecture shown in Figure 4.31. Internally, another Web service manufacturer can choose totally different approaches, which does not matter to the consumer as long as the interfaces are known. For the plug-and-play integration of content services this is, for instance, the WSRP interface.

4.3.2   Further Necessary Standards

Data about resources (e.g., users, learners, computers) are often stored in directories. *Directory services* in general maintain information often read and only rarely written. Nowadays, directory services are frequently used to maintain network resources; provisioning servers can be seen as a special type of directory service. Directory services are often organized as trees to allow an efficient discovery of their resources. The objects stored inside such a tree can be defined very flexibly, based on the needs of the application domain at hand. Objects can refer to one another to model correlations between two or more of them.

Most directory services offer a proprietary interface and query language to execute operations on their resources. To cope with this heterogeneity, the *Service Provisioning Markup Language* (SPML [Rol03]) has been provided as a framework for executing provisioning requests which in turn manipulate or obtain relevant data from resources called *Provisioning Service Targets* (PST). PSTs can include relational databases, applications, LDAP (Lightweight Directory Access Protocol) services, or any other system that may offer relevant information. For the elearning scenario described here, data maintained by PSTs include particularly learner profiles. In the following, an overview of the SPML standard is given. As the modeling of user profiles can be carried out in various ways, the data model is not explained here, but in Chapter 5.9. SPML requests are encoded as XML documents and sent by a *Requesting Authority* (RA) to the provisioning server that is able to receive and process SPML documents. To achieve this, it has to implement an SPML interface called *Provisioning Service Point* (PSP). The request is then executed on the data of the PST.

SPML requests are based on XML schemas that have to be defined by the PSP to publish information about the structure of the resources and objects stored inside the directory. The schemas define object attributes and their data types. Each operation requested by an RA is related to a data object defined in a schema. To make a request, an RA must hence be aware of the schema. To obtain relevant schema information, an RA can use the *schemaRequest* operation to ask the provisioning server for the desired schema. Apart from this method, the PS has to implement the basic SPML methods *add*, *modify*, *delete*, and *search*, and each operation comes with request-response elements to define the communication flow.

To allow operations on the data stored inside the directory and to check access rights of other Web services, it is necessary to have an authentication mechanism to control user rights. The *Security Assertion Markup Language* (SAML [HM02]) offers a way to perform this by using common Web technologies. SAML defines a protocol that builds on XML-based requests and responses and is a framework for the exchange of security information concerning people or computers. This includes information about authentication, attributes of people or computers, and access rights to resources defined by an authority. SAML itself is not an authority, but a transport protocol for assertions that cover information about identities, attributes, and access rights. SAML assertions can be combined with other transport protocols, in particular SOAP.

One of the fundamental application domains of SAML is the area of Cross-Domain-Single-Sign-On (CDSSO). Traditional Web-based elearning platforms often use cookies for the control of learner sessions. However, as cookies can only be read by the same computer or domain, they are not appropriate in the Web service context since services may be provided by many different servers or institutions. The basic ideas of the CDSSO have already been sketched above. How the SAML standard can be enhanced to be used with Web services and particularly in a service-oriented elearning system to check authentications will be presented in Chapter 5.2.1.

4.4   The Customer View

The customer view of a service-oriented elearning environment can be subdivided into two dimensions. These are the same as stated with the physical architecture used for the LearnServe system. On the one hand, this is the end user that consumes offerings, and, on the other hand, the consumer of the Web services from a technical perspective (i.e., the portal or other clients).

In the best case, end users do not notice that the elearning platform offered to them is a compilation of functionalities from several remote servers. This can be achieved by a uniform user interface offered by the portal or any other Web service client that is used to consume the services. Even the presentation of content is integrated in this interface since the WSRP standard offers information on how to present the content, but still leaves some design options for the client platform to do so (e.g., colors and stylesheets).

For consumers, the flexibility of using content services to be found anywhere on the Web and the possibility to search outside of closed systems are the most important advantages. The plug-and-play possibility of WSRP content services makes them free to choose any content without having problems with the import. In addition, content is always up-to-date since changes are visible immediately after their release.

As shown in Figure 4.31, customers have a higher flexibility to use clients that are able to consume Web services. However, the organization of elearning on the foundation of Web services leads to complex clients since they have to implement a couple of functionalities like, for example, WSRP in order to display the content as it was intended by the author. This is why the portal approach for the public use of offerings in tertiary education seams to be the most likely way to implement the client. The learner just needs a browser and thus a thin client to access the portal. For tertiary education within a company, even other clients are appropriate.

4.5   The Provider View

From a provider's perspective the offering of Web services has a couple of advantages - both technically and economically. Technically, the services can run on a server of the provider, which makes an administration and maintenance very efficient and easy. The provider does not have to care about hardware or operating systems of the customers since the systems are not installed on the customers' machines. Moreover, the Web services approach bears an efficient way to offer products for the provider. Updates of applications and content can easily be made by just changing the offerings on the server in case the interface stays the same. These changes are visible for all users of the environment immediately, and no additional distribution costs will have to be paid.

In general, the optimization of processes in the value chain is a key factor for the survival of enterprises. The Web-services approach provides a way for organizations that offer elearning software to concentrate more and more on their core competences by offering only those parts of the software of which the respective enterprise has special know-how, technologies, or abilities that are very valuable for a learner and not imitable for competitors. Then, by using modern Internet technologies, several of these companies are able to combine their abilities to produce offerings very efficiently. These combinations of enterprises need obviously not be transparent for a customer who interacts with such an organization. Thus, a virtual elearning platform with offerings of many providers may arise. In fact, the virtual compilation is one of the most important advantages for the

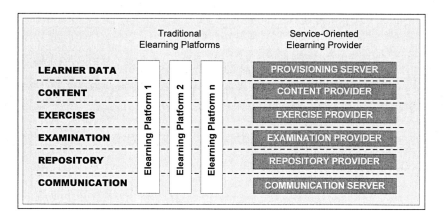

Figure 4.32: Specialization of elearning providers.

customer since the platform appears as a single product, but with the most powerful features.

The concepts of combinations of core competences are generally known as virtual companies. Virtual companies are flexible in their configuration and able to change partners on demand to optimize the output for the customer. Although the concept of a virtual company was discussed already about 20 years ago [Por85], elearning manufacturers still concentrate only on their core competence in limited areas. The traditional form of elearning platforms can be described as vertical since each platform implements all functionalities that are necessary for an elearning platform. The service orientation leads to a horizontal organization of elearning offerings, as shown in Figure 4.32.

A special provider is the manufacturer of the consumer portal, for example, the LearnServe Consumer Portal, which is of course not a Web service provider. By selecting and aggregating Web services for learners and offering additional application logic, they can provide offerings that provide greater value than the sum of the parts. By selling access to elearning Web services, providers generate income. The new organization of the offerings demand new business models since a service rather than a software that has to be installed on machines of the customers is sold. Accordingly, Chapter 6.2.1 will offer an economic overview of the changes and challenges that appear for providers to be considered in business models.

The compliance to standards in the field of Web services is critical for all providers. If a provider does not adhere to all of the standards mentioned it is very difficult to include the Web service, and additional programming has to be executed on the consumer side.

4.6 Related Work

A couple of projects exist that either address the reuse of learning functionality in a non-distributed fashion or the realization of distributed elearning environments. This section describes the most important projects and states differences to the LearnServe approach. Four different approaches can be found in the scientific literature:

1. The realization of a single platform based on the service paradigm. Different parts of the application are encapsulated as services and are integrated by a client application.

2. The realization of an elearning platform in an organization with clearly defined boundaries. These approaches try to reuse functionalities and are commonly not based on the use of Web services.

3. The offering of stand-alone elearning functionalities. This includes in particular stand-alone repositories.

4. The provision of services for elearning on the Web. These services are based on technologies known from the field of distributed systems and are publicly accessible.

Like in the chapter about distributed systems and middleware, the following descriptions do not consider object-oriented approaches (OO approaches) for reasons mentioned there. Of course, several of the systems still to be mentioned may use the OO paradigm in the implementation.

Peer-to-Peer (P2P) networks generally provide distributed and cooperative file-systems. Typically, they are non-hierarchical and community-driven, but have central mechanisms for a peer to take part in the network. Edutella[17] [NWQ+02] and LionShare[18] are two well known P2P networks in the area of education. They foster the exchange of learning objects. As the above-mentioned P2P communities work on metadata like LOM, these search facilities can also be used to search for learning services. However, as Web services are normally not exchanged physically, the typical exchange functionalities of the P2P community cannot be used.

Grid computing is also beginning to enhance the elearning field, mainly in two directions. This is firstly the support of supercomputing facilities to enable complex calculations, e.g., while executing learning content (see, for example, [NSD+05, WGG+05, NG04,

---

[17]http://edutella.jxta.org/
[18]http://lionshare.its.psu.edu/

GFH+03, PV03, Pan03]). The other application domain of grid computing in elearning is its use for community services that use the existing grid (see [BRE+02, BVV+04]). Grid services are based on the Open Grid Service Architecture (OGSA)[19] and are basically Web services. Thus, the current research in the field of elearning grids can be interpreted as enhancements of the work presented in this thesis and provides, for example, powerful communication services.

4.6.1   Closed Platforms Based on the Service Paradigm

In early 2001, ActiveMath[20] was introduced to support the learning process in mathematics. The system consists of three major parts that are encapsulated and communicate via XML-RPC, a predecessor of SOAP. Accordingly, the internal communication of the software is realized in form of Web services, but does not use SOAP. Its Web services are only accessible for special clients; and, actually, the system is not going to be opened for all Web service clients on the Web. It is going to be migrated to SOAP within the LeActiveMathEU project in future [LW05].

Carnegie Mellon University is working on an elearning system that is based on SOAP Web services and aims particularly on an adaption of content for learners [BR03]. The core of the system is made of several agents that implement the interface for the users. These agents interact with Web services providing services like user management, tracking, and content management. A central repository is to decide which learning objects are sent to the presentation agent. In comparison to the LearnServe approach where content is stored in a distributed manner, content in this system is stored centrally. Apart from that, there is a very tight coupling of the agents to the services. Agents on the consumer side do all the communication and also initialize tracking. In consequence, it is easy to enhance the system by adding new services or agents, but owing to the tight coupling it is difficult to offer the services for a public reuse on the Web.

[SCL+03] describes an approach that implements the communication of the SCORM RTE instance with the LMS based on SOAP messages. As SCORM does not define how this communication has to be executed, the approach is SCORM conform, but makes the client software very complex because it has to download an additional API adapter. The common SCORM implementation uses simple Java or JavaScript for the communication process. The system Isoph Blue[21] is a full-fledged LMS that can be integrated into portals by means of Web services. However, it is a tightly coupled all-or-nothing approach that

---

[19]http://www.globus.org/ogsa/
[20]http://www.activemath.org
[21]http://www.isoph.com

heavily depends on the client. It is thus comparable to the system offered by Carnegie Mellon University. Details about the internal implementation are not presented and plug-and-play integration of content is not possible.

4.6.2 Approaches to Reuse Elearning Functionalities Within an Organization

The second CampusSource Developer Conference held at the University of Muenster in 2004 stated the demand for an integration of open source elearning platforms and a reuse of functionalities owing to the problems in financial and personal resources [GDB04b]. The resulting approach is based on the Model Driven Architecture (MDA) and realizes a system by combining models representing the desired functionalities to one elearning platform. The approach works well within the boundaries of one organization, where functionalities can be selected before learners work with the system. An integration of new functionalities afterwards leads to a new compilation which cannot be done by a learner. The result of the compilation is one LMS, which does not provide the flexibility necessary in tertiary education. From an integration perspective, the LearnServe approach is totally different from the MDA approach. LearnServe focuses on service offerings publicly available, which can be integrated at runtime by learners. The MDA approach focuses on the development of one LMS for a company that includes the most suitable building blocks.

Another open source approach trying to integrate elearning platforms within one enterprise is presented by [BWM04] within the OLS (Open Learning Suite) project. OLS wants to integrate existing elearning applications that are installed in one enterprise via Web services to achieve a common look-and-feel. The approach will be realized by means of wrappers, but neither were the wrappers nor the architecture or services of the system defined when the paper was written. Instead, this has been mentioned to be future work. [GDB04b] already stated that the integration of several open source systems within one company via Web services leads to huge administration work, since all systems including the integration interfaces have to be maintained by the enterprise. The approach is only feasible if all systems have to be used at the same time.

The Open Knowledge Initiative (O.K.I. for short [OKI02, Atw04]) is designing an architecture and specification to foster the reuse and exchange of modular elearning components. O.K.I is based on an architectural view of a campus in higher education or an enterprise. The interfaces are implemented in Java and published under an open source license. Other implementations may be offered in C++ or C# and may also be implemented in a service-oriented manner. Components that adhere to the tightly-designed and standardized application interface (API) can be plugged into the existing learning infrastructure. The approach is comparable to the MDA approach as it focuses on campus or enterprise-wide systems, but uses proprietary APIs rather than models.

The Collaborative and Sharable Learning (CoSL) system developed at the University of Missouri-Kansas City offers an educational middleware based on XML [LG02]. CoSL is the core of an infrastructure composed of local Learning Component Systems (LCS). All LCSs have interfaces called "ports" specified in XML. The interface specifications describe the properties of the component in a way comparable to IDLs. Agents use the ports to support the communication between the components of this architecture. The general architecture reminds one of the general CORBA architecture but uses a proprietary XML protocol. The entire communication is established through the Learning Channel, to which all components are connected.

LeAP (Learning Architecture Project) aims at the integration of existing applications within the Tasmanian Department of Education. It builds on the foundation of several existing platforms. It should be able to integrate these platforms to build flexible learning offerings. It is based on a "service-oriented" approach without giving any further technical details. It is thus comparable to the OLS project.

4.6.3 Stand-Alone Elearning Functionalities

Stand-alone elearning functionalities that are offered independently of LMSs include in particular authoring tools and repositories. As this thesis does not discuss authoring tools, the following description will concentrate on repositories. Different repositories already exist in the area of elearning that might provide the facility to be used in the service-oriented architecture. The most promising ones will be sketched in the following and reasons will be given why these repositories are not optimal for use within the LearnServe architecture.

The iLumina[22] repository provides a centralized register and references content on distributed servers. However, iLumina is not based on Web services, which makes an integration of content for a distributed environment difficult. The OLR (Open Learning Repository) references content stored on distributed servers, but is not accessible via Web services [DNW+01] either. The LORAX[23] repository provides a central content management facility ("The Exchange") to store and publish content. A detailed specification is given how

---

[22]http://www.ilumina-dlib.org
[23]http://www.thelearningfederation.edu.au/

to access this repository via Web services to search for and to retrieve learning objects. LOs are delivered in form of PIFs by the central "Exchange". Although this repository can be accessed via Web services, the physical delivery of PIFs is only suitable for LMSs (see Chapter 5.3).

Edutella and POOL, both based on SUN's JXTA platform, are used in peer-to-peer (P2P) networks. POOL is a distributed architecture of learning-object repositories, while Edutella [NWQ+02] supports the exchange of information about learning objects based on RDF, but provides no support for the exchange of content itself. Edutella offers a Query Exchange Language (QEL), which can be used to connect heterogeneous metadata repositories built on RDF. To enable a peer to take part in the network, wrappers are used to convert queries as results from QEL to the local query format of the peer and vice versa. Mediators provide coherent views of the data in the sources by performing reconciliation of the data representation provided by wrappers. P2P works fine in closed communities but needs a broker in open communities so that a new peer can take part in the network. Particularly crucial is also the definition of a wrapper for the formats used in Edutella.

CAREO[24] (Campus Alberta Repository of Educational Objects) aims at creating an on-line repository of learning objects and a community that both creates and supports such objects. The objects within this repository can be stored in a centralized or distributed way; and access to the repository is given by a Web-front-end or an XML-RPC mechanism. However, SOAP is not yet fostered and metadata cannot automatically be extracted from existing Manifest documents, which makes a registration more expensive.

Several features from the architectures described above can be used to realize a repository in the service-oriented environment. The basic idea to reference content on distributed servers and the ability to search within the registered content via a Web service provide the solution needed in LearnServe owing to the Web services architecture of all building blocks within the entire environment.

4.6.4 Provisioning of Services for Elearning

CORBAlearn is a system developed by the University of Vigo, Spain, [ALF+01]. As the name of the system implies, CORBA and its object-oriented distributed computing capabilities are used to develop an elearning application. The use of CORBA ought to allow an easy inclusion of new software and to reduce the time-to-market for new developments. A second system called "SimulNet" based on CORBA and comparable architectural ideas

---

[24]http://www.careo.org

is explained by the same authors [AFL+01]. A third approach using CORBA is explained by [TF02]. The shortcomings of CORBA have already been discussed before and resulted in the conclusion that CORBA-based elearning systems cause difficulties owing to their underlying architecture and are thus not suitable for the implementation of an open, service-based elearning environment.

The project "AdeLE" (Adaptive e-Learning with Eye-Tracking [GGM04]), initiated by the University of Graz, Austria, develops an elearning system aiming at an adaptive elearning solution based on real-time user behavior. It is centered around three main components that can interact in a service-oriented way and support Web services and Java-based technologies. The components are a Profiler System, an Adaption System, and an LMS. In contrast to many other elearning implementations, the Adaption System is the central component of the entire system. It receives data from the Profiler System and controls the LMS. The latter is to present content created by the Adaption System. Although the system's components are encapsulated, they can provide added value for an elearning implementation. Any content provider may use the Adaption System to change content for particular users. The approach can provide additional functionalities to any service provider, but, in contrast to LearnServe, AdeLE still uses a centralized LMS. The WIESELfederation approach is comparable to AdeLE because it creates courses for learners based on requests. The central LMS communicates via Web services with the WIESELfederation engine [RFP05], which is the counterpart to the AdeLE Adaption System. The WIESELfederation engine communicates via Web services with repositories that send suitable SCOs. The SCOs are combined to a course package (i.e., a PIF) and sent to the LMS. Although some of the communication is based on Web services, WIESEL still uses traditional LOs that are not based on Web services. On the other hand, it is conceptually possible to call the Adaption System or the WIESELfederation components in a service-oriented platform to enhance its capabilities. A third system that is very similar to WIESELfederation is introduced in [Fu03]. It describes a "student-centered course authoring system environment" (SCASE) that interacts with repositories via Web service calls. Matching content is combined to a course. The latter has to be reviewed by instructional designers and is afterwards sent as a package to an LMS to be presented to a learner. Apart from these systems, it is worth mentioning that the COW project [VP03] and the FlexEL system [LHW+01] use workflow management to deliver content. Although not based on Web services, these approaches are comparable to IMS Simple Sequencing and the combination of Web services via BPEL4WS.

Several articles sketch the underlying idea of how to create an elearning environment based on Web services. One of the first papers [Che02] from the University of Bergen, Norway, introduces the idea of implementing elearning Web services and sketches a top-down division of centralized elearning platforms. However, the paper gives neither architectural nor implementation details. [BES03, Sch02d] offer ideas to provide an architecture of services for teaching. The abstraction in these papers is very high, and several issues are mentioned, but not explained in detail. The user management, the problem of presentation, or the tracking, and other components are shown as black boxes. Each of them are implemented by a Web service without any further explanations, neither for the internal nor for the external architecture. Basically the same idea is sketched by other authors in [XYS03, LSD03, WZ04, AK04, Asa04]. However, they do not offer detailed information either. The OEPortal approach [HY05] addresses the reuse of learning objects by means of WSRP. Traditional learning objects are converted into WSRP portlets. Although OE-Portal addresses the integration at a presentation level, it suffers from the very important integration of tracking data. A concept how tracking activities executed by traditional SCOs are converted into portlets or into the presentation on the consumer is not given.

The elearning framework (ELF[25] [TCA+05]) is a joint project of UK's Joint Information Services Committee (JISC) and Australia's Department of Education, Science and Training (DEST). It has recently begun its work by providing a service-oriented framework for modular, Web-services-based elearning services. It does not make any assumptions about the implementation of services. The framework is intended as a starting point for discussion. Some partners have just started to implement services, but the core functionalities like tracking, CDSSO, and a plug-and-play content integration, as proposed in this thesis, are not implemented. However, the LearnServe services could be published under the umbrella of the ELF framework, although it is more fine-grained than the LearnServe services identified after the top-down division. Of course, ELF services could also be used in LearnServe as soon as they are available. High-level descriptions similar to ELF without any interface definitions or implementation details are also provided by [IMS03d] and [Sun03].

The approach described in [QJ04] provides Web services based on two-dimensional Scalable Vector Graphics (SVG)[26] to offer user-facing Web services. The architecture was initially developed for a variety of applications and is now transfered to the elearning domain. The main focus of the work is on collaboration services that can also be used for elearning. The approach does not describe what kind of Web service standard is used nor does is care about elearning standards. In addition, the use of SVG implies that the client application is able to render this graphical information, which makes the client very complex.

---

[25]http://www.elframework.org
[26]SVG is a W3C standard. Details can be found at http://www.w3.org/Graphics/SVG/

[Ste05] describes a distributed architecture for laboratory-based elearning applications. Although the title of the work implies the use of a technique known from the field of distributed systems, the integration of the remote platforms is achieved by wrappers. The latter are implemented in PHP and combine dynamic Web pages, and the description of services is done by means of a proprietary language. In consequence, it is a proprietary solution that works fine in this particular case. [Bab01] describes a distributed laboratory system based on Java RMI for remote calls. The system consequently depends on the programming language.

4.7 Summary

The general service-oriented view of an elearning platform offers the fundamental understanding of the relations within a distributed organization. To define reasonable service providers, the chapter has started with a subdivision of a hypothetical web-based elearning platform into several self-contained building blocks. The core elearning building blocks have been further subdivided on the basic definitions of LTSA to define reasonable elearning providers. The subdivision has resulted in four overall providers. These are the content provider, the repository, the provisioning server, and communication functionality providers. Several additional Web services that have initially not been implemented to be used in elearning could also be included into the environment.

A process modeling has expatiated the external architecture of a distributed elearning system. In particular, it has presented the message flow between the servers interacting in the entire environment. Some additional requirements like security and CDSSO have resulted from the interactions. These requirements have been explained thereafter. In addition, the WSRP approach has been introduced to enable presentation-oriented Web services. The chapter has concluded with the customer's and the provider's view of the environment and with projects addressing the reuse of system functionality in elearning. These approaches have been sketched and differences to the LearnServe approach have been pointed out.

The essential parts of the LearnServe system are pictured in the "Learning-Services L", shown in Figure 4.33. It comprises the fundamental findings from Chapter 3 and Chapter 4 and can be interpreted as the overall model for Web-service-oriented elearning environments. In contrast to frameworks like ELF, it is coarse-grained and includes standards. The "L" is centered around the users of the system and is based on XML and the specifications SOAP, WSDL, and UDDI. Several additional standards are used owing to specific requirements. These are, on the one hand, WSRP for presentation-oriented services, and, system. In addition, tracking services can be accessed by all other services. They will be constructed in the next chapter on the foundation of SCORM RTE. Based on this stack, several application Web services and the consumer applications will also be created in the next chapter. These services can use additional standards like LOM and BPEL4WS. As shown in Chapter 4.6, grid technology can also be used by these services. Grid approaches are discussed in the scientific literature and have been mentioned before. They will be not addressed in the next chapters. The users of the environment can access the Web services by various applications including authoring tools and special consumer platforms. These applications call the Web services on demand.

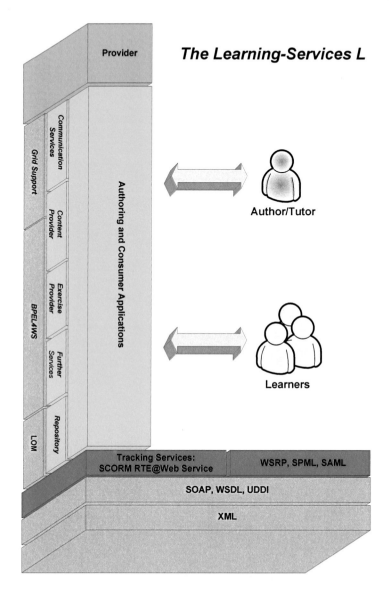

Figure 4.33: The "L" symbolizes service-oriented elearning.

Chapter 5

Realization of Elearning Web Services

The previous chapter has described a top-down approach to identify services that are necessary to implement a distributed elearning system. These services have been mapped to the LTSA standard to show their context in the entire architecture. This chapter will introduce the internal architecture and, in particular, a detailed description of the interfaces of the services. It will focus on the core and basic learning services. Implementations of communication services like the email service already mentioned before can be found on the Web and reused in the environment. Each service provider will be described by its conceptual interfaces and the underlying data model. The interfaces will be characterized by a function name and signature. These characteristics will be presented for all functions in the form of tables. The physical realizations of services depend on design decisions and are not really important as long as the services realize the specified interfaces. The physical components used to implement the LearnServe services will be sketched for the sake of completeness. The descriptions of the interfaces in the form of WSDL documents will be referenced in the tables and can be found in the Appendix.

For each server, a graphical model will be introduced that shows interfaces with their names as circles (see, e.g., Figure 5.9). Depending on the color of a circle, it represents a standardized service interface (white circles, e.g., SPML and SAML service interfaces) or a proprietary interface (black circles, e.g., UserLogin of the provisioning server). Components and applications using the Web services will be pictured as black boxes to show possible connections. Interfaces in blue are more general and can be used by various components, which will not be shown. First, the chapter will describe the LearnServe Repository (Chapter 5.1), followed by the LearnServe Provisioning Server (Chapter 5.2), the LearnServe Content Provider (Chapter 5.3), the service-oriented exercise provider in the form of a wrapper of the xLx system (Chapter 5.4), and the LearnServe Consumer applications (Chapter 5.5). The chapter will also show and explain some screenshots of the LearnServe Consumer Portal (Chapter 5.6) and will evaluate the LearnServe system (Chapter 5.7).

5.1   LearnServe Discovery Services

Discovery services in general build the central facility for users and developers of distributed systems to search for functionalities to be included in their systems. Systems based on Web services use a UDDI directory to discover services. In the LearnServe case, a UDDI directory is used for non-elearning-specific functionalities and to find additional repositories covering learning services. As explained above, UDDI searches through its data structures and in referenced documents. A user of a client application can access the standardized search mechanisms offered by UDDI as Web service to include additional functionalities. The latter can be found and afterwards integrated into the client. In the LearnServe case, for instance, they include the Google Web service or the Amazon Web service as presented in Chapter 4. As the UDDI search is a standardized functionality and, therefore, already sketched in Chapter 3.6.2, it will not be explained any further here. As already discussed in Chapter 4.2.3.4, the UDDI directory could be used for the discovery of Web services that provide content, but several shortcomings in that particular case lead to a development of a specialized repository. However, it is possible to adopt basic concepts of the UDDI directory in order to build a repository for elearning Web services because UDDI has proven to be useful for the discovery of Web services in general. The LearnServe Repository, explained in Chapter 5.1.1, basically searches through LOM metadata. The main functionality of the LearnServe Repository can be enhanced by semantic descriptions, as will be explained in Chapter 5.1.2. In a first step, the semantic descriptions can improve the search results of the repository; however, with the development of semantic search engines in future, these descriptions can also be stored on the (remote) servers of the content providers. A semantic search engine can then crawl the descriptions and offer search functionalities independent of a special elearning repository. This approach is comparable to the decentralized description of Web services used in WS-Inspection, but the semantic approach is much more powerful. Figure 5.1 offers an overview of the discovery approaches used in LearnServe.

An elearning repository serves as central lookup mechanism for learners, authors, and reviewers. These user groups have different motivations to access the functionalities of an repository.

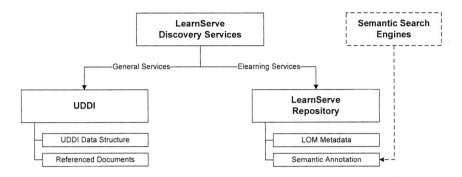

Figure 5.1: Overview of discovery approaches.

- Learners search for material for their education. The content has to be suitable for their needs, subject area, interests, and budget.

- Authors search through the data to reuse content for own learning materials. In addition, authors want to store information about their content in the repository.

- Reviewers search for material to evaluate the latter.

In comparison to traditional elearning repositories handling learning objects and their metadata, Web services providing content cannot be moved physically into a repository. This is typical for common repositories that provide search mechanisms on and a download ability for traditional learning objects (see Chapter 4.6.3). In a service-oriented environment, a referencing of content Web services is needed to guide the seeker to the service.

5.1.1   The LearnServe Repository

According to the activities mentioned above, a repository has to offer search functionalities and content metadata management functionalities. Administration functionalities are not described here since they normally are executed on the local server and are not offered as Web services.

Figure 5.2 shows the conceptual architecture of the LearnServe Repository, which provides a store for information about learning Web services. This storage is to cover particularly LOM metadata (in relational and XML form, see below) and information about the owner of the data sets. It offers interfaces to search for content and to publish and

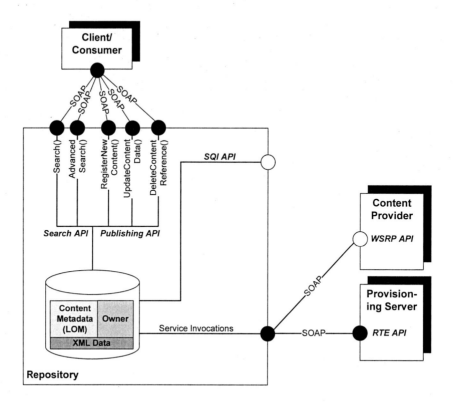

Figure 5.2: Conceptual model of the LearnServe Repository.

maintain metadata about content. In addition, it offers an interface that is compliant to the specification of the "Simple Query Interface (SQI)[1]" to enable other repositories to query data and search for information that is stored within the LearnServe Repository. As this interface is not LearnServe-specific, details are omitted and can be found in [SMD94, SMA+05].

For the purpose of publishing, an author just includes the desired Web service (*regis-terNewContent*, see Table 5.1) into his or her client, transfuses a copy of the Manifest document created by an authoring tool to the LearnServe Repository, and publishes the content as a Web service on a server of his or her choice.

---

[1]SQI is not standardized yet, but the contributors taking part in the specification process make the effort very powerful. SQI is partly sponsored by the CEN/ISSS Workshop on Learning Technologies. Several institutes are currently taking part in the work on SQI, like Ariadne, Educanext, Celebrate, Edutella, Elena, EduSource, ProLearn, Universal, and Zing.

Table 5.1: Function RegisterNewContent()

Name:	**RegisterNewContent()**
Function Call:	string return_value = RegisterNewContent(ManifestType Manifest)
Manifest:	The Manifest document created by an authoring tool.
Return Value:	The ID of the new content reference on the highest aggregation level or FALSE.
Type:	Technical, data-oriented Web service
LTSA Mapping:	Not part of LTSA.
WSDL File:	Appendix A, Listing A.2

The Manifest includes all necessary metadata and structuring information needed for search and content retrieval. The service implementation of the LearnServe Repository extracts the necessary information into a database. This includes particularly the metadata of the content at different levels of aggregation and the organization of the content itself, i.e., the dependencies within the content [ADL04b]. Information about the content is stored in the database in two different ways: on the one hand, parts of the Manifest document themselves are stored to enable a search on all specified metadata information; and, on the other hand, the implementation maps the most important attributes of the clearly structured data schema of the valid XML (Manifest) document to a relational data schema. This enables a fast search for content on a search request of a user. The most important LOM data fields to be mapped into the relational data model are selected on the basis of the descriptions provided in [VJ02]. However, a couple of attributes are exchanged owing to their importance for a service-oriented implementation of the content. Installation remarks as offered for content in LOM are obsolete since content does not have to be installed or imported into the consumer platform. Other attributes like the typical age range, difficulty of content, and annotations for reviews are added because the open nature of the content makes these data fields important for learners who search for content. The following metadata elements explained in detail in [IEE02] are mapped into the relational database schema:

- from "General": Identifier.Entry, Title, Language, Description, Keywords, Coverage, Structure, AggregationLevel,

- from "Life Cycle": Version, Contribute.Entry[2],

---

[2]The attribute Contribute.Entry covers the institution or author that has built the content.

- from "Technical": Format, Size, Location, Requirement.OrComposite.Type, Requirement.OrComposite.Name, Requirement.OrComposite.MaximumVersion, Requirement.OrComposite.MinimumVersion, OtherPlatformRequirements, Duration,

- from "Educational": InteractivityType, LearningResourceType, TypicalAgeRange, Difficulty, TypicalLearningTime, Description, Language,

- from "Rights": Cost, CopyrightAndotherRestrictions, Rights.Description,

- from "Annotation": Entity, Date, Description.

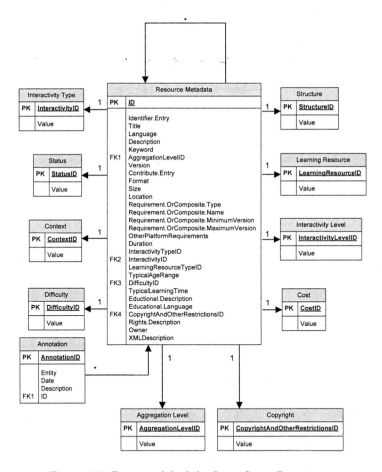

Figure 5.3: Data model of the LearnServe Repository.

In addition, the data model has a data field "Owner" to store the publisher's userID
(to be gained from the LearnServe Provisioning Server by means of the SPML interface,
see Chapter 5.2) and a data field "XMLDescription" to save the corresponding XML
fragment of the metadata of the content building block in the database. SCORM CAM
[ADL04b] defines metadata to have a <lom>-root element at each level of description
within the entire content structure. Furthermore, metadata have to be encapsulated in
an <imscp:metadata>-tag when they are included into the Manifest document to meet
also the IMS's requirements. In consequence, the extraction process is straightforward to
almost all data elements within the data model; the latter is shown in Figure 5.3. The
dependencies within the content, i.e., the content structure, are modeled by a hierarchy
on the table "Resource Metadata". The latter includes the LOM descriptions for each
resource described within the document as specified by SCORM. One of the central attributes is the element "Location", which stores the access point for the content. A couple
of attributes can only have well-defined values, which are referenced by foreign keys from
the table "Resource Metadata".

Table 5.2: Function UpdateContentData()

Name:	**UpdateContentData()**
Function Call:	string return_value = UpdateContentData(string ID, ManifestType Manifest)
ID:	The ID of the content to be updated.
Manifest:	The updated Manifest document created by an authoring tool.
Return Value:	TRUE or an error message depending on the success of the update operation.
Type:	Technical, data-oriented Web service
LTSA Mapping:	Not part of LTSA.
WSDL File:	Appendix A, Listing A.2

Information about content can only be updated (via the *UpdateContentData* service, see
Table 5.2) and deleted (via the *DeleteContentReference* service, see Table 5.3) by the
publisher who referenced the content initially. For this, the publisher UID stored in the
database is compared to the userID of the requesting user. All activities have to be verified
using the concepts of the CDSSO.

One of the important functionalities of any repository for learners is the search function
in all registered contents. The LearnServe Repository provides its search functionality

Table 5.3: Function DeleteContentReference()

Name:	**DeleteContentReference()**
Function Call:	string return_value = DeleteContentReference(string ID)
ID:	The ID of the content to be deleted.
Return Value:	TRUE or an error message depending on the success of the update operation.
Type:	Technical, data-oriented Web service
LTSA Mapping:	Not part of LTSA.
WSDL File:	Appendix A, Listing A.2

as a Web service. Different general studies have analyzed Web searching strategies of people and have come to the conclusion that the average search query in Web-based searches consists of no more than two keywords (see [JP00] for a review on these studies; see Google Website[3] for an overview of actual top keywords). In consequence, a simple search interface enabling a user to key in a couple of keywords is appropriate in most cases, although it may not result in an optimal search result. To enable a more precise definition of keywords, the LearnServe Repository also allows the definition of keywords for special LOM attributes. The specification uses the name of the attribute and the keyword comparable to *Google's Query modifiers*[4], for example, the phrase "Title:SQL" would only return results having the phrase SQL in its title. Table 5.4 presents the signature of the basic search function.

Search results for this basic search functionality of the LearnServe Repository include the number of results, the ID of the resource, and the following LOM attributes:

- from "General": Title, Language, Description,

- from "Life Cycle": Version, Contribute.Entry,

- from "Technical": Location,

- from "Educational": TypicalAgeRange, Difficulty, TypicalLearningTime,

- from "Rights": Cost.

---

[3]http://www.google.com/press/zeitgeist.html
[4]http://www.google.com/help/operators.html

This small selection covers enough information for a learner to decide whether the content is interesting. In particular, the results can be displayed for the user in a way nowadays common for search engines, e.g., Google[5] or AltaVista[6] (see also Figure 5.28).

Table 5.4: Function Search()

Name:	**Search()**
Function Call:	searchresult return_value = Search(string keywords)
keywords:	A simple string that covers keywords used for the search.
Return Value:	A structure covering the most important attributes of the matching metadata. This includes Title, Language, Description, Version, Contribute.Entry, Location, TypicalAgeRange, Difficulty, TypicalLearningTime, Cost, the number of results, and an identification of the resource.
Type:	Technical, data-oriented Web service
LTSA Mapping:	Query (Q), Catalog Info (CI) Extensions: Learner Query, Learner Catalog Info
WSDL File:	Appendix A, Listing A.2

The LearnServe Repository offers a second search interface that accepts documents according to the LOM standard to support advanced searches. This enables a specification of search queries at a very detailed level with well matching search results. The document has to be transformed on the server of the LearnServe Repository into a query that has to be executed on the metadata of all registered data sets. Although this search offers better results, it is not appropriate for most users as the LOM specification is very complex (see [IEE02]). This advanced search functionality can also be used, for example, for a more detailed search after the presentation of the results of the basic LearnServe search functionality. It can be offered by another link that refers to the more detailed search functionality and only restricts the search to the ID of the content. In this case, the entire metadata of the content is returned. Table 5.4 shows the signature of the basic search function, while Table 5.5 refers to the one of the advanced search.

The LearnServe Repository may also invoke Web services on the content provider side owing to two reasons. On the one hand, a WSRP producer has to offer the *Service Description Interface* to publish additional information about the producer and the services offered. A repository may intend to store some of these data sets to enhance the description of the learning services that are already registered. On the other hand, the

---

[5]http://www.google.com

[6]http://www.altvista.com

Table 5.5: Function AdvancedSearch()

Name:	**AdvancedSearch()**
Function Call:	LOM return_value = AdvancedSearch(string ID, LOM lom)
ID:	The ID of referenced content to obtain metadata of an exact specified resource.
lom:	LOM document that covers values of attributes to be used in the search process.
Return Value:	A structure covering the entire LOM metadata of the matching entries.
Type:	Technical, data-oriented Web service
LTSA Mapping:	Query (Q), Catalog Info (CI) Extensions: Learner Query, Learner Catalog Info
WSDL File:	Appendix A, Listing A.2

LearnServe Repository checks the availability of registered services in a periodic cycle. This can be achieved by sending a SOAP request to the provider. If there is a response without an error message, the service is still available.

The LearnServe Repository also invokes the RTE API of the LearnServe Provisioning Server to gain additional information about the learner, for example, about his or her learning preferences, to optimize search results.

The overall process of searching for learning content in the service-oriented LearnServe environment is organized as described in the following. A user keys in keywords and submits the form to the consumer platform, which calls the search Web service of the LearnServe Repository. The LearnServe Repository uses the CDSSO information to obtain additional information about the learner from the LearnServe Provisioning Server. Afterwards, the search is executed on the metadata of the registered learning contents taking into consideration the user's restrictions, keywords, and preferences. The results of the search returned by means of a SOAP response message to the learner include all matching contents with information about the content. This information is extracted from the metadata as defined above. Afterwards, the user requests additional information about a certain content by using a link within his or her presentation page that invokes the advanced search functionality on the LearnServe Repository server. The detailed information that is returned is displayed for the user who decides to use the content and requests the content. The entire communication between the consumer, the repository,

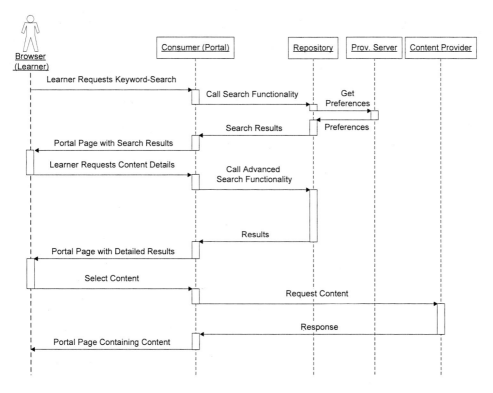

Figure 5.4: A learner searching for content.

and the content provider is performed by means of SOAP messages and shown in Figure 5.4.

The main advantage of a distributed storage of content is an easy upgrade and correction of content because the author has only to replace special (commonly just small) parts of the content without changing anything in the repository if the metadata of the content stays the same.

All repositories, no matter what kind of architecture is implemented, have the problem of verifying the quality of the registered content. Actually, this problem can at the moment only be solved by human beings. The LearnServe environment supports an accreditation of content that is explained in Chapter 5.3.

The implementation of discovery functionalities as Web services offers also an advantage for content developers. Authoring tools can support the service-oriented reuse of content by including the search functionality of the LearnServe Repository directly into their ap-

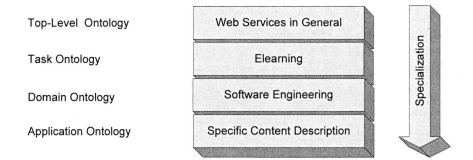

Figure 5.5: Semantic content service description.

plications. An author is then able to use the remote functionality as if it was implemented locally within the authoring application.

5.1.2   Semantic Description

This chapter illustrates how the use of ontologies can support an advanced mechanism to search for learning services. Only the basic ideas are sketched here as the entire concept is explained and discussed in detail by [Sch03]. In the context of knowledge sharing, the term *ontology* means a specification of a conceptualization. Accordingly, an ontology is a description of the concepts and relationships that can exist for an agent or a community of agents [Gru93].

A semantic Web service description can be constructed in four major steps [KKR03]:

1. Define model,

2. find task ontology,

3. specify domain-specific ontologies,

4. derive application ontology.

This incremental approach defines a structured way and enables the reuse of already existing ontologies. Each step gives a more precise description of the Web service by (re)using or creating ontologies (see Figure 5.5). The first step defines a model for the description of Web services in general. For this purpose, the OWL-S [OWL03] language (formerly known as DAML-S) has been developed. It is a top-level ontology that offers a uniform and well-accepted model. Since this ontology has a broad focus, the second step defines a task ontology for a certain domain. As the LearnServe Repository has to provide search mechanisms to find Web services offering elearning content, the domain of those services is elearning. Thus, the task ontology specializes the top-level ontology to a specific application and is also called service-category ontology. The third step includes existing ontologies or creates new ones which carry the descriptions of a Web service in a concrete application domain. For an elearning service that presents content, this step specifies the domain, for example, whether the Web service contains content about computer science, biology, or musicology etc. According to the sample course to prepare for the CIAD, the focus in this subsection will be on software engineering as part of the modules "Build Internet Applications". The last step creates an application ontology and uses the concepts of the top-level, task, and domain ontologies.

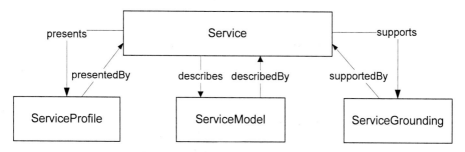

Figure 5.6: Main parts of OWL-S.

Top-Level Ontology

OWL-S is used as top-level ontology language for describing the general Web service, as indicated in Figure 5.6. In OWL-S, a Web service is an instance of class *Service* and has the properties *presentedBy*, *supports*, and *describedBy*. Class *ServiceProfile* offers a description of the service, which can be used to discover a service, whereas class *Service-Model* contains information about the way a service works. Detailed technical information on how a service can be used is provided by the class *ServiceGrounding*. As learners are interested in the discovery process, this thesis concentrates only on the *ServiceProfile*. OWL-S does not determine a fixed representation of a service in *ServiceProfile*, but provides a way to define profiles for specific application domains. This can be achieved by task ontologies, and exactly such an ontology will be presented for the elearning Web services in the following.

Task Ontology

The task ontology for elearning Web services merely considers those services responsible for the provision of learning content. They are simplified for a better understanding here by concentrating on the most important characteristics of the ontology. As shown in Figure 5.7, two items have to be modeled in order to build the ontology: the learning content, on the one hand, and the learning service profile as specialization of the OWL-S *ServiceProfile* class, on the other hand. The learning content can be modeled on the foundation of LOM, as presented in Chapter 2.2. Several RDF approaches exist for modeling LOM (see, e.g., [NPB03, BN04]). The model described here uses a LOM description in OWL having a class *LearningObject* to represent the content related to an instance of the class *Author* via the *hasAuthor* relation. Although the content described by the ontology cannot be seen as a tradtitonal learning object but as a Web service, the concepts of LOM can still be used. LOM is centered around the concept of a learning object, which, in consequence, leads to the labeling of the class *LearningObject* to achieve an exact modeling of the LOM specifications. An author is characterized by attributes *hasName* and *hasEmail* which point to the XML Schema data type *string*. Author information can be found in LOM in the "Lifecycle" subsection. The properties *requires*, *isRequiredBy*, *hasPart*, and *isPartOf* are used to model content as well as structure dependencies and can be extracted from the LOM portion named "Relation". The technical format (corresponding to LOM section "Technical") and the category of the content (corresponding to LOM section "Classification") are described by properties *hasFormat* and *hasCategory*. It must be emphasized that the values of these properties are not restricted in order to enable a categorization of learning content by referencing classes of (domain-)ontologies of additional descriptions. This subsection will only focus on the usage of *hasCategory* and will use an existing specification for the area of software engineering.

Apart from class *LearningObject*, class *LearningServiceProfile* as a specialization of class *ServiceProfile* is the central concept in the ontology. Its modeling is similar to the modeling of the class *Profile* in OWL-S and contains information about the provider of the service in question, the functionality of the service, and information about special nonfunctional characteristics of the service. Information about the provider is captured by the property *hasProvider*. The provider is described by the property *hasName*, which is of the type *string* (i.e., the XML Schema data type string). Functional characteristics of the content learning service are a specialization of *functionalParameter*, and are modeled by the concepts *input* and *output*. In addition, the ontology has a non-functional property *hasPrice*, which is of the data type *float*.

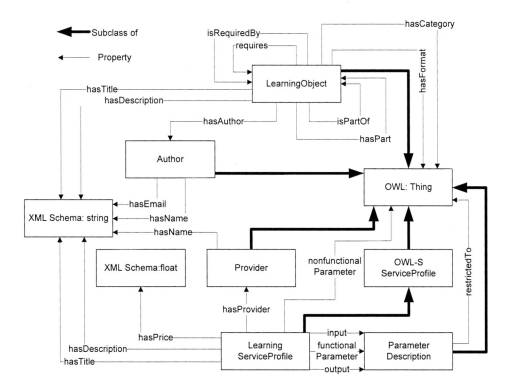

Figure 5.7: Simplified task-ontology for elearning content Web services [Sch03].

Domain Ontology

The task ontology enables a characterization of a learning Web service by categorization. Properties *hasFormat* and *hasCategory* are not restricted. This enables a classification by existing systems. As the example intends to focus on learning content for software engineering intended to be used in the CIAD course, the system of the Software Engineering Body of Knowledge (SWEBOK)[7] can be used for this purpose. SWEBOK, created by specialists, is a well-accepted classification in the field of software engineering. It covers ten areas of the software engineering domain and contains about 300 topics. [Sch03] has modeled a SWEBOK ontology in OWL which uses classes to represent areas and topics referencing properties *hasName* and *hasDescription* of the XML Schema data type *string*. The hierarchies are modeled by subclasses.

In the last step, distinctive information for a certain system can be modeled in an application ontology. After modeling the overall ontology, the representation of a given

---

[7]http://www.swebok.org/

content learning Web service is an instance of *LearningServiceProfile*. This can be found in [Sch03].

The search for a learning Web service based on a semantic matchmaking will generally provide better results because all the hits without an exact match will also be recognized. The results can be classified according to how closely a given query matches the learning Web services to be delivered. The search query can be interpreted as a restriction on the characteristics of a potential learning Web service. Thus, the services provided as the result of the query can be interpreted as the set of all services that do not "contradict" the query. This means that the result set is much bigger than the one of an exact match of characteristics of service metadata. [LH03] also specifies five classes of possible results feasible for content learning services. The class of "exact results" contains all services that have an equivalent description of concepts compared to the query. Class "PlugIn" is slightly less precise and contains all services that represent generalizations of the query. Traditional repositories without a semantic annotation are usually not able to provide results other than exact matches. Class "Subsumption" contains all the results that are specializations of the query. Although "PlugIn" and "Subsumption" are less precise than the exact match, they can still offer useful information. For instance, if a service with a certain description is not found, the requestor might want to use a more general one. In the software engineering field, this may be the case if the learner searches, for example, for the content about a certain process modeling language. If no adequate service is found, he or she may prefer a more general learning Web service. The same is possible if the search for process modeling does not result in exact matches, but may offer services about a special process modeling language. In this case, the results of class "Subsumption" are helpful. In general, requestors and providers may formulate their requests and offerings in a more imprecise way than it was initially intended in order to find other results in addition to the exact match they are looking for. The two additional classes not mentioned yet are "Intersection" and "Disjoint". Both of them are not very interesting as they do not match a query well. "Intersection" contains all the results that match the query to a certain degree; otherwise, the result ends up in the class "Disjoint".

As already sketched above, the semantic descriptions can also be stored on the remote servers of the service providers. In future, semantic search engines will be able to crawl these documents and enable a search functionality that is comparable to search engines in use today [ASF05]. As semantic search engines use ontologies, the concepts explained above can be used by these search engines, too.

5.1.3   Physical Architecture

The LearnServe Repository is implemented on the basis of an Apache Web server. The communication is based on SOAP messages marshaled and unmarshaled by a NuSOAP component[8]. The entire application functionality is implemented using PHP and data is stored in a MySQL database. It further offers WSDL documents for a download via HTTP. The physical architecture of the LearnServe Repository is pictured in Figure 5.8.

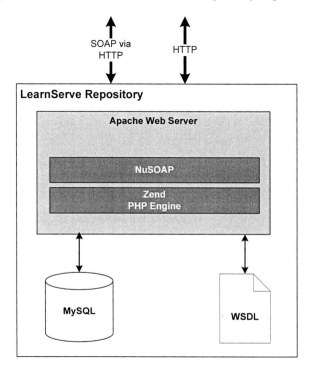

Figure 5.8: The physical architecture of the LearnServe Repository.

---

[8]NuSOAP is a set of PHP classes provided on http://sourceforge.net/projects/nusoap/

5.2   The LearnServe Provisioning Server

In the entire architecture, the provisioning server is the central instance that maintains the personal data of all learners and of other users of the system. Its functions can be classified into the central coordination of the CDSSO and the maintenance of profile and tracking data.

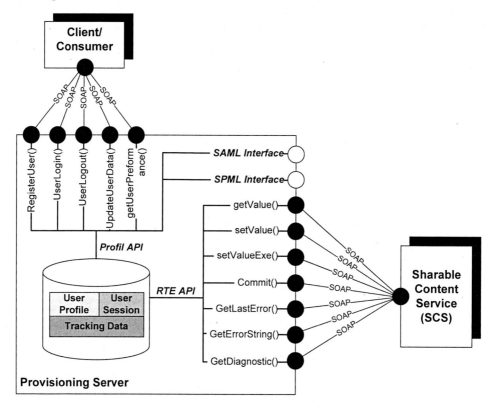

Figure 5.9: Conceptual model of the LearnServe Provisioning Server.

Figure 5.9 shows the conceptual model of the LearnServe Provisioning Server. Its data is subdivided into three parts: the user profile, the user tracking data, and the session data necessary for the CDSSO. The API to be used by other Web services consists of four parts: the RTE API for tracking data, a general Profile API for manipulating user related data, and the SAML and SPML interfaces for complex data manipulations. The RTE API for the service-oriented platform and the general Profile API are explained in the following and are proprietary for the implementation of the LearnServe Provisioning

Server. The SAML API as well as the SPML API are implemented as defined by the respective standard (see Chapter 4.3.2).

5.2.1   Cross-Domain-Single-Sign-On

The following description stresses the external architecture and message flows of the system used to implement the Cross-Domain-Single-Sign-On (CDSSO), as introduced in Chapter 4.2.3. The enhancements of the messages in the SOAP header sent within the entire system are important to identify the user on every server involved in the activities. For the sake of clarity security mechanisms are not mentioned again.

A user who does not have a profile on the LearnServe Provisioning Server has to create a new one first. It is a simple activity: the user has to key in certain information which is transferred to the LearnServe Provisioning Server by means of the *RegisterUser* function. Details are omitted here; the description of the function is shown in Table 5.6.

Table 5.6: Function RegisterUser()

Name:	**RegisterUser()**
Function Call:	string return_value = RegisterUser(User user)
user:	Includes necessary data to create a new user profile.
Return Value:	A string indicating if the profile was created (TRUE) or an error string (e.g., "UID already exists").
Type:	Technical, data-oriented Web service
LTSA Mapping:	Not explicitly part of LTSA, but related to Learner Process (LE).
WSDL File:	Appendix A, Listing A.4

For a person, the first step to use the distributed elearning functionalities is to key in a user identification (UID) and a password. Both password and UID are transmitted to the *UserLogin* service of the LearnServe Provisioning Server for validation. Table 5.7 shows the signature of this service. If the user data is correct, a SAML assertion is created and stored in the data space of the LearnServe Provisioning Server. This assertion can later on be used for the CDSSO of other services. The assertion comprises at least the UID of the user. The response of the *UserLogin* service is a SAML artifact to the consumer that is henceforth used in each Web service call to verify the access rights of the user in question. In the service-oriented case, as assumed here, the artifact consists of a unique token and also carries the URI of the LearnServe Provisioning Server to announce this address to all other servers that participate in the system. The artifact acts like a reference to the assertion on the LearnServe Provisioning Server. The token in LearnServe is technically generated by an MD5-encryption of the username. In general, the way how the token is generated is up to the implementation of the provisioning server since it is the only instance in the entire system to be able to interpret the token. All other peers in the system must only be able to extract the two parts from the entire artifact to be able to contact the provisioning server.

Table 5.7: Function UserLogin()

Name:	**UserLogin()**
Function Call:	artifact return_value = UserLogin(authenticate user)
user:	Includes UID and password. The UID identifies the user. It is a unique identification code that is stored inside the database of the LearnServe Provisioning Server to be able to identify a learner. The password is a sequence of characters used to determine that a user requesting access to the system is really that particular user.
Return Value:	A SAML artifact comprising a unique identification token for the new user session and the URI of the LearnServe Provisioning Server. If the authentication failed, FALSE will be returned as token.
Type:	Technical, data-oriented Web service
LTSA Mapping:	Not explicitly part of LTSA, but related to Learner Process (LE).
WSDL File:	Appendix A, Listing A.4

The artifact in combination with its corresponding assertion implements the CDSSO because all services can rely on the first authorization if the referenced assertion for an artifact exists. Based on these concepts the services can also implement a role concept. Although roles are not explicitly included in the artifact, the service provider can decide which user is allowed to access which service.

The login sequence of a user is shown in Figure 5.10 in the upper part. The use of the artifact is shown in the middle part. The artifact is added to the optional part of the SOAP header of all messages that are sent inside the system. It can be used by all involved servers to request the assertion stored on the LearnServe Provisioning Server via the SAML interface to check at least the UID and hence to verify the identity of the user. After the user logged in, he or she requests a functionality that is implemented as a Web service. The consumer intercepts the request and adds the artifact to the message that is afterwards sent to the server of the provider of the requested functionality. As

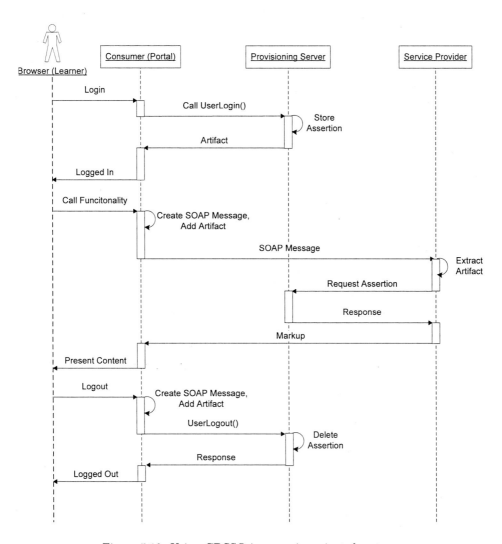

Figure 5.10: Using CDSSO in a service-oriented system.

the requested service is protected, the provider has to validate the token that is included in the artifact of the SOAP message. The provider extracts the artifact and uses the URI to contact the SAML interface of the LearnServe Provisioning Server to request the assertion of the user referenced by the token. As the assertion includes at least the UID of the user, the provider can check the access rights of the user.

The logout procedure is shown in the lower part of Figure 5.10. This function does not have any parameters because the artifact references a certain assertion on the LearnServe Provisioning Server. Upon arrival, the LearnServe Provisioning Server deletes the assertion. In consequence, servers are not able to request the assertion anymore and the CDSSO validation fails and the Web services are not being executed after a request. The signature of the *UserLogout* function is shown in Table 5.8.

Table 5.8: Function UserLogout()

Name:	**UserLogout()**
Function Call:	string return_value = UserLogout()
Return Value:	TRUE or FALSE will be returned depending on the success of the logout activity.
Type:	Technical, data-oriented Web service
LTSA Mapping:	Not explicitly part of LTSA, but related to Learner Process (LE).
WSDL File:	Appendix A, Listing A.4

5.2.2   Tracking

As shown in Chapter 4, tracking activities can be performed every time a learner interacts with a provider. The SCORM Run-Time Environment specification (SCORM RTE, see [ADL04c] and Chapter 2.2) defines the requirements for launching content objects establishing communication between LMSs and SCOs and managing the tracking information that can be communicated between SCOs and LMSs. Assets are not able to communicate with LMSs. These aspects create an environment that satisfies several of ADLs "ilities" (see Chapter 2.2), which build the conceptual starting points and define high-level requirements for all SCORM-based elearning environments. One of the major goals is the possibility to move content objects that are able to communicate from one LMS to another without a modification to their communication attempts. In the Web service environment, this movement is not necessary anymore because the content is presented by a Web service on demand. The central LMS is subdivided into a provisioning server, content providers, and repositories, which can be accessed via Web service interfaces. No matter what concept is chosen to implement a provisioning server, it has to offer several interfaces for the communication process that include particularly the communication of the content as specified by SCORM RTE, for a storage of data about the performance of a learner, as well as interfaces to maintain the master data of learners.

The main definitions of SCORM RTE encompass a common API (Application Programming Interface) and a data model. The API defines the functions that can be used in the communication process of the content and the LMS, the data model specifies the data that may be exchanged. In its simplest terms, the API is merely a set of functions that a SCO can rely on being available. How these functions are implemented is of no importance for the SCO as long as the API adheres to the semantics of the interface defined. The responsibility to find the API of the LMS as well as the initiation of all communication processes falls on the content building block. This means that the LMS acts only in the moment the content building block contacts the LMS, and there is currently no mechanism to initiate calls to functions implemented by content. The response sent by the LMS is purely generated in response of a request by a consumer.

The specification defines the data that is passed between a SCO and an LMS. This data is used as parameter of functions calls and is to be represented as character string, although SCORM RTE defines data types to be used for the internal representation inside the LMS. The function names and parameters are case-sensitive and are to be exactly expressed as defined in the SCORM RTE specification.

The communication model between a SCO and an LMS as defined by SCORM RTE corresponds with the typical communication model of Web services. Web service providers offer functionalities by publishing WSDL documents and offering the interfaces to start their activities in the moment a consumer requests a service. In the service-oriented elearning case, this means that a remote function on the LearnServe Provisioning Server is activated by sending a SOAP message to the corresponding interface, and the LearnServe Provisioning Servers responds with a corresponding SOAP message. In particular, the request message can include tracking data sent by a content block to be stored on the LearnServe Provisioning Server. The LearnServe Provisioning Server itself does not start any communication. SCORM RTE exactly defines which response has to be sent to a certain request including error-codes in case anything went wrong. Details about the error-codes and response messages can be found in [ADL04c]. The representation of data sent between the content and the LearnServe Provisioning Server in form of character strings reduces the complexity of the definition of the interfaces. All parameters will be defined as simple character strings and have to be interpreted by the corresponding service implementation as stipulated by SCORM RTE.

The decomposition of the former central LMS has some implications on the sequencing of content for the learner. Some data structures of the SCORM RTE specification have an impact on the navigation and sequencing. However, as the maintenance of content and the maintenance of user data are handled by different servers, the content server has to request data from the LearnServe Provisioning Server in order to make decisions concerning sequencing and navigation.

In the following, the API, the communication with this API, and the data model for the service-oriented elearning will be explained. The modeling follows the SCORM RTE specifications as far as possible. However, some implementation details and data model details differ from the standard because the service-oriented paradigm requires changes. The content block that is allowed to communicate to an LMS is called SCO in SCORM. As no physical objects are exchanged in the service-oriented environment, SCOs do not exist. Instead, a *Sharable Content Service (SCS)* builds the smallest unit that can communicate with a tracking instance on a provisioning server. The notion of an SCS is introduced in detail in Chapter 5.3. At the moment, it can be seen as a service-oriented SCO. Because the server of the content provider initiates the tracking process, as will be explained below, particularly an identification of the SCS in question has to be transmitted each time the communication takes place owing to the stateless nature of Web services.

The connection to the LearnServe Provisioning Server by an SCS is based on two major regulations. On the one hand, each SOAP message in the entire system carries the SAML artifact for the CDSSO process. This artifact includes the URI of the LearnServe Provisioning Server in order to check the learner's authorization. The URI can also be used by the provider of an SCS to contact the LearnServe Provisioning Server; in other words, the LearnServe Provisioning Server is already known to the server of the SCS. Accordingly, the API is already discovered and one major requirement of the SCORM RTE specification covered. The second regulation is the strict definition of functionalities according to the SCORM RTE specification. Thus, the server of the SCS can rely on the definitions of SCORM RTE. In addition, all descriptions of the remote services are described by WSDL documents that are published by the LearnServe Provisioning Server.

Tracking information about learning activities can be seen as simple *getValue* and *setValue* function calls on the data maintained by the LearnServe Provisioning Server and initiated by the provider of an SCS. These functions build the core of the entire communication between an SCS and the LearnServe Provisioning Server. SCSs use these data transfer methods to direct the storage and retrieval of runtime data from and to the LearnServe Provisioning Server. The calls have to be enlarged by an identity of the SCS that interacts with the LearnServe Provisioning Server. An additional identification of the learner to whom these tracking data belong is not necessary since all SOAP message carry the SAML

Table 5.9: Function getValue

Name:	**getValue()**
Function Call:	string return_value = getValue(string SCS, string element)
SCS:	Value SCS identifies the SCS. It is a unique identification code that is stored inside the database of the LearnServe Provisioning Server to be able to assign data exactly to an SCS and a learner. The SCS is only able to get data stored about itself or general information about the learner in question.
element:	Element identifies the data model element requested.
Return Value:	The method returns the value as string or an error code as defined by the SCORM RTE specification.
Type:	Technical, data-oriented Web service
LTSA Mapping:	Learner Info (LI), Learning Preferences (LP) Extension: Learner Info (D to R)
WSDL File:	Appendix A, Listing A.4

artifact identifying the learner. In the following, the signatures of the two most important functions of the service-oriented environment are explained in detail.

The *getValue* function requests information from the LearnServe Provisioning Server. This includes information on the general data model to find out which data can be stored on the LearnServe Provisioning Server as well as concrete values of data fields stored about an SCS that corresponds to the actual learner. The signature of the *getValue* function is shown in Table 5.9. The *setValue* function is used to request the LearnServe Provisioning Server to store data (see Table 5.10). In addition, a function *setValueExe()* is offered that has an additional parameter identifying the learner to whom the data belongs. This function is used by tracking interactions that are not invoked by the learner, but belong to a certain learner. The exercises, for example, are corrected by a human tutor. The tracking data is written after the tutor stored the results of the corrections (see also Chapter 4.2.1). The function *setValueExe* is not defined by SCORM and details are not presented here because it is equal to *setValue* except for the additional parameter. The signature of the function is shown in Appendix A, Listing A.4.

A third data method is the *Commit* function that only demands the identification of the SCS as parameter. Commit requests the LearnServe Provisioning Server to store data in the persistent data store if it uses a caching of data. If there is no caching, the function call has no effect. Again, TRUE and FALSE are the possible return values of this method.

Table 5.10: Function setValue

Name:	setValue()
Function Call:	string return_value = setValue(string SCS, string element, string value)
SCS:	Value SCS identifies the SCS. It is a unique identification code stored inside the database of the LearnServe Provisioning Server to be able to assign data exactly to an SCS and a learner.
element:	Element identifies the data model element requested.
value:	Parameter "value" is the value of the element requested.
Return Value:	The method returns TRUE or FALSE depending on the success of the storage of the data specification.
Type:	Technical, data-oriented Web service
LTSA Mapping:	Behavior (B), Learner Info (LI) Extension: Learner Info (D to R)
WSDL File:	Appendix A, Listing A.4

If errors occur during the processing of the above-mentioned services, the data methods have already returned the error-code or FALSE. The SCORM RTE specification defines three support methods to obtain information about errors. The methods *GetLastError* and *GetErrorString* receive the SCS identification as input parameter and return the last error-code or the last error-string respectively. In addition, a *GetDiagnostic* function having two input parameters (the SCS identification and an implementor-specific value) returns a character string with the diagnostic information requested. This function is not defined any further in SCORM and is a provisioning-server-specific value.

The data model of the LearnServe Provisioning Server is shown in Figure 5.11. It is subdivided into two main parts. The upper part of the data model covers the learner's profile and the session data and is made of four entities. This data only slightly changes, whereas the lower part of the data model covers the tracking information written during learning activities. It is up to the SCS how often and in how much detail this data is written, however, in comparison with profiles, tracking data changes often.

The central table "Learner" of the profiling part stores the basic data about a learner like first and last name, email address, address, and banking details for the accounting of learning material. Learners give this information during the registration process (see Table 5.6), and updates on these data sets are rare. A learner can have one or many learning

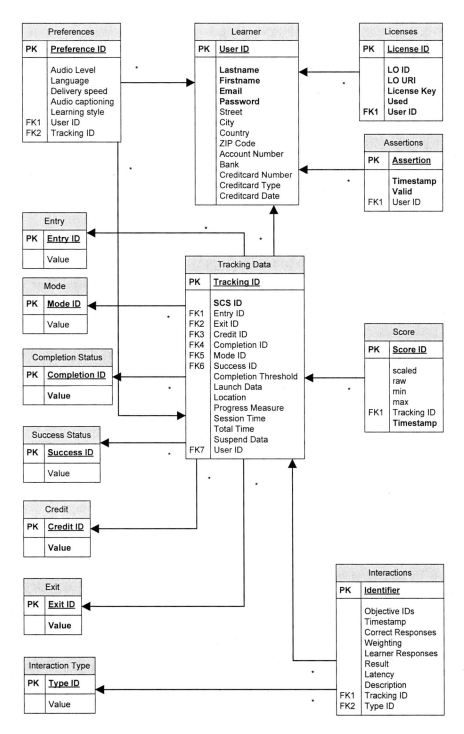

Figure 5.11: Data model of the LearnServe Provisioning Server.

preferences as defined by the SCORM RTE specification. The foreign key to a tracking data set and thus to an SCS is not mandatory and is only necessary if a learner wants to define certain preferences of a single SCS. More common is the case that there is no foreign key and only one learner's preferences data set, which describes the default setting for that learner. SCORM RTE does not define how these preferences are found; either can the learner state this information or an intelligent mechanism implemented inside the LearnServe Provisioning Server can set it. In the following it is assumed that the learner stated the information. In addition to the data defined by SCORM RTE, the table covers an attribute "Learning style" indicating if the learner likes to learn on definitions or by solving exercises etc. This information can have an impact on the decision which SCS is to present to the learner if the author of the SCS has defined different learning styles for the same content.

Licenses cover a certain allowance of the learner to use content and can be interpreted as the learning assignment of a learner. They are defined on a coarser grained granularity than the SCS. A license normally covers material that is made of several SCSs. A license is characterized by a server URI (the address of the Web service that presents the content) and an identification of the learning material it belongs to. In addition, the license is encoded by a certain string ("License key") that can cover, for example, a hash value of the identification and the duration the learner is allowed to use the content. This string is encoded by the instance that issues the license; and the LearnServe Provisioning Server does not have to interpret the meaning of this license code. Instead, the LearnServe Provisioning Server sends the license code to the requesting content server on demand. This server has to interpret the license key and has to decide whether to present the content to the learner. If the content will be presented, the flag "used" has to be turned to TRUE to indicate that the license was used by the learner. Depending on the type of license the learner is later allowed to access the content again. This depends on the interpretation of the license key by the content provider. License information is manipulated using the SPML interface.

Table "Assertion" keeps data about user sessions. An assertion is used by the CDSSO mechanism of the entire system to verify if a learner has started a learning session and has authenticated by a password and a user login. The SAML interface is used to access this data.

The lower part of the data model covers the tracking data and is modeled according to the SCORM RTE specification. It is thus explained only roughly here; details can be found in the SCORM RTE specification. The central table "Tracking Data" of the model covers information that always belongs to an SCS and a certain learner. If the SCS stores data, there is exactly one data set for each learner/SCS combination. Several attributes that belong to a tracking data set can only have predefined values. These values are defined by the SCORM RTE specification and are stored in the tables "Entry", "Exit", "Mode", "Completion Status", "Credit", and "Success Status". The "Success Status" data model element, for instance, indicates whether the learner has mastered the SCS. The way how the SCS determines its status is outside the scope of SCORM. The SCS could base this decision on a certain percentage of interactions being passed, a certain percentage of objectives being met, a total score for a test or quiz compared against a mastery score, etc. The value indicates the overall success status for the SCS as determined by the SCS author. The value space of these state values is bound by SCORM to three possibilities by the following restricted vocabulary tokens:

- "passed": the learner has passed the SCS. It indicates that a necessary number of objectives were mastered or a necessary score was achieved.

- "failed": the learner has failed the SCS. It indicates that the learner did not master the necessary number of objectives or that a required score was not achieved.

- "unknown": no assertion is made. This signals that no applicable assertion indicating the success status can be made.

Similar definitions can be found for all the attributes mentioned above. The information about the score which a learner achieved for the work on a certain SCS is closely connected to the "Success Status". It covers the minimum and maximum values and the value achieved as well as a scaled element that covers the overall performance of the learner for this SCS. The interactions data model element defines a set of learner responses that can be passed from the SCS to the LearnServe Provisioning Server. Interactions are intended to be responses to individual questions or tasks that the SCS developer wants to record. Interactions can be thought of as a collection of information (interaction data).

When interactions are requested to be set, the LearnServe Provisioning Server does not have to execute any activity apart from storing the data. The "Interactions" data model element can be used by an SCS particularly for journaling.

The LearnServe Provisioning Server also offers a simple functionality to obtain information about learner's learning activities. It returns all "Success Values" stored for a learner. The learner is identified by the CDSSO mechanism. The functionality has consequently no parameters. More complex queries can be made by a client implementation using SPML.

Table 5.11: Function getUserPerformance

Name:	**getUserPerformance()**
Function Call:	Performance performance = getUserPerformance()
performance:	The data structure encompasses all data sets with the identification of an SCS and the value of the SCORM "Success Status". It gives a broad overview of the learning success.
Type:	Technical, data-oriented Web service
LTSA Map-ping:	Learner Info (LI), related to Learner Entity (LE)
WSDL File:	Appendix A, Listing A.4

5.2.3   Physical Architecture

Figure 5.12 shows the physical architecture used for the LearnServe Provisioning Server. It is centered around open source implementations of the most important building blocks necessary to implement the specified interfaces of the LearnServe Provisioning Server. The most important part of the server is the Apache AXIS implementation that is an open source implementation of the SOAP specification. Apache AXIS is integrated in form of servlets into a servlet container like Apache Tomcat. Tomcat offers an HTTP server that receives and sends SOAP messages and serves additional requests, for example, the download of WSDL documents that describe the interfaces of the LearnServe Provisioning Server.

The SAML and SPML interfaces use open source implementations offered on the Web in form of Java programs. The profile API and the RTE API are implemented in form of Java programs that interact with an Oracle 9i database via a JDBC connection.

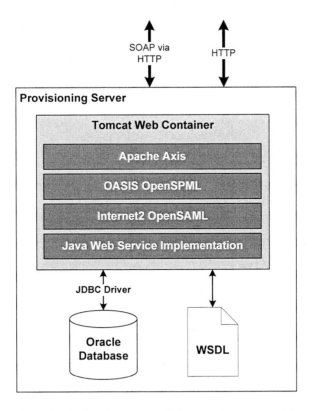

Figure 5.12: The physical architecture of the LearnServe Provisioning Server.

5.3 Learning Content Web Services

The offering of learning material as a Web service has to fulfill at least two functions. On the one hand, the presentation information to be sent to the consumer in order to display the content in the correct manner. On the other hand, traditional learning objects have to communicate with an LMS in order to track the learners' activities based on a client-side SCORM API instance. This API is now offered by the LearnServe Provisioning Server in a service-oriented way. The content on the client side is not able to connect to these Web services, but tracking data must still be stored. Both aspects are covered by the realization of the basic LearnServe Content Provider. Mediators in turn can combine learning material to courses that are especially designed to populate content checklists for learners. They use other manufacturers' content services to offer their added value. Mediators as a special form of content providers are introduced in Chapter 5.3.3.

5.3.1   Basic LearnServe Content Provider

As explained in Chapter 2.2, traditional learning objects adhering to the SCORM specification are physical files containing SCOs and Assets that are copied and exchanged
between LMSs. They consist of content resources and an API implementation used by
SCOs to connect to the LMS and store tracking data on the latter.

To build learning "object" Web services, a content provider has to implement an interface
to support Web services. This interface is used to offer content in a service-oriented way;
there are several different possibilities to achieve this. However, the general idea is always
the same and has been already sketched above: the content stored in a database or in an
XML file has to be extracted and enriched by presentation information; afterwards, one
or more SOAP messages carrying the content and the presentation information has or
have to be constructed. These SOAP messages have to be sent to the consumer platform
to display the content to the learner. In principle, there are three ways to realize this,
which will be explained in the following:

1. If the device on the consumer side has capacities to execute transformations, two
   data-oriented Web services can be used to send, on the one hand, the raw content to
   the consumer and to send, on the other hand, a stylesheet containing presentation
   instructions, see Figure 5.13a. The consumer has to extract the necessary information from both SOAP messages; moreover, the stylesheet and the content have to
   be processed and transformed to display the output for the learner. This solution
   is proprietary and has to be implemented for each consumer. It is not conform to
   the standard of WSRP and turns the consumer into a complex application.

2. The second scenario uses a mixture of presentation and data-oriented Web services.
   In this case, the consumer machine receives a data-oriented message containing the
   raw content of the learning section, but it does not receive a message with presentation instructions. Instead, it sends the content in a SOAP request to another (third)
   provider of presentation Web services. This provider is in charge of combining a presentation stylesheet with the content. Afterwards, the consumer machine receives
   a SOAP response message from the presentation provider containing the content in
   an already presentable format, as proposed by presentation-oriented Web services,
   see Figure 5.13b. The advantage of this approach is the fact that the consumer
   platform is able to set additional information for the preparation of the content for
   presentation. This additional information is included in that message which is sent
   to the provider of the presentation Web service. However, network traffic increases
   owing to additional communication steps. It is also doubtful if the content provider

can be separated from the stylesheet provider since the structure of the content and, thus, the stylesheet depends on the implementation of the content provider. This makes this second approach very difficult to be implemented.

3. Processing the entire transformation on the server of the provider is the most likely form of conversion. After a consumer's content request, the server of the provider extracts the required content from its database and converts the raw content to a presentation-oriented response message using a stylesheet, as shown in Figure 5.13c. This can be achieved, for example, by means of XSL stylesheets with a corresponding XSLT transformation [Kay00]. The entire transformation can easily be implemented in a WSRP-conform way since the provider defines the SOAP message to be sent to the consumer completely. For these reasons, this approach is used for the realization of the basic LearnServe Content Provider; it is explained in the following.

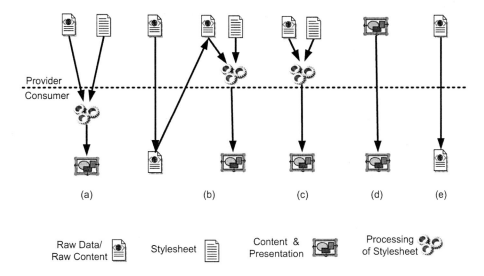

Figure 5.13: Possibilities to provide learning material as Web service.

Apart from the already-mentioned methods, there are two other simple possibilities to access learning material via a Web service; they are mentioned for the sake of completeness. The approaches are limited in their ability to be used via a plug-and-play integration because they are data-oriented. Although the presentation of the content is included in the message, the first one is a data-oriented procedure, as shown in Figure 5.13d. After the consumer's request the content provider returns a Packaging Interchange File (PIF, see Chapter 2.2) as MIME-attachment to the SOAP message or as binary code within the message. The PIF includes everything necessary for an LMS to present the content to a learner. However, this is only possible because an LMS knows exactly what to do with a PIF file. Web service clients which are not LMSs are not able to handle the file in the correct manner as long as there is no additional application code that can handle the PIFs. Conceptually, this approach is not different to the traditional (physical) exchange of learning objects since it is an import of the PIF to the consumer platform and, hence, a copy of the resources containing the learning content. The second possibility is shown in Figure 5.13e. It returns the raw content as data-oriented Web service in a SOAP message in response to the consumer request. If there is a clear (didactical) understanding of the message format on the consumer side, the latter is able to construct the presentation without any presentation information provided by the server. However, this can only be assumed in closed environments and does not provide an acceptable solution for an open environment.

The implementation of the API instance to communicate with tracking services offered by the LearnServe Provisioning Server or another tracking service implementation can conceptually be realized on the client side (i.e., browser or consumer) or on the content provider side. The implementation on the client side can be attained in two ways.

1. The first one is to include ECMAScript (or JavaScript) or any other application code in WSRP markup fragments to connect to the tracking service of the provisioning server used by the respective learner. This ECMAScript code has to be executed on the learner's browser. Although this approach is in line with typical SCORM implementations, its realization is very difficult in the Web service environment since the browser has to invoke a Web service on the provisioning server. SCORM defines that content (i.e., a SCO) is to contact the tracking mechanism, but the way to implement this in a service-oriented environment is very complex using ECMAScript. The use of the latter is generally (even within traditional SCORM-conform learning objects) questionable since it forces the user to enable ECMAScript on his or her browser. This makes the use of elearning not browser-independent and may also lead to security problems. In addition, learners with advanced programming skills may be able to inspect the code transferred to the browser to manipulate their learning success.

2. The second client-based approach implements the Web service invocation on the consumer. This implies a certain intelligence on the consumer platform because it has to evaluate learner activities.

However, to realize a plug-and-play integration of content, it is most likely that a content provider interacts with the provisioning server used to maintain the tracking information of the respective learner. This is feasible due to the following reasons.

1. The content provider has to implement a Web service interface anyway. It can also be used to store the tracking information.

2. The content provider is aware of the provisioning server owing to the CDSSO mechanism. Consequently, the demand to find the tracking interface as specified by SCORM is already satisfied.

3. The content provider is able to evaluate learner interactions with the content. The only design decision to be recognized is the one that the interactions with the provider have to be as frequent as tracking information ought to be transferred to the provisioning server (see below).

4. On the client side (i.e., a browser of the end user or a consumer), no complex activities have to be executed. The consumer merely has to communicate with the content provider and request markup information to present the content.

In conclusion, the mechanism to provide learning material as Web service in LearnServe is implemented in form of common WSRP messages. These messages are completely constructed by the LearnServe Content Provider and sent afterwards to the consumer, as explained above. Tracking the learner activities is executed by the LearnServe Content Provider after learner interactions with the latter. In consequence, content is very flexible and can be plugged into every common WSRP client.

The overall process of using learning material as Web services is organized as presented in the following (see also Figure 4.15). After searching for content in a Web-services-based repository, for example, the LearnServe Repository, the latter returns a link and information about matching content Web services, i.e. portlets, to the consumer. If the learner then decides to access certain content, the consumer sends a SOAP message with a WSRP *getMarkup* request to the Web service interface of that content provider to receive the first part of the content. The signature of the WSRP getMarkup function is shown in Table 5.12[9]. The content provider has to check if the user owns a valid license. This is executed by an SPML request on the provisioning server to send all valid licenses that correspond to the content. The result covers all valid licenses and the content provider can check if the learner is allowed to use the material. The content is logically divided into several "presentation" pages that can be interpreted as content to be displayed and tracked at

---

[9]For simplicity, the signature of this functionality is only described by data types.

Table 5.12: Function getMarkup()

Name:	**getMarkup()**
Function Call:	MarkupResponse = getMarkup(RegistrationContext, Portlet-Context, RuntimeContext, UserContext, MarkupParams);
RegistrationContext	Contains information related to a particular registration of a consumer with a producer, e.g., a reference handle to their relationship.
PortletContext:	Supplies portlet information that was pushed to the consumer.
RuntimeContext :	A collection of fields used in transient interactions between the producer and the consumer, e.g., a session ID for referencing state on the producer.
UserContext:	Supplies end user specific data to operations, e.g., an end user profile. It does not include user credentials like userID and password.
MarkupParams:	A set of fields that is needed to visualize the markup on the device of the end user, e.g., information if the channel to the client is secured.
Return Value:	The MarkupResponse type contains in particular the returned markup and fields related to this markup.
Type:	User-facing, presentation-oriented Web service
LTSA Mapping:	Multimedia (M), Learning Content (LC), Locator (L)
WSDL File:	Appendix A, Listing A.5

once. For this reason, content which is presented to the learner and which is communicating with a tracking instance implemented by a provisioning server is called *SCS*. This
means *Sharable Content Service* according to SCORM's SCO (Sharable Content Object).
SCSs are still composed of several Assets as defined by SCORM; they represent reusable
building blocks. Several SCSs can be composed to build a complex learning material
service (i.e., a class or course), which is conceptually an SCS again. The content provider
can contact the provisioning server to write tracking data via the *setValue* function, as
explained in Chapter 5.2. The content provider sends a SOAP message including the
content and the presentation information of the SCS to the consumer. If the consumer
platform is a Web portal, SCSs can be presented to learners via common Web pages that
can be displayed by a Web browser. However, as SCSs are WSRP conform, they are very
flexible and can also be interpreted by other consumer applications, for example, on a
mobile device with a proprietary end user program. The entire process is shown in Figure
5.14. Each additional part of the content is sent after a call of the next SCS and the
getMarkup operation by using links in the displayed presentation pages. Normally, the
learner does not recognize any difference to traditional Web-based runtime systems. The
links that point to the next part of the learning service (i.e., the next SCS) have to be
rewritten by the WSRP consumer, and invocations of the links have to be handled by the
WSRP consumer before the SOAP message can be sent to the content provider.

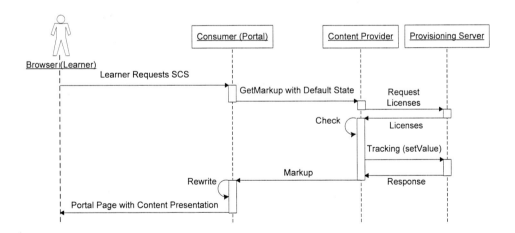

Figure 5.14: Service-based content presentation.

The presentation pages of the content Web service include the structure of the content
and the latter itself comprising graphics, sounds, video, etc., which can be attached as

MIME objects to the SOAP message. The logical organization of the presentation generated by the LearnServe Content Provider is shown in Figure 5.15. The structure of the
content is displayed on the left hand side as it is common in elearning platforms today.
Depending on the definitions of the author and on didactical reasons, this structure may
consist of links that can be used by a learner to navigate within the content services.
Another definition may include only those parts of the content structure that ought to be
visible for the learner owing to didactical reasons defined by the author. The extent of this
structure can vary with each call of the Web service. Technically, each content building
block refers to an SCS. By clicking on one of the links included within the structure, a
server interaction is initiated, which enables the LearnServe Content Provider to execute
a tracking of data and a selection of new content for the learner. The content structure
can easily be attached to the content in form of a tree on the left hand side of the page
to enable a navigation between SCSs. The entire message is conform to the WSRP standard and can hence be interpreted and displayed (didactically) correctly by the consumer.

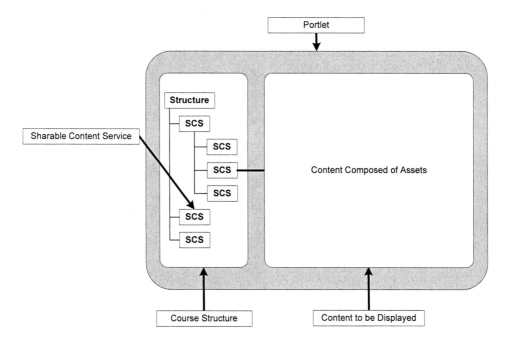

Figure 5.15: LearnServe's SCS presentation to learners.

The consumer has to rewrite all-included links within the content to reroute user requests
to the LearnServe Content Provider. Every selection of a link in the material or index is

Table 5.13: Function accreditation.

Name:	**accreditation()**
Function Call:	string return_value = accreditation(string SCS, string review)
SCS:	Parameter SCS identifies the SCS.
review:	Review keeps the comments of the reviewer.
Return Value:	The method returns TRUE or FALSE depending on the success of the storage of the data specification.
Type:	Technical, data-oriented Web service
LTSA Mapping:	Not part of LTSA.
WSDL File:	Appendix A, Listing A.3

intercepted by the consumer, rerouted to the LearnServe Content Provider and tracked afterwards. Since no displaying action has to be taken in the core tracking process, this message flow is performed by a data-oriented Web service (by calling the *setValue* operation as defined in Chapter 5.2).

In a more advanced scenario the content selection for a special kind of learner on the provider side can be influenced by the learner's profile. One learner may, for instance, prefer theoretical material, whereas another learner wants to start with some examples about the use of the covered material. To cope with this, the LearnServe Content Provider can query the RTE API of the LearnServe Provisioning Server as a reaction to an incoming consumer's request message. The LearnServe Content Provider can then call the (data-oriented) Web service to gain information about the learner's preferences provided by the learner's profile (by calling the *getValue* Web service as defined in Chapter 5.2). The corresponding information is stored in the field "Learning style" in the data model shown in Figure 5.11. According to the response message sent by the LearnServe Provisioning Server, appropriate content for the learner can be selected. The different SCSs that can be used alternatively within a course and their selection rules have still to be defined by authors in advance. However, with the evolution of the semantic Web and intelligent agents as well as semantic search engines, the platform of the LearnServe Content Provider will hopefully be able to execute the selection process automatically in future. This includes both the personalization and the contextualization of learning material. A semantic approach to annotate SCSs in order to support this automatic selection has already been introduced in Chapter 5.1. The SCS approach in combination with the semantic annotation offers the opportunity to support the automatic selection in the future. The entire

Table 5.14: Function bookContent.

Name:	**bookContent()**
Function Call:	string license = bookContent(string SCS, Bank bank)
SCS:	Value SCS identifies the SCS.
bank:	Covers bank information like account number, bank, name of learner, or credit card informations like card number, card type, card date.
Return license:	A unique code generated from the username and a validation date or FALSE.
Type:	Technical, data-oriented Web service
LTSA Mapping:	Not part of LTSA.
WSDL File:	Appendix A, Listing A.3

system is already very flexible and enables a use of SCSs that are anywhere on the Web. In contrast to this flexible selection, current adaptability approaches are typically limited to single learning platforms.

Reviewers can accredit content by means of the *accreditation* functionality, explained in Table 5.13. It is a comment that belongs to a certain SCS. LearnServe supports only the accreditation on the basis of entire structures. This means that the comments belong to the top level in the Manifest hierarchy. An incoming review is stored directly in the Manifest document. Afterwards, the new Manifest can be sent to the LearnServe Repository in order to update the metadata for the content.

To obtain a license for a certain content, a learner has to book this content. This can be achieved by means of the function *bookContent*, as shown in Table 5.14. It receives the identity of the SCS and payment information of the user. The payment information can be used by the LearnServe Content Provider to process the payment. Afterwards, a unique license is generated by means of a hash-function, the username, and a validation date. If a learner afterwards requests content, the license can be checked easily be means of these aspects.

Figure 5.16 shows the conceptual model of the LearnServe Content Provider. It has to offer a WSRP interface to enable an access to the SCSs. In addition, an authoring interface has to be provided. As there are many authoring tools available that can be used to create and store content in the database of the server, this interface is not described in this thesis. The LearnServe Content Provider accesses in particular the RTE API of

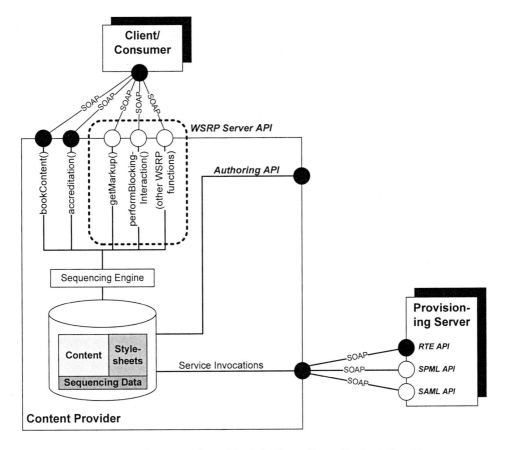

Figure 5.16: Conceptual model of the LearnServe Content Provider.

a provisioning server used by the respective learner to track interactions and the SPML and SAML interface in order to check access rights. To retrieve content in the intended way, the sequencing engine controls and executes the process of building the output for a learner.

Figure 5.17 shows the data model of the LearnServe Content Provider. It is designed in order to fulfill two goals. This is, on the one hand, a reuse of existing documents as provided by the SCORM specification (i.e., in particular the Manifest document) and, on the other hand, a flexible internal reuse at different levels of content granularity. This includes the reuse of Assets, SCSs, and stylesheets.

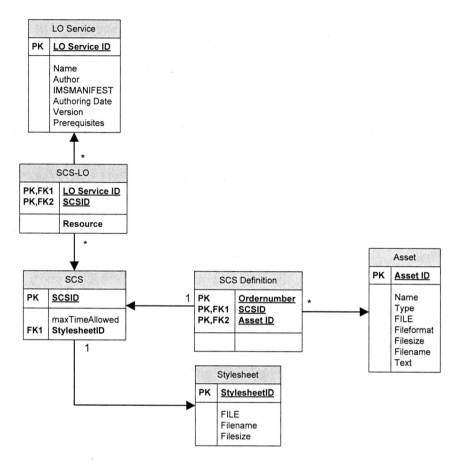

Figure 5.17: Data model of the LearnServe Content Provider.

The central concept as explained above is the SCS which is related to exactly one stylesheet. The stylesheet is an XSL document that is stored inside a database field "FILE" of the type BLOB (binary large object). The table also stores the original name and the size of the XSL file. This information is used if an author has to download a stylesheet from the server.

An SCS may have a maximum time to be displayed according to the SCORM definitions. Several Assets build an SCS, and Assets can be used in different SCSs. An Asset is characterized by its name and its type (text, graphic, animation, etc.). If the Asset is not a text, it is stored within a BLOB database field "FILE" and is described by its file format, filename, and file size. It can have additional descriptions that are stored in the text field. If the Asset is a text, the latter is just stored in the text field offered in the Asset table.

The sequence of several SCSs builds a complex learning service. The latter is still described by the Manifest document that is stored as an XML file in the BLOB field "IMSMAN-IFEST". All information necessary to be stored about content is part of this file. This includes particularly the (LOM) metadata and the sequencing information as well as the references to the SCS resources. The latter are mapped to the "LO Service" and to an SCS to connect names with IDs of the data sets. Only a couple of data sets are stored separately in the database to ensure a faster access to those pieces of information. For all additional accesses to information contained in the Manifest document, it has to be parsed by an XML parser.

5.3.2 Physical Architecture

The physical architecture of the LearnServe Content Provider is centered around the WSRP producer implemented in form of a Java library called WSRP4J[10]. The content and the stylesheets are stored inside an Oracle database (version 9i). After a request, the content and a corresponding stylesheet are extracted from the database. A Sablotron XSLT engine is to enrich the content by executing a transformation on the raw content and the stylesheet. The sequencing engine has to add the structure of the course to the content, as defined by the author. The entire content block is passed to the WSRP producer, which uses the Apache Axis implementation to send the SOAP message to the consumer.

The Apache Axis is embedded as servlet into the Tomcat module, which is itself part of an Apache Web server. The WSRP interfaces are described by WSDL documents, as defined by OASIS. These documents can be downloaded via HTTP. The WSDL documents can be found in Appendix A, Listing A.5.

---

[10]http://ws.apache.org/wsrp4j

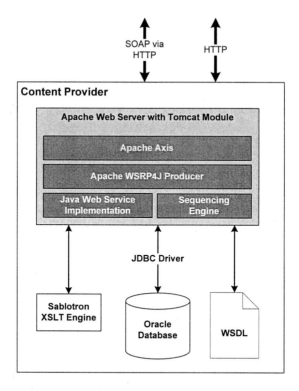

Figure 5.18: Physical architecture of the LearnServe Content Provider.

5.3.3 Mediators

The previous subsection has described a single server providing content as Web service. As already mentioned above, the concepts of SCSs enables to use resources offered anywhere on the Web by invoking the services on demand. A *mediator* in elearning can be seen as a special type of content author who offers courses made of content, which may have even been created by other manufacturers. A mediator can be, for example, an organization creating courses which are compliant to checklists defined for learners participating in tertiary educational programs, for example, for the CIAD course of Figure 1.1 mentioned above. In this case, they provide their added value for learners, for instance, by populating checklists with concrete SCSs. The learner relies on the knowledge of the mediator and is afterwards (hopefully) well prepared to pass the examinations of the course. Normally, mediators are independent manufacturers and try to train learners to pass certain exams offered by examination institutions.

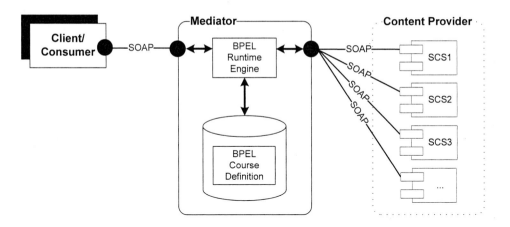

Figure 5.19: Conceptual model of a mediator.

Elearning courses in traditional, centralized environments are often made of several (physical) learning objects. A mediator reuses existing learning objects and combines them to a new course. This is performed physically by copying files containing the content and by defining the structure of the new course by means of using, for example, IMS Simple Sequencing. Afterwards, the course files are packaged into an IMS Packaging Interchange File that can be exchanged over the Web and plugged into any LMS if both the LMS and the course adhere to certain standards. In particular, it is now possible for a learner to buy these PIFs from the mediator to get the content of choice. It is worth mentioning that a combination of content already stored inside a platform does not necessarily require to copy files, but to reference them. In any case, a reference to content outside the LMS is normally not possible.

A mediator in a Web-services-based environment has different tasks to cover as learning material is not physically available, but implemented as SCSs and provided on demand by remote servers. This means that the mediator has to combine service calls rather than files. The execution order of the services cannot be controlled by an LMS because it does not exist. Instead, the mediator defines course structures that have to be controlled by the mediator itself or by any instance being able to import and execute these course definitions. As content is offered as a common Web service, BPEL4WS (see Chapter 3.6.5) can be used to define elearning courses based on Web services. These courses themselves are Web services. A (BPEL) runtime engine has to control the invocations of the Web services and has to keep track of the state of the learning sessions for different learners who might use the same service.

Technically, the integration and execution of processes described by BPEL can be implemented in various ways. Normally, the Web services are integrated into a Web portal that serves as an access point for the learner and can include and use several Web services of different providers. If this portal is able to execute processes described by BPEL documents, the mediator may offer and sell the BPEL-course description to be downloaded and executed by the BPEL runtime engine of the portal. However, as a runtime environment for BPEL is a complex software, this option is not the best choice because it cannot be assumed that every learner access point is able to execute these processes.

Content providers can also offer courses that are made of several content services. As the courses are described by metadata just like learning objects and come with a WSDL description, the implementation of the courses via a BPEL description may not be obvious for learners. Again, BPEL can be used to control the order of the content service execution. Therefore, it makes a description via IMS Simple Sequencing obsolete.

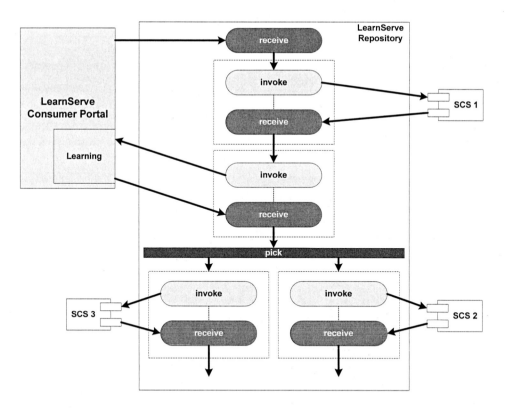

Figure 5.20: Execution of a course built from several content services with BPEL.

Figure 5.19 shows the conceptual model of an independent mediator. This can be, for example, an additional instance in the entire distributed organization or an already existing one like the LearnServe Repository. The latter is a central lookup platform in the distributed organization and covers metadata about many content services. This knowledge can easily be used by authors to offer courses from various manufacturers through a combination of different SCSs. Thus, a repository in general is a good instance to serve as a mediator. To achieve this, it has to be enhanced by a BPEL runtime engine to execute course descriptions. It further has to store the BPEL course descriptions on its server and provide WSDL descriptions for learners to access the courses. Metadata of these courses have to be stored into the database of the repository and can then be found by learners via the common search functionality. The combined courses technically look like single content services for learners, although they cover more topics.

Using BPEL, courses can be defined by graphical tools such as the ORACLE BPEL Process Manager[11]. Accordingly, authors of courses do not need a special authoring tool for elearning to glue the existing SCSs together. Although graphical assistance helps the course author to manage the creation of courses, basic knowledge about Web services is necessary if a mapping of data between SCSs of different manufacturers has to be defined. In addition, authors of courses must have distinct knowledge about the domain to be learned to select appropriate SCSs.

Figure 5.20 describes a sample scenario of a course program executed under the control of the BPEL runtime module, which is an enhancement of the LearnServe Repository. The first step in the overall processing is the selection of the course by a learner. This step is not pictured in the figure, but is a prerequisite to receive the address (URI) of the course Web service in question. After the selection of the course, the LearnServe Consumer calls the desired content service of that course. It is a Web service using a BPEL process description to combine several SCSs to a course. The outermost structure is a sequence to call the content services step by step in a pedagogically useful order. The first invocation is a call of the SCS 1 that delivers content from provider 1. The repository forwards the results to the LearnServe Consumer to present the content to the learner. After the learner has finished learning the content of SCS 1, the LearnServe Repository receives a message from the LearnServe Consumer to continue. Owing to the definition of the course author, the next content to be learned by the learner is part of SCS 2 or SCS 3 depending on some conditions defined by the author of the course. The BPEL runtime engine uses existing data to figure out which service to call.

The CIAD sample course can also be described by means of BPEL and executed like

---

[11] see http://otn.oracle.com/bpel

mentioned before. The pick activity models alternatives for the first and third module. The condition specifying the selection of SCS 2 or SCS 3 in Figure 5.20 or even in the CIAD sample can be based on different data sets. On the one hand, this can be the result of an activity executed by a learner while using SCS 1. On the other hand, it can be a condition that decides whether a learner needs more information covered by SCS 1 in order to deepen the learner's knowledge. It is also possible that the BPEL process queries the user preferences by invoking the *getValue* Web service offered by the provisioning server maintaining user data. In this case, the condition may consider the learner's preferences to decide which content service ought to be executed. This can be, for example, a more theoretical content for a certain learner, whereas the same topics presented in a more practical way may be the more suitable solution for another learner.

5.4   Exercise and Examination Web Services

The OASIS WSRP specification enables the implementation of interactive Web services with session persecution and time limits for different users as presentation-oriented Web services. This functionality makes it also possible to develop exercises for the learners in a comparable way as described for the LearnServe Content Provider.

In general, exercises and examinations can be interpreted as special content to be included into a course. In consequence, they are SCSs like any other content building block, but include at least one additional interaction with the server of the exercise provider. This interaction takes place at the very moment the learner submits his or her solution. The granularity of the SCSs of exercises and examinations is not fixed and can include one or several exercises. The interpretation of an SCS in this context is comparable to the one of content presentation and can be seen as "content to be presented at once".

In the following, the handling of exercises, based on the xLx system, is described. Although the concepts are described for this particular system, the basic ideas are more general and can be implemented for any exercise provider.

5.4.1   xLx Wrapper

Exercises are provided within the "Submit Section" of the xLx system, as explained in Chapter 2.4.4. The xLx system displays only one exercise to a learner at once. Accordingly, the SCSs of the xLx system only encompass one exercise per *getMarkup* request. Figure 5.21 presents the conceptual architecture of the xLx system to provide exercise services. The basic functionality of the xLx "Submit Section" is still the same,

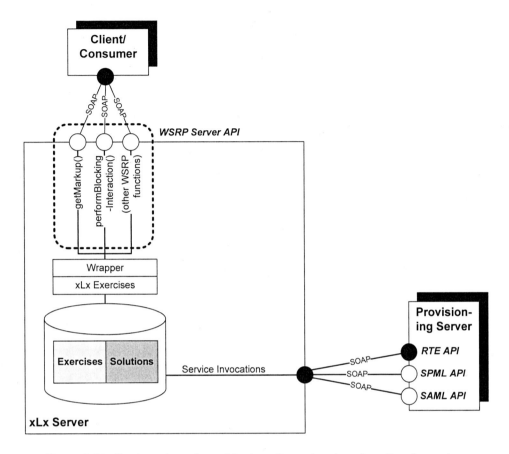

Figure 5.21: Service-oriented provisioning of exercises based on the xLx system.

but the presentation of exercises and the submission of solutions is handled through a special wrapper program. The wrapper interrupts the incoming requests and outgoing responses and enables a conversion of the original xLx-Web-based communication into a Web-services-based communication using SOAP messages and the WSRP standard. The outgoing HTML pages containing the exercise presentation are converted into WSRP-conform messages. In turn, the incoming requests are mapped to the corresponding functionalities. The model in Figure 5.21 merely shows the two most important interfaces of the WRSP producer. In addition, a booking interface could be included like in the LearnServe Content Provider. However, the actual version of xLx does not support licenses. This is why the interface is not implemented here.

The xLx platform stores solutions in a database. In addition, the tracking RTE API of the LearnServe Provisioning Server has to be called two times. This is, on the one hand, in the moment the learner submits the solution. The tracking data set now indicates that the exercise has been solved by the learner. The second time the xLx system has to call the RTE API of the LearnServe Provisioning Server is after the exercise has been corrected. In xLx, this is typically performed manually. The only automatic correction of the xLx is applied for multiple-choice questions. In this case, the points achieved for the solution can be stored on a provisioning server at once. If anything has to be corrected manually, the RTE API is called after the tutor has corrected the learner's solution. In both cases the *setValueExe* function is used owing to the initiation of the interaction by the xLx system. For example, it sets the value "success status" (see Chapter 5.2.2) of the corresponding exercise to "passed" if a learner gets more than 50% of the maximum points.

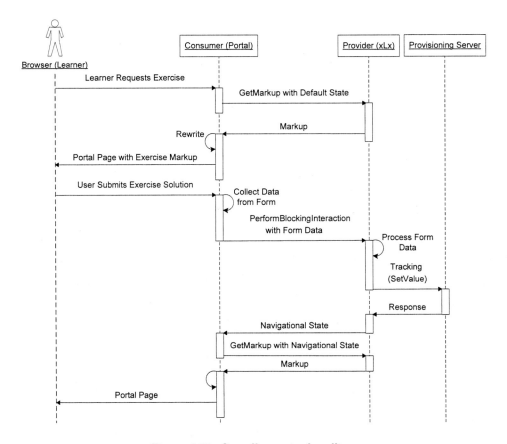

Figure 5.22: Overall exercise handling.

The xLx system is a full-fledged exercise platform and includes a Web-based authoring interface. The latter is not shown in Figure 5.21. Although the exercises are now handled as Web services, the legacy Web-based authoring interface of xLx can still be used to create exercises. Figure 5.22 shows the sequence for the overall handling of xLx exercises in the LearnServe environment. The learner uses a common Web browser to access the LearnServe Consumer Portal and requests an exercise. One exercise can be interpreted as an SCS and can contain Assets like texts, graphics etc. This request is forwarded by the consumer in a SOAP message to the xLx system. The message contains the *getMarkup* function call to receive the presentation information of the exercise. The xLx system generates the markup with the necessary Assets and responds by means of a SOAP message. After the consumer has received the message, links and names of forms have to be rewritten by the consumer. Then the page is presented to the learner and contains, for example, a text field to enter the solution of the exercise.

The learner keys in the solution into the text field and submits the solution. The submission is interrupted by the consumer and does not go directly to the xLx system since it is not a SOAP message so far. Instead, the consumer receives the submitted solution, collects the data (i.e., the solution) from the message and sends a *performBlockingInteraction* request in a SOAP message to the xLx system. This operation is to send user interactions and form data to the producer. The producer can change the state of the portlet and perform additional activities. In this case, the xLx system processes the message and extracts the solution from the SOAP message. Afterwards, it sends some tracking information to the LearnServe Provisioning Server (e.g., the "success status" after an automatic correction of multiple-choice exercises). The provider's response sent via a SOAP message to the consumer can include additional information for the consumer. In this case, a new *Navigational State* is transmitted. The producer expects the consumer to include the latter into the following *getMarkup* request. This request is then executed by the consumer, and the new page is displayed to the learner after the xLx system has returned the markup.

Table 5.15[12] shows the signature of the *performBlockingInteraction* function, as defined in the WSRP specification [KLT03]. The latter function and the *getMarkup* function, already explained in Chapter 5.3, are the most important WSRP definitions to implement exercises and examinations in a service-oriented way. Further details to these definitions can be found in [KLT03] and will not be explained in detail here because the functionalities are used as defined in the standard. Playgrounds are conceptually not different from exercises. They provide an interface to key in data, for example, in form of SQL statements. This data is transmitted to the xLx system and executed. The results of the executions are

---

[12]For simplicity, the signature of this functionality is only described by data types.

Table 5.15: Function performBlockingInteraction()

Name:	**performBlockingInteraction()**
Function Call:	BlockingInteractionResponse = performBlockingInteraction (RegistrationContext, PortletContext, RuntimeContext, UserContext, MarkupParams, InteractionParams);
RegistrationContext:	Contains information related to a particular registration of a consumer with a producer, e.g., a reference handle to their relationship.
PortletContext:	Supplies portlet information that was pushed to the consumer.
RuntimeContext:	A collection of fields used in transient interactions between the producer and the consumer, e.g., a session ID for referencing state on the producer.
UserContext:	Supplies end-user-specific data to operations, e.g., an end user profile. It does not include user credentials like userID and password.
MarkupParams:	A set of fields necessary to visualize the markup on the device of the end user, e.g., information if the channel to the client is secured.
InteractionParams:	Specific fields to invoke the performBlockingInteraction. This includes, in particular, form data submitted by the end user.
Return Value:	The BlockingInteractionResponse includes particularly either items returned or another URL the end user ought to be redirected to.
Type:	Interactive, presentation-oriented Web service
LTSA Mapping:	Multimedia (M), Learning Content (LC), Locator (L)
WSDL File:	Appendix A, Listing A.5

returned to the learner. Accordingly, playgrounds use the same interaction pattern with a *getMarkup* call to provide content and input form to be displayed, and interact with the xLx by means of a *performBlockingInteraction*.

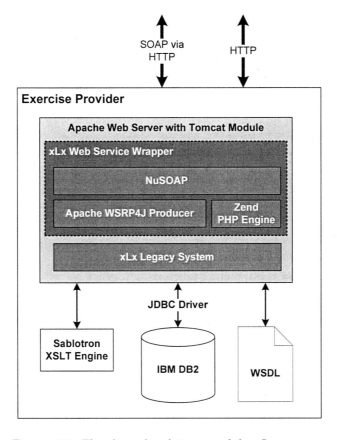

Figure 5.23: The physical architecture of the xLx wrapper.

5.4.2 Physical Architecture

The physical architecture of the wrapper (shown in Figure 5.23) is influenced by the overall architecture of the xLx system. The latter is based on an Apache Web server with a PHP Zend engine. The Apache server also includes a Tomcat module to execute servlets used for special functionalities within the xLx architecture. However, as the basic interactions and functionalities are based on PHP, the SOAP requests and responses are handled by a

PHP SOAP engine called NuSOAP. The basic WSRP functionalities are again included via the WSRP4J implementation and communicate with the NuSOAP engine.

WSDL files are stored on the Apache Web server and can be downloaded via HTTP requests if necessary for a developer. They are conform to the common WSRP WSDL documents.

5.5   Client and Consumer Platforms

Client and consumer platforms offer a single-point of entry for a user of the service-oriented elearning environment. These platforms integrate the remote service and present interfaces for users in a uniform look-and-feel. Client or consumer platforms can be already-existing platforms like elearning platforms, ERP systems, or new applications. For authors even authoring tools can serve as a client application that includes the learning Web services directly. This can, for example, be the search functionality of the LearnServe Repository to support the author's work.

A consumer platform for learners is typically implemented in form of a Web portal. In this case, the end user only needs a Web browser to access the portal to consume the learning services. Other client platforms, on the other hand, can directly consume the Web services. Client platforms can be stand-alone applications that implement the graphical user interface for the services and additional functionality or an existing ERP system that uses the services. Web services can also be called by mobile devices if they have an online connection. Conceptually, they can have a browser to access a portal to consume services, or they can have an application that is able to consume the services directly.

All applications, no matter what kind is implemented, ought to use at least the services offered by the LearnServe Provisioning Server. These services are technical services and users normally do not want to select or change them. However, a platform can offer the ability to change the provisioning server. Owing to simplicity reasons for users, they also ought to provide a search functionality for services through including UDDI search services (UDDI Inquiry API). In the elearning case, it is also helpful for inexperienced users to provide at least basic functionality to find learning services, i.e., the integration of search functionalities provided by the LearnServe Repository, and to offer non-elearning-specific services like the Google and Amazon services. In other words, for inexperienced users the platform ought to include all services that are not content services. For content services, the platform has to be able to consume WSRP messages in order to display content in a correct manner.

The platforms also ought to enable a flexible inclusion of services for users. This inclusion can be interpreted at two different levels. On the one hand, it ought to be able to include new functionalities, for example, an additional search functionality of a semantic search engine once it is available as a Web service. On the other hand, a learner ought to be able to build courses by combining Web services. To attain this, the platform has to save the learner's course definitions.

In the following, the LearnServe Consumer Portal is explained in more detail. It implements a classical Web portal that is able to consume Web services and has the special characteristics as explained above. Afterwards, an enhancement of the OpenUSS system for the Web service use is sketched. Stand-alone applications that are able to consume Web services have a similar structure like the LearnServe Consumer Portal but have to implement the graphical user interface. They are not discussed here any further.

5.5.1 The LearnServe Consumer Portal

The basic functionalities defined in the previous subsection are integrated into the Learn-Serve Consumer Portal, as shown in Figure 5.24. It is implemented in form of a common Web portal that can be accessed by the user via a Web browser. Conceptually, the portal has to be able to consume data-oriented and presentation-oriented (WSRP) Web services. For both kinds of Web services it implements service-invocation interfaces: a general Web service interface, and, on the other hand, a WSRP client. The Web server is the general interface for the user and presents the graphical user interface in form of HTML pages.

As users of the portal ought to be able to include functionalities on their own, the portal has to store connections to these Web services. It has to distinguish between two kinds of services to be integrated:

1. Functionalities like the Google or Amazon Web services are directly offered to the user via a graphical user front-end.

2. Content, exercise, and other learning services can be bundled to courses to be consumed by a learner.

Connection information about both kinds of services are stored inside a database. As course definitions of learners only need to handle sequences because learners already decide about the order of the content in the moment they select a certain service, the order of the course is directly stored within the database. This does not mean that there is no choice for learners since options within material are implemented by the content provider.

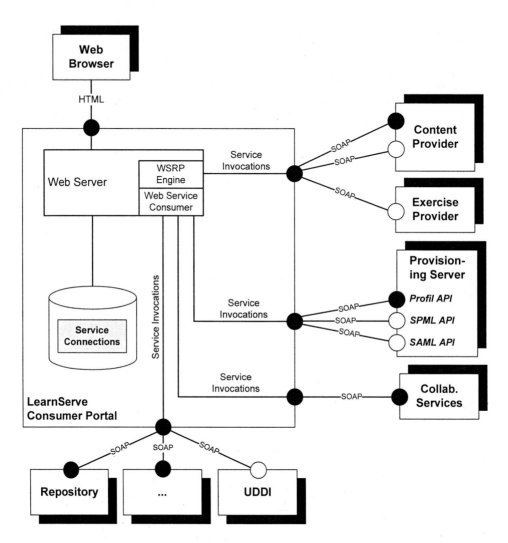

Figure 5.24: Conceptual model of the LearnServe Consumer Portal.

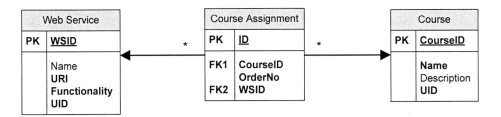

Figure 5.25: Data model of the LearnServe Consumer Portal.

In the easiest case the learner selects just one service offered by a mediator, e.g., the course CIAD. In this case, decisions about the learning path are handled in the moment of learning. This is also the case if the learner selects content from different mediators. In the sample course to prepare for the CIAD exams, each class can be offered by another mediator. In this case, the learner defines a course on the client platform and decides which classes to learn. He or she takes exactly four of the six classes in any order preferred. Within each class there can be still options controlled by the respective mediator.

Figure 5.25 presents the data model of the LearnServe Consumer Portal. It is capable of storing the connection to a Web service in the Table "Web Service". The Web service is defined by its URI, an optional name, and the user identification (UID) of the user who included the service. In addition, the flag "functionality" defines the way how services are to be to presented. It can be displayed as functionality (like the Google Web service) in the main menu of the platform. If it is not a functionality, the LearnServe Consumer Portal interprets the service as part of a course. Courses can be created by learners and are stored in the table "Course" with a name, a description, and the identification of its owner. The table "Course Assignment" stores the Web services that are part of a certain course and their order.

The physical architecture of the LearnServe Consumer Portal is based on the "uPortal"[13] open source application. The uPortal is an effort of several universities to implement a sharable portal using Apache Web server, Tomcat, Java, XML, XSLT, and J2EE. Most importantly, it already implements the WSRP consumer interface and offers abilities for producing graphical user interfaces. Additional functionalities are implemented using the Java programming language. Data is stored in a MySQL database.

---

[13]http://www.uportal.org

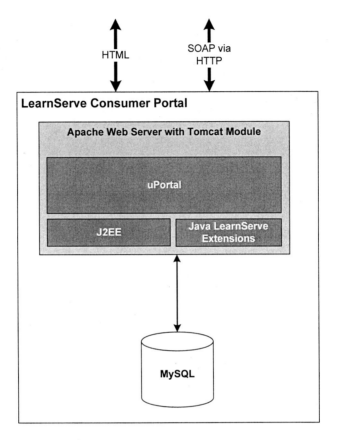

Figure 5.26: The physical architecture of the LearnServe Consumer Portal.

5.5.2   OpenUSS Integration

The implementation of a new consumer portal as explained before is an expensive task. Although most of the functionalities are included in form of Web services, implementation tasks still have to be executed. The more likely case for the use of elearning Web services is the integration into existing platforms like WebCT, xLx, or OpenUSS. The OpenUSS platform, already introduced in Chapter 2.4.3, builds a perfect foundation to implement the client platform owing to several reasons:

1. OpenUSS is an open source software. The source codes are available and developers are allowed to add components needed for the Web service consumption.

2. Implementations of these necessary components (explained below) can be distributed under the open source license again. In consequence, every instance of OpenUSS can benefit from an enhancement.

3. OpenUSS is implemented on the foundation of J2EE. Several Java libraries exist that simplify the development of the necessary components. Particularly, the Apache Axis implementation can be reused to enable the SOAP communication with the remote services.

4. OpenUSS offers a user management that can serve as the central instance for the CDSSO. This means that services check access rights against the OpenUSS database. A Web service interface has to be implemented to enable these validations.

5. Existing data structures can be used to store the tracking data sets of the learners sent by the LearnServe Content Providers or LearnServe Exercise Providers. However, the tracking interfaces have to be implemented by the OpenUSS system.

6. OpenUSS offers an outstanding set of communication functionalities for interactions with learners, other learners, or tutors. The functionalities can, of course, be used and need not to be included from remote servers.

Figure 5.27 pictures the enhanced architecture of OpenUSS to consume elearning Web services. The architecture is based on the one described in [GDB04a]. The new components are dark-gray shaded. In particular, content services and exercise services are included into the system. Conceptually, these components are "Extension Components" as shown in the figure, but technically they are realized by the "Service Component" "WSRP Consumer" because the latter is to invoke the services. In addition, discovery services can be used to find the elearning services.

In order to use Web services, the OpenUSS platform has to be enhanced by a SOAP engine. In this case, Apache Axis is used. The incoming SOAP messages can be data-oriented or presentation-oriented depending on the remote server. Presentation-oriented messages are sent by the content and the exercise providers. To display these messages for a learner, OpenUSS has to be enhanced by a "Service Component" to handle WSRP messages, i.e., a consumer implementation that can be realized by means of WSRP4J.

To serve as the central instance for the CDSSO, OpenUSS has also to be enhanced by an interface to provide adequate functionality. This can be achieved in a comparable manner to the LearnServe Provisioning Server by means of OpenSAML. The tracking of learner activities can be also attained by a simple Web service, as explained in Chapter 5.2. OpenUSS has to offer at least a *getValue*, *setValue*, and *setValueExe* service as well as an internal matching algorithm to map SCORM data fields to OpenUSS data fields.

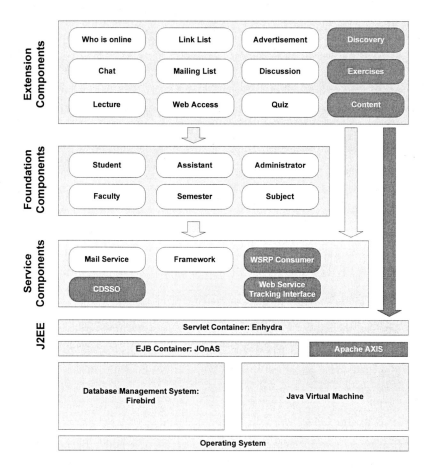

Figure 5.27: Enhanced OpenUSS component architecture according to [GDB04a].

5.6   Usage of LearnServe

The LearnServe Consumer Portal is to integrate the services and offer an interface for users. As already explained before, the learner does not recognize that most functionalities are included by Web service calls. The portal is subdivided into three parts, namely a menu bar on the top of the page, a menu bar at the bottom of the page, and the middle section to display the interfaces of the services. The menus depend on the services included. However, some of the options are predefined like the course management and the logout. Others have been selected by the learner like the playgrounds included in the top menu.

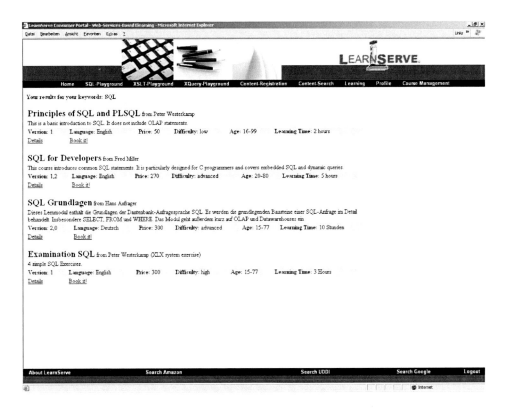

Figure 5.28: Search results in the LearnServe Consumer Portal.

Figure 5.28 shows the results of the search Web service offered by the LearnServe Repository. The learner has invoked this service by selecting the "Content Search" functionality.
Afterwards, he or she has entered a keyword. In this case, the learner has searched for
content on "SQL". The results of this search are displayed in a way common for search
engines today. The portal presents all attributes that have been specified for the simple
search functionality in Chapter 5.1.1. The advanced search functionality can be invoked
by selecting the link "Details" presented with each content block. The link "Book it!"
requests the booking functionality offered by this service, and the necessary information
would be transferred to the booking service. The license obtained from the booking service
is stored within the learner profile.

The LearnServe Portal organizes content in courses. All content services have to be assigned to a course in order to be used. A learner can maintain courses by using the simple
"Course Maintenance" functionality, as shown in Figure 5.29. A learner can create a new

Figure 5.29: Course selection.

course by using the "New Course" link. The creation of a new course is very simple and not shown in this thesis. A learner just needs to key in a course name and a description. All existing courses are listed in the "My Courses" section (see Figure 5.29). Courses can be edited or deleted by using the respective links. Content can be assigned to a course by using the "Assign Content" link. This assignment is shown for the CIAD course in Figure 5.30. All content licenses that have been bought but not yet assigned to a course are listed on the left-hand side. Content can be assigned to a course by selecting the latter and using the arrow button. In the same way, content can be removed from a course.

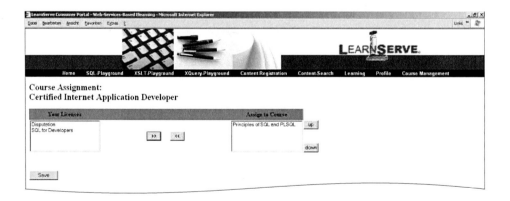

Figure 5.30: Course assignment.

The order of the course-building blocks can be changed by selecting content and using the up and down buttons. As already mentioned before, LearnServe supports only a sequence of content at this definition level since a learner has to pay for each content building block and completes consequently his or her choices prior to the payment.

The learning process is initiated by selecting "Learning" in the menu. Afterwards, a selection screen is displayed which has a similar design like the one shown in Figure 5.29. The learner selects a course to be learned, which is afterwards displayed. Figure 5.31 shows the presentation of content in the LearnServe Portal. The content is presented as defined in the WSRP message. Since the displayed content has been requested from the LearnServe Content Provider, its format is exactly as specified in Figure 5.15.

The left-hand side of the content displays the structure of the content. Each link is a reference to an SCS to be requested from the LearnServe Content Provider. One SCS is presented on the right-hand side of the screen. It is a simple explanation of the PL/SQL functionality.

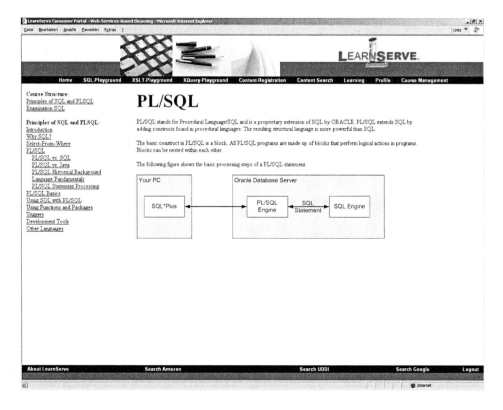

Figure 5.31: SCS presentation in the LearnServe Consumer Portal.

5.7   Evaluation of LearnServe

Technically, the implemented LearnServe environment fulfills the specifications of Layer 3 of the IEEE LTSA standard. LTSA flows have been mapped to the service functionalities in the previous chapters.   Only the flows *Interaction Context (IC), Locator (L)* (from *Coach* to *Delivery*), and *Assessment (A)* are part of the internal implementation of the LearnServe Content Provider (resp. the Exercise Provider) and are not connected directly with a function. Owing to its LTSA-conform architecture, LearnServe can be seen as a full-fledged elearning platform. Indeed, from a learner's perspective the system does not appear as a distributed environment since the consumer platforms integrate the services and offer their user front-ends in a uniform look-and-feel. Consumer platforms may be implemented in form of Web portals, as an extension of already-existing open source solutions, as stand-alone desktop applications, or services can even be integrated into existing ERP company platforms.

However, the selection of services by the learner is a non-trivial process. The decision in the LearnServe architecture to use technical and user-facing services reduces this process to only those services covering any kind of learning material. The technical services are already selected and included by the provider of the consumer platforms, although it is conceptually also possible to let the user select these services. The possibility to select learning services offers, on the one hand, a lot more flexibility to choose from content than in traditional, monolithic, and centralized platforms. On the other hand, the learner has to decide which kind of content fits his or her needs. This decision is not easy.

In a service-oriented elearning environment it is difficult to integrate collaboration services like chat-rooms, document-sharing services, or forums, not from a technical perspective, but from a learner's perspective. Owing to the nature of these functionalities, they are typically used by closed communities discussing very specialized topics. A learner has to integrate very specific services to benefit from the latter. There are several possibilities to achieve that:

1. The learner decides which collaboration service to integrate. This approach is only possible for advanced learners.

2. The provider of the consumer platform integrates the service. This approach is difficult owing to the open nature of the environment. The provider cannot decide which service is suitable for a certain learner. However, the provider may offer help to find an adequate collaboration service for a learner.

3. The content authors provide links to the collaboration services that are related to the topics covered. These links can be included, for example, within the introduction of the course. This is a very helpful way for the learner and ensures that the interactions within a particular collaboration service really are about the content covered in the learning material.

4. Mediators offer the collaboration services as added value, which is also a very elegant way.

The quality of search results largely depends on the quality of metadata describing the learning services. This problem does not occur if content is assigned to learners by tutors, but occurs if learners search for content on their own. This problem is not unique for a service-oriented environment, but increases because learners do not search in closed systems anymore. Both the learner's search query and the author's metadata have to be created very carefully.

Some problems occur when a distributed system is used, not only if it is used for elearning. These are, on the one hand, the problems of trust, privacy, and security, and, on the other hand, the problems of quality and availability of services. The first type of problems can be addressed by technical specifications as explained in Chapter 4.3.2, but each server included in the entire environment must contribute in these approaches. In addition, learners must trust providers of user management functionalities that they do not provide access for unauthorized people to private data. The availability of services can be checked by automatic procedures, for example, by a repository, as explained in Chapter 5.1.1. In addition, a content provider has to ensure that services can be accessed as long as learners may have valid licenses.

The second type of problems is also addressed by technical specifications and efforts. Several approaches aim at the quality of service. This includes Quality-of-Service models, Web-service policies, Web-service testing etc. However, they address only the technical quality of the service. The quality of the content presented by services is even more important for learners since they do not (want to) care about technical issues. This problem can at the moment only be solved by reviewers who can provide statements about the quality of content.

Technically, the implementation of Web services is independent of platforms, programming languages, and operating systems. The use of portlets for the presentation currently implies the use of Java for the implementation of the services because there are only three powerful implementations available: BEA WebLogic, IBM Gridsphere, and Apache WSRP4J. As portlets can be used in any application domain, this situation will change in future.

The strategy of implementing the tracking interactions on the content provider's server solved many difficulties in realizing of a SCORM-compliant runtime environment on the learner's side. However, it implies that the content provider's server is able to connect to the provisioning server. Owing to the CDSSO, the URI of that server is known, but the tracking interface of the provisioning server is crucial. The LearnServe Provisioning Server uses an interface that is closely related to the SCORM definitions because there are no common specifications or standards in the Web-services field for tracking yet. The ELF initiative rises the hope that common definitions will be developed in future. Currently, there is just a collection of possible services without detailed definitions to be developed in future. The adoption of the LearnServe interfaces may be acceptable for a broad community of developers since a couple of them are based on the widely-accepted SCORM definitions. If there will be no definition of a common interface, a content provider should be able to use various kinds of interfaces offered by typical provisioning servers. Content providers can define certain restrictions within the metadata and state which provisioning server works fine.

5.8   Summary

This chapter has explained the realization of elearning providers for the LearnServe environment. For each server, the internal architecture and interfaces have been described. In addition, one physical architecture for each server has been presented.

The chapter has started with a description of the LearnServe discovery services supporting the search process for learning services. As the UDDI repository is not sufficient for the search process within LOM metadata, an additional repository adapting the basic UDDI ideas has been presented. Furthermore, a semantic annotation for learning services has been explained. This annotation can be used in the future by semantic search engines to index learning services.

One of the core functionalities of the entire environment is implemented by the LearnServe Provisioning Server. This server deals with the Cross-Domain-Single-Sign-On process and is in charge to maintain user and tracking data. The tracking interface is used by the LearnServe Content Provider. The latter presents learning material in a service-oriented way to learners and stores tracking information on the LearnServe Provisioning Server. The presentation uses the WSRP standard to display the content in the intended way. The LearnServe Exercise Provider is a special content provider and uses the same approach. It is implemented as a wrapper of the xLx system.

Consumers can be implemented in a huge variety of ways. Two implementations have been explained in more detail. This has been, on the one hand, an extension to the OpenUSS system, and, on the other hand, the realization of the LearnServe Consumer Portal. The usage of the latter has been presented briefly before the chapter has ended with an evaluation of the LearnServe environment. Table 5.16 summarizes the key differences between the realizations of traditional and service-oriented elearning.

Table 5.16: Key differences between traditional and service-oriented elearning.

	Traditional Approach According to SCORM	**LearnServe: Service-Oriented Approach**
Platform	Centralized LMS	Decentralized offerings of content and functionalities
Client/ Consumer	Often Web browser or special application	Every Web service client, integration in existing applications possible
Content	Sharable Content Object	Sharable Content Service
Content Distribution	Physical copy of PIF	Service invocation on demand (only one copy)
Content Import	Physically	No import, Web service call on demand
Content Update	On each server that stores the content, may be expensive and time-consuming	Only once on the server of the content provider, updates are immediately visible for everybody
Mediator	Offers PIFs for import	Coordinates Web service invocations
Control Flow Description	IMS Simple Sequencing	BPEL4WS (IMS Simple Sequencing still possible)
Learner Tracking	By content on client side	By content provider, no consumer interaction with tracking service
Exercise Exchange	Within PIF	No exchange, Web service call on demand
User Session Maintenance	By LMS, normally by means of cookies	By provisioning server using CDSSO by means of SAML

Chapter 6

Perspectives

Web services can be used in different organizational environments to build distributed elearning systems. In the following, three different organizational environments are described with their potentials for the use of elearning Web services. Thereafter, a couple of economical aspects are discussed from both a provider's and customer's point of view: they arise with the horizontal organization of learning offerings as sketched in Chapter 4.5.

6.1 Organizational Perspectives

The use of Web services for learning can be offered in different organizational environments. The latter determines organizational aspects, which will be explained in the following. Basically, three levels can be distinguished:

1. Web services are offered for public use on the Web and learners freely use these offerings for education.

2. Web services can be used in small companies to provide flexible learning platforms.

3. Web services can be used in big companies to integrate existing learning platforms to a new learning portal.

The first approach has been described in the previous chapters and will be sketched only shortly here. Web services used in an open environment have to be integrated by a powerful consumer application, e.g., a portal. The latter has to be very flexible to allow the use of Web services with different kinds of WSDL interface definitions. The use of portlets enables an easier integration and a presentation in the intended form. Basic functionalities have to be offered for a user, as described in Chapter 5.5.

The second approach is not very likely because small companies would only need one LMS to train all employees. To reduce development costs, a company LMS can be connected to content providers on the Web to include additional material or offer employees the possibility to include content on their own. In addition, Web services can be used to integrate the platform with an existing application, for example, to exchange user data with enterprise systems or to include content services in ERP systems to enable a training-on-the-job. However, an integration of different, existing platforms within a small company is not very likely, as explained by [GDB04b]. It leads to high administration efforts and is expensive for the company. The elearning market study provided by the European Union [Mas05] also states that relationships of companies and manufacturers of elearning products last very long. Consequently, it can be assumed that a company only uses one LMS.

The situation is different for very big companies with several autonomous departments. Often, these departments can decide on their own which kind of software to employ. Taking this kind of company for granted, the use of Web services in a big university is explained here. The distribution of elearning products within a university is extremely different. While several institutes have just started thinking about elearning, other institutes already use elearning products for a couple of years. [GDB04a] proposes a bottom-up deployment strategy for OpenUSS for an entire university with about 40,000 students. The strategy is based on a stepwise introduction beginning at a single institute and moving forward to the faculty. In the last step, OpenUSS should be used in the entire university. Although this is a desirable objective because students must then only use one system during their entire time at university, the approach faces a lot of difficulties. In particular, several different systems are currently in use and elearning content has been developed on a variety of platforms. The latter include systems that do not adhere to standards and specifications enabling an easy import of content and exercises into OpenUSS. As decisions about learning platforms and other software applications are often made by each institution on its own, the approach is probably only successful if legacy systems can be integrated into OpenUSS.

Figure 6.1 shows the conceptual model of a single university environment centered around OpenUSS. The latter is enhanced by a Web service interface, as explained in Chapter 5.5.2. It further implements the provisioning services as it already includes a user management, which can easily be reused. This functionality could also be implemented by the LearnServe Provisioning Server, which would have to be integrated into the entire environment in this case. All existing platforms are enhanced by Web service wrappers.

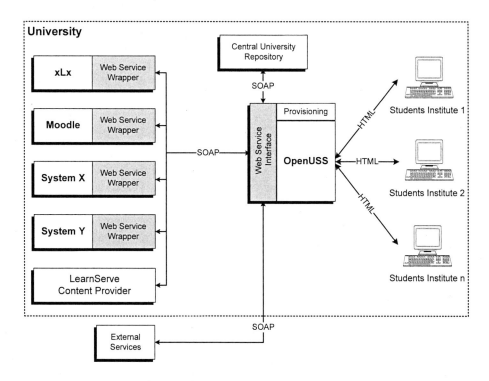

Figure 6.1: OpenUSS as university-wide integration platform.

They have to provide their learning functionalities as WSRP services. Tracking data sets are also sent to the OpenUSS platform. In addition, services from other manufacturers offered on the Web can be included if it is necessary for institutions. Figure 6.1 shows the integration of xLx and Moodle into OpenUSS. This enables learners to use OpenUSS to solve exercises, to learn content offered by Moodle, and to use at the same time communication facilities of OpenUSS. Learners do not even notice that they work on three systems as all functionalities are offered within the front-end of OpenUSS.

Technically, the integration within clear boundaries, e.g., within a university or company, has the advantage that the integration platform is centrally maintained. All interfaces can be implemented according to well-defined specifications. The integration platform offers contextualization and personalization opportunities for learners and institutes.

All learning services are registered in only one repository serving as the central lookup facility for both students and teachers. Additional functionalities may be offered by a company-wide UDDI.

6.2   Economical Perspectives

The organization of publicly available services cannot be assumed to be free of charge. In universities and companies content may be offered for employees and students for free, but for the open offerings on the Web it is more likely that learners will be charged.

Business models for elearning are typically developed on the basis of centralized platforms. Both content and platforms are distributed in form of physical software products. Web services turn these functionalities into real services. In consequence, new business models have to be developed for these offerings. The following subsections expatiate the special business perspective of elearning Web services and point out differences to the traditional business models. It is worth mentioning that certain indices for a controlling of learning platforms can still be used in the service-oriented environment. For the use of content, they mirror the real use as there is only one service on the Web. Consequently, some indices may be more precise than in the use of traditional learning systems. Details about the controlling of LMSs can be found in [GBD+04].

6.2.1   Provider View

The development of elearning products is generally similar to the development of any commercial product: the commercialization of goods has to generate certain revenues in order to cover at least the expenses of its production. Beyond that, it should generate some profit in order to hedge for the financial survival of the company offering the product. A detailed strategic planning of activities and actors is essential for such a financial survival. This planning is supported by business models that describe specific parts of economics relevant for the corresponding products and the company. These parts are represented by single models that are suitable for an understanding of the interconnections and effects present in the market [HB03]. A very common definition of a business model is given by [Tim98], who describes it as

- an architecture for the product, service, and information flows, including a description of the various business actors and their roles,

- a description of the potential benefits for the various business actors, and

- a description of the sources of revenues.

According to this definition, a business model describes the material, information, and service flows between enterprises and their environment as well as in the inside of the enterprise. In addition, it comprises the revenues that can be generated.

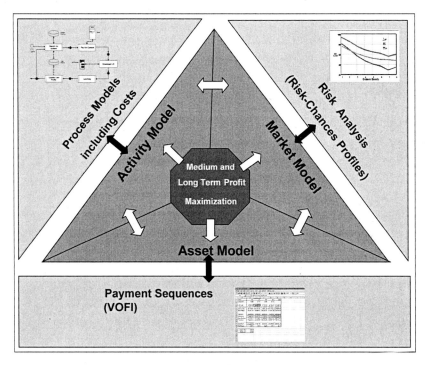

Figure 6.2: Framework for the evaluation of business models (according to [GBB04, HB03]).

The generic description of [Tim98] was the foundation for the development of three interdependent partial models that have been introduced in [HB03]. These are the *Activity Model*, the *Market Model*, and the *Asset Model*. As an essence of different approaches, particularly suggested by [Tim00] and [Wir01], these partial models build a framework for the creation of business models. They have to be considered and harmonized with each other to generate maximum revenues in the medium or long term (see inner part of Figure 6.2). As the inner model is not able to display, calculate, and evaluate the profit of a business model, it has been enhanced by [GBB04] by adding methods known from investment appraisal to each of the partial models. The methods can be used to calculate key data at different levels of interest as pictured in Figure 6.3. Indeed, the approach is able to determine key data like the total-cost-of-ownership (TCO) or the return-on-investment (ROI). The key data and its relevant information is calculated by a stepwise procedure. As shown in Figure 6.3, the costs of different processes are the foundation to quote the financial ratios at the budget level. These data are in turn used to calculate the

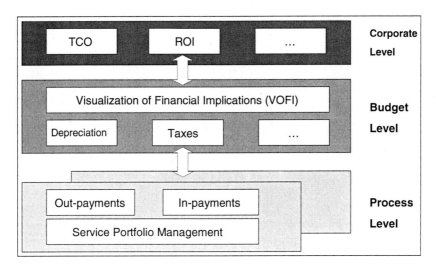

Figure 6.3: Conceptual framework for evaluating the financial consequences of service portfolio management [BL04].

key data for the corporate level. Although both authors used the framework to develop or evaluate elearning business models, the pictured framework is more general and can be used in various kinds of businesses. Figure 6.2 shows this enhanced framework.

The broadest concept covered by the framework is the Market Model that describes the structure of the (elearning) market with its actors and their roles. The Activity Model is to show the (elearning) activities that have to be carried out by providers of elearning products. Finally, the Asset Model pictures the revenues of the activities and the costs that incur. All models will be explained in Chapter 6.2.1.1 for the case of elearning Web services. The objective of all activities of an elearning provider is to maximize the profit in the medium or long term.

The actors, their roles, and the costs of the activities during the development and distribution of elearning products according to a certain business model can be analyzed by means of process models. Event-driven process chains (EPCs [KNS92]) can be used to analyze the costs of the activities (Out-payments) [GBB04], but also other process models can be employed here, for example, Petri nets [Rei01]. The evaluation of the revenues (In-payments) has to consider uncertainties of the market. This can be achieved by a suitable risk analysis [Her64] that pictures different revenues of a certain business model under various circumstances of the market. The periodical payments can be consolidated by means of so-called VOFIs (*Visualization Of Financial Implications* [Gro93]), which make a flexible, clear, and extensible calculation possible. At this step of the calculation, even taxes, depreciations etc. can be considered to get the key data at the corporate level that can be extracted from the payment sequences. Based on VOFI, the key data at the corporate level (ROI, TOC, etc.) can be calculated if desired, as indicated in Figure 6.3.

6.2.1.1 Business Models for Elearning Web Services

Several projects for the development of centralized elearning platforms and elearning content funded by public investors are currently reaching the end of their development phase; as a consequence, a market strategy has to be implemented to ensure the survival of the findings and developments. Research has been undertaken to build business models for these platforms (see, e.g., [HB03, LS04, GBB04]). The provision of elearning Web services differs in many respects from what has been described by these authors in the field of business models for elearning. Although general frameworks can be adopted, the point of origin is different because every provider has to own or at least rent hardware and software to offer services and provide them on demand. Several additional issues have to be recognized in order to offer elearning Web services to hedge the financial survival of the provider. This section is intended to describe the overall situation for different service providers and to exhibit aspects that have to be considered when developing a strategy for the provisioning of services. Neither will a general business model for these providers be constructed nor will a sample model to be adopted by a company delivered because each provider has different starting points and most of all different cost structures for hardware, software, and employees. In addition, the functionality of a service has a huge influence on the price that can be achieved on the market as well as on the acceptance of the service by consumers. Nonetheless, a sample calculation for illustration purposes with fictitious data will be given for a certain elearning service. In the following, each of the partial models that have been introduced in the previous section will be described at a meta level with a special focus on the provision of elearning services.

Market Model for Elearning Web Services

On the one hand, the market model describes the demand of a certain product and, on the other hand, the competition that is present in the market. The demand portion shows which products will be ordered in which quantity. The competition and the demand depend on special characteristics of the product offered. Thus, in the remainder of this section relevant markets for elearning services are described, but no concrete models will be developed for a certain service.

Life-long learning is a phrase that characterizes the situation of most employees in companies of all business sectors. In fact, continuous learning is a key presupposition to be successful on the job and to keep the job. This kind of learning means more than only updating knowledge in a certain field an employee is an expert in, but includes also striving for additional qualifications in areas related to that field. Today, it is impossible for employees to have an overall knowledge in a certain area. Computer science is a good example for this. It is impossible to be an expert in all the fields of software engineering, operating systems, administration, and databases etc., but a basic understanding of all subjects is necessary. Of course, experts in each subject have to improve and update their knowledge permanently.

Thus, an employee has to learn very special topics continuously during his or her work life and update basic knowledge for related topics. Clearly, costs, location, quality, and time spent on learning are important factors that all drive the selection of courses. Particularly, location and timing problems can be solved by using elearning courses. Open service-based environments as developed throughout this thesis give learners additionally a considerable flexibility to optimize the learning process regarding selection, quality, style, and costs of content.

Content to be consumed by learners has to be developed by domain experts. This content is published and subsequently requested by learners. Several companies are providing professional services to build content and to offer content even for an anonymous market. For learners as well as for authors, the technical form of the content does not play a key role as long as it is easily accessible. As shown in the previous chapters, applications that provide content can be implemented based on Web services. This enables an easy integration and an extended possibility of reuse. In this form, not only can learning content be used in other platforms, but also system functionalities (i.e., there is no need to have a full-fledged elearning system, but only an access client). As a consequence, the learner does not have to use content that is offered by a closed platform, but can search globally on the Web for learning services. Content providers are in turn able to offer their content to a much bigger community of learners compared to the use of closed systems. There is also a demand of integration platforms that can be implemented in the form of Web portals or as stand-alone applications that may even be usable on mobile devices. In addition, there is a market for exams since course programs often end up with a certification that is obtained after the corresponding examinations have been passed successfully. Web service providers for these exams will hence show up. They may be closely related to the authors that produce learning content. For example, mediators will provide material for the CIAD sample course of Figure 1.1 and have at the same time the allowance to offer exams for this course.

In the field of content, these mediators can combine existing material, exercise services etc. into high-level courses or classes. Although there is still a market of content suppliers and content requestors, a mediator adds another dimension of consuming content between himself and content authors since the mediator itself is now a requestor and able to negotiate conditions. Often these courses or classes need some form of accreditation, typically given by external organizations that offer quality assurance.

The use of any software application and learning in particular demands a certain support for upcoming questions. For learning services, this tutoring can be offered at an organizational level (technical support and advice services for the choice of material) and at a content level to answer questions about the content to be learned.

In conclusion, the market for elearning content and special services like playgrounds and Labs is much bigger than in traditional elearning and offers an enhanced flexibility for learners. However, as a specialization on certain parts of a platform means that cross-functionality advantages that could compensate disadvantages in other functionalities are obsolete, competing manufacturers have to be observed all along since an exchange of services by a learner is possible at any time because of a another, better service.

Activity Model for Elearning Web Services

Actors in the field of elearning services comprise learners or consumers of services and providers of services. A special type of provider is a mediator who is at the same time a special type of content consumer. Technically speaking, the new service is just another service with more functionality. For example, the bundling or composition of content services leads to a new content service that has to be handled by the learner exactly as each simple service of the bundle. This is why mediators are not described in detail in the following, but can be seen as common content providers.

According to [HB03], elearning providers have to carry out certain activities in order to produce and install elearning platforms for customers. Although these activities are described for inhouse systems, the activities have also to be carried out by elearning Web services providers. However, as will be shown next, the center of the activities is different.

The general activities that can be found in the field of elearning manufacturers do not vary considerably from those that have to be carried out by manufacturers of other products. In general, a manufacturer has to design the product first. For this product, the price that can be achieved in the market has to be determined. Pricing and product design have to be carried out for all kinds of services, although the design of services is not as complex as for

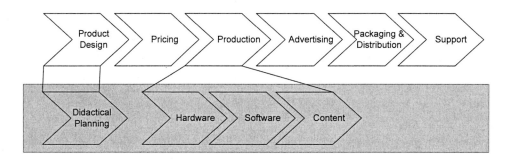

Figure 6.4: General activities in production and distribution.

an entire elearning platform since the service only covers a small part of the functionality of a complete platform. In the special case of elearning, the product design also has to consider didactic planning, and the production phase the development of content. As these two activities might have a big influence on the costs of the offerings, they are considered separately in this description. Clearly, only some of the service providers have to carry out this work, e.g., the providers of the content services. Others who may also have to do this planning are providers of exercise services, which can be seen as a special case of content services. In the end, advertisement has to be devised to offer the learning functionalities to learners, and the services have to be made available via publication in a repository and via distribution (as Web service). Support for learners and service users is important to help using the offerings. A high-level model of the entire activities is shown in Figure 6.4 that highlights the specific parts for elearning in gray. Parts of the model are described in more detail in the following.

The situation for hardware and software is different from that of traditional elearning manufacturers. In the latter case, particularly hardware is offered by special vendors that might even do not have to be elearning specialists. Software has to be installed at the customers servers. In particular, LMSs as well as third party systems [HLV+02] necessary for the learning have to be bought and installed for the customer, i.e., in most cases a company that wants to train employees. For elearning Web services, the situation is different. Although there has to be a computer with a client application at the learner side, there is no need to install servers on the customer side to provide the functionality of a learning platform. Instead, all services are offered on remote machines that are maintained and run by service providers. The likely case would be that the integration platform is offered by another provider (e.g., by a "learning center") and can be accessed via a Web browser. In this case, neither additional software nor any additional hardware is needed by the learner. The learner just needs an Internet connection and a computer with a browser. In any case, the providers of the services have to develop and offer software (i.e., the service) and hardware (i.e., the machine that hosts the service) in order to do their business.

Manufactures of goods often have to advertise their products. This is also relevant for elearning services since the platform is open and learners can include services according to their own preferences. Advertising can be placed directly by sending material to a learner or indirectly by using the central look-up mechanism, in most cases the repository that serves as an index for all available elearning services. This is where the learner searches for content, courses, and additional offerings. Of course, each provider has to perform also some advertising to integrate the own services to services of other providers. Here, the most important platform is the repository because learners access it directly.

Next, goods have to be packaged and distributed after a customer has bought them. For a digital service, there is no packaging since there is no distribution in the physical sense. Instead, Web services are based on messages exchanged between the services. The complexity of the messages sent by the service providers to the client system varies accordingly to the type of service. Most services just need to send data-oriented messages with result sets of the processing of the service (e.g., the *getValue* and *setValue* functionalities). Content services must send presentation-oriented messages. However, the costs for distribution are negligible as network traffic is cheap even for presentation-oriented messages.

Support has to be given during the after-sales phase. For the learner, the provider of the integration system has to offer support, as the learner normally does not recognize that most of the functionality is provided by Web services. In turn, each service provider has to offer support to the provider of the service platform.

Figure 6.5 summarizes the activities and typical elearning Web services as well as the effort of carrying out the activities. The inhouse provider is shown as reference in the very left column of the figure and can be interpreted as a company that offers a complete elearning platform that has to be installed on a computer of the customer. As mentioned above, nearly all service providers have to offer hardware and software. A special case is the integration platform that can be a Web portal or a client software to be installed on a learner's device. For example, this device can be a mobile client. Thus, hardware is not needed to provide the integration service. The coloring of the activities shows the intensity of the respective activity of the providers.

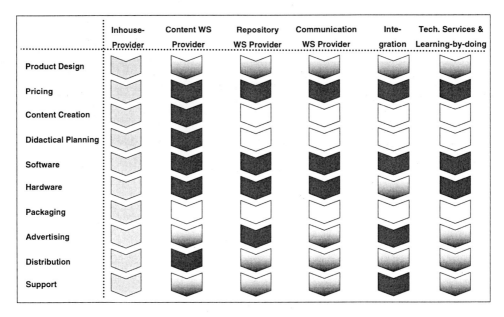

Figure 6.5: Overview of the activities of typical elearning service providers.

Price Discrimination for Elearning Web Services

To maximize the profit from the sale of products, it can be useful to pattern prices depending on external circumstances. In general, price discrimination means charging consumers different prices for the same product or service in order to increase profits [Mef00, Phl83, Var89] and it is one of the basic concepts in microeconomics. It is even possible that some products are sold with a loss in order to benefit from complementary relationships of products (the profit of the complementary product has to cover the loss) [Mef00]. Pricing is important to calculate and manage the profit a product can generate on the market. The market model has to consider reactions of the market owing to different prices. An important foundation is a good estimation of the dependencies between price and demand. The mechanism of price discrimination works particularly well if the demand curve for output is decreasing, i.e., the demand increases if a product is sold for lower prices. At large, this can be observed on the Web for digital products or digital services. Unlike non-digital products, the mechanism of price discrimination on the Web has to cope with problems of anonymity because it is often not possible to set individual prices for customers owing to the fact that their identity is not known [BH03b]. Instead, customers can live in any country and may buy only one product at a certain reseller in his or her lifetime. Six basic models for a pattern of prices and their usability for elearning Web services are going to be discussed next [Mef00].

The value of the same good is subjective for different people. This means that different customers will pay different prices for the same good. This fact is covered by a price discrimination where the *price varies by customer*. In this case, the price usually depends on certain characteristics of the customer, such as age, gender, or professional status. However, in practice customers try to use their bargaining power, which makes the situation more complex. On the Web, the situation is even more difficult as it is hard to prove certain facts given by customers. If a transaction between a customer and a reseller is completed electronically, it is nearly impossible to check the age, gender, and other personal characteristics of people they pretend to be. For elearning Web services it is difficult to argue why prices ought to vary on personal characteristics of customers because all learners consume identical products and may have the same benefits. In addition, the fact of the learners' quasi-anonymity makes the allocation of a transaction to a certain price very difficult. If an allocation of a service invocation is possible, the authentication is expensive since the identity has to be verified every time the service is called (via CDSSO mechanisms) because the calls are usually stateless if no corresponding mechanisms are implemented. Thus, this kind of pricing is only feasible if learners build a closed community and everybody has to be identified in a reliable way.

An often-practiced price discrimination is *according to the quantity sold*. This type is sometimes called *second-degree price discrimination* in literature. Normally, larger quantities are available at a lower unit price. For Web services in elearning this type of price discrimination can be used in particular for services that enable hands-on experience. For example, the SQL playground of the xLx system provides an interface for the learner to submit SQL queries which are then executed on a (commercial) database system. Second-degree price discrimination models for xLx could now determine that prices vary depending on the number of queries a learner has submitted (pay-per-use). If he or she has submitted more than a certain number, the unit price for all queries may be decreased. Although the system has to authenticate the learner each time a query is submitted, the learner can still keep a certain anonymity as only the number of queries for a learner determines the price and not personal learner's characteristics. However, this pricing strategy is only useful for special services. It does not make sense to charge learners depending on the number of hits they execute on the same learning content because learning may require different navigation paths inside learning material for different learners.

Another type of price discrimination is *based on the location the consumer buys the product*. Typically, locations can be classified into cities or countries, but even smaller units are possible and depend on the market strategy of the vendor. For non-digital goods arguments for varying prices are, for example, freight charges or different taxes. However, this argumentation is not reasonable for digital goods and digital services provided on the

Web since transport costs do not incur for digital goods. Although a price determination based on the location of a learner may be reasonable, it is very difficult to detect the location of a learner. Particularly for learners from the developing countries it is reasonable to offer learning material for lower prices, but technically it is difficult to allocate a learner exactly.

The fourth type of price discrimination is *based on the time a service is consumed*. This is a very common model in the field of telecommunication, where companies charge higher prices during the business hours owing to a more frequent use of their capacities. However, overtime working can also lead to higher price structures for services in other fields. The variation of prices of elearning Web services depending on the time a learner uses the material is generally speaking hardly feasible because it is one of the key characteristics of elearning to be time-independent. If a company charges different prices for certain periods, it is very difficult to argue why.

Yield management [Mef00] initially designed for services is another differentiation based on time. The difference to the time-based price discrimination is that the moment of consumption is (much) later than the moment of buying a license to consume a service. For example, airlines use yield management for flight prices to control capacities on airplanes. For elearning services yield management can be used to influence the time of booking courses to control capacities for special courses.

Price discrimination *based on the quality of a product* is strictly speaking different from the ones mentioned above. If the quality of elearning material or courses varies, it is impossible to regard the material as the same product or course. Instead, it ought to be seen as different material with similar content, but also with a different field of application. Thus, it is another product with a different price and is mentioned here for the sake of completeness.

A special type of pricing strategy is *bundling*, which may often be applicable to mediators. Although it is not comparable to the other cases because bundling looks at more than one product, it is an interesting way to capture consumer surplus in the field of elearning. Usually, material is not sold in units of learning objects, but in units of courses or classes, which are bundles of multiple learning objects. Looking at elearning services, the courses or classes are also provided as services. In addition, they can be combined with hand-on experience services like the aforementioned playgrounds to form a unit of study. If a learner takes the entire bundle of services from one provider, prices may be lower than booking each learning service and practical-experience service separately.

Asset Model

A central feature of a business model is the asset model that describes the financing of
a business activity. Revenues paid for a certain service can be direct or indirect. Direct
revenues are characterized by the payment of the consumer of a service to its provider.
Indirect revenues are not paid by the consumer of the service but by a third party. Figure
6.6 shows the most important revenue types for elearning Web services; some additional
ones are described by [BBS04].

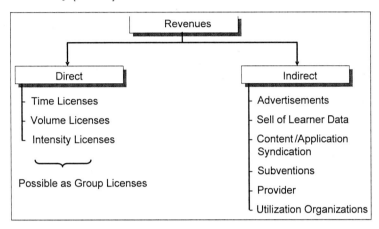

Figure 6.6: Overview of relevant types of revenues.

Direct revenues can be classified into time licenses and volume licenses. Time licenses
allow the use of a service in a predefined time slot as often as the consumer likes. Volume
licenses, on the other hand, allow the use of a service for a predefined number of times. If
this number is 1, the model is often called "pay-per-use". Time licenses for the definition of
semesters and a pay-per-use license for the accounting of uses are appropriate for elearning
services. In addition, a mix of the two models can be used that allows a certain number of
invocations during a predefined period, e.g., if a playground can be used during a semester
a certain number of times. Other models such as the accounting for the execution time
are not suitable for elearning services since learning of predefined content ought not to
depend on the procession time (CPU-time) of the server. This model called intensity-
license seems to be only reasonable for the use of third-party systems like SQL databases,
but is unfair because learners with a greater breadth of understanding have to pay less
than others.

The most common form of indirect revenues are advertisements. For elearning services
advertisement can be used in form of banners on the integration platform, as building

blocks delivered with the Web services responses, or even in form of direct product placements in the learning content. The sale of learner data to third parties or organizations is also a possible source of revenue. These data sets have been recorded during the learning sessions and could already have been prepared and formatted for statistical analysis. However, depending on the contracts between a learner and a service provider, it might be not legally to sell these learner records.

Content and application syndication is a very useful model for Web services. An integration platform provider, e.g., a learning center, can use external services and (learning) content on his or her platform and pays a certain amount of money to the provider of the service. For a user (or a learner) of the integration platform the content or applications does not appear as if it is external content.

A common model for indirect revenues for educational organizations are subventions that are paid by national or international funds, e.g., the European Union (EU). Several of these EU support programs exist in the field of elearning. The objective of these payments is often to foster special projects, research, or to open new jobs.

Indirect revenues can also be paid by Internet providers. In the elearning case, a certain Web service is only accessible for learners if the IP addresses of their Internet provider is allowed to use the services. Thus, a Web service provider only enables the access if the Internet provider pays. Although the use of the Internet might even be more expensive for the learners because the Internet providers will forward the additional costs to the learners, the revenues are indirect because the money the service providers get is not directly paid by the learners. Another indirect revenue model uses Utilization Organizations that charge learners fees for using Web services. A special amount of that money is forwarded to the author of the service or to the service provider. This model is leaned on the model used for the public performance of music, where the organizers of the performance have to pay money for the music to a utilization organization (e.g., the German GEMA) which in turn pays money to the composers.

6.2.1.2   A Sample Calculation

The following example of an online course for becoming a CIAD presents a sample calculation for a provider of a content service. In order to obtain this certification, a student has to learn different aspects of database systems and software engineering, as shown in Figure 1.1. The classes as well as an examination are composed into a course that has an overall duration of one year. Before a learner can use the content of the course, he or she

has to pay for the entire program, which is handled by a license, as described in Section
5.3.

Activity and Asset Model: For the sake of simplicity, it is assumed that the costs
for hardware and software have already been calculated with another service and can
therefore be ignored here. The content is provided on a machine with an already-existing
Web service front-end. Consequently, the provider only has to author the content at
the beginning of the period of the course (time t=0). The authoring is calculated with
90,000 €, and the course is offered for three years in an unmodified version. The costs for
the authoring are paid to one third of internal funds, the rest of the money is credited
by the bank with an interest rate of 12.00%. The course is a complex one consisting of
many learning services and only a couple of competitors exist. However, there are a lot
of customers, although the price for the course is set to a fixed amount of 1,000 €, which
has to be paid in advance by the learners.

Market Model: The analysis of the market forecasts 50 learners in the first year (t=1),
42 learners in the second year (t=2), and 20 learners in the third year (t=3); it is assumed
that this number is decreasing over time owing to emerging competition in the field of
elearning Web services. In the second year, 32 learners have paid the regular price of
1,000 €, but 10 learners have received a special price of 820 € since the company they
work for has bought a bundle for ten learners and got a discount (price discrimination).
The resulting payments are shown in Table 6.1.

The money earned in year t=1 is used to pay the interest to the bank and to pay off a part
of the credit. The same happens in year t=2, but as there is still money left after paying
off the credit, it is put in a financial investment with an interest rate of 8.00%. After three
years the net balance is 42,611 €. The overall strategic decision to invest the money in
an elearning course as calculated before is thus positive if the following condition holds:

> The net balance after the overall duration of the course has to be bigger than
> the amount of money that can be earned by using financial investments.

Thus, in the example the internal funds of 30,000 € could have been invested for 8,00%:

$$42,611 \geq 30,000 \left(1 + 8.00\right)^3 = 37,791.36$$

As this condition holds in the example, the provision of the course leads to a higher income
for the provider in comparison to a financial investment. On the foundation of this VOFI,
further key data (ROI, TCO, etc.) can also be calculated.

Table 6.1: Calculation of elearning course using VOFI.

	t=0	t=1	t=2	t=3
Series of Payments	-90,000.00 €	50,000.00 €	40,200.00 €	20,000.00 €
Internal Funds	30,000.00 €			
Standard Loan				
+ Credit Intake	60,000.00 €			
- Redemption		42,800.00 €	17,200.00 €	
- Debtor Interest		7,200.00 €	2,064.00 €	
Financial Investment				
- Reinvestment			20,936.00 €	21,675.00 €
+ Disinvestment				
+ Creditor Interest				1,675.00 €
Net Funding	0.00 €	0.00 €	0.00 €	0.00 €
Balances				
Amount Borrowed	60,000.00 €	17,200.00 €		
Amount Reinvested				
on Financial investmentl			20,936.00 €	42,611.00 €
Net Balance	**-60,000.00 €**	**-17,200.00 €**	**20,936.00 €**	**42,611.00 €**

6.2.2 Customer View

The customer views of the use of elearning Web services have to be subdivided into two subgroups: the end user (learning in the spare time) and companies offering workplace education. Obviously, both groups benefit from flexible offerings and can choose content and functionalities from a variety of manufacturers. The open market may also lead to lower prices and a higher quality of products owing to competing offerings. However, the monitoring of the success of elearning activities is different for the groups. An end user is interested in passing the course. A controlling of in-payments and out-payments is normally not performed. This situation is different in the workplace education where companies are interested in financial key data in addition to the simple passing or failing of courses by employees. As Web service providers use licensing models, out-payments can easily be discovered. The latter process may be simpler than in traditional elearning offerings since hardware, software, and administration costs are much easier to calculate owing to the thin software structure on the consumer side. Common models that are currently discussed in the scientific literature like ROI, elearning balanced scorecards, or house of quality to measure the success of elearning can still be used in the service-oriented environment. Details can be found, for example, in [ES05].

6.3 Summary

This chapter has discussed three kinds of models to use Web services for elearning. It is particularly useful to integrate services in an open environment or within big companies that have to maintain several learning platforms. Smaller companies normally only have one LMS. However, all of them can integrate services offered on the Web to provide flexible platforms. Service providers have to develop new business models in order to be successful on the market. Several aspects of these models have been discussed, for example, the market, asset, revenue, and pricing model. The chapter has also shortly mentioned the economical perspective of service costumers.

Chapter 7

Conclusions

The starting point for the development of the distributed elearning environment "Learn-Serve" has been the inflexibility of traditional, monolithic, and centralized elearning platforms. The latter resemble one another to a large extend. However, a reuse of functionalities and a flexible reuse of content in the traditional systems is uncommon and often difficult, if it is possible at all. Existing elearning standards aim at a reuse of content, but a number of systems exist that do not adhere to these standards.

To solve these problems, this thesis has realized a Web-services-based elearning environment that consists of several remote service providers. Although Web services create an overhead owing to their message-based communication [WCL05], it is reasonable to build the environment on this technology owing to the general advantages of Web services. To identify elearning service providers, a top-down division has been executed on a hypothetical elearning platform. First, several general functionalities have been identified; thereafter, based on the IEEE LTSA standard another top-down division of the special elearning functionalities has led to several providers. The resulting service providers are relatively coarse-grained and offer functionalities that are self-contained, for example, a user management. In consequence, each realized LearnServe service provider constitutes a complete and independent unit having everything needed in itself and can be exchanged flexibly. A further subdivision of the identified providers as proposed by ELF is a design decision and would offer more functionalities as independent services but would at the same time make application communication more complex.

The elearning community just has started to think about Web services. Frameworks like ELF have just been created to be discussed. They are based on a very fine-grained definition of services. The top-down approach executed in this thesis resulted in coarse-grained implementations that aggregate several of the fine-grained services of ELF. This is reasonable since data elements of learners should not be distributed across several service implementations. For example, authentication data and tracking data correspond to a single user and present a complete identification of a person with all characteristics. As soon as real services rather than mere concepts are available for a broad community of learners, the effects will be positive for both, learners and providers. On the one hand, the market will offer more courses for a learner to choose from, and, on the other hand, the reuse of content and the reuse of functionalities have a positive economical effect for providers. In particular, a mixture of free and commercial services would be possible on one consumer platform. This cannot be realized within the organization of traditional platforms as open source platforms are incapable of using system functionalities from commercial platforms. It is also possible to realize an easy integration of elearning services and business applications to support a "learning-on-the-job" as proposed by [VH04, WG05]. New business models have to be developed for the provision of services as they have different characteristics than learning objects of elearning software. Several of these ideas have been discussed throughout this thesis.

Chapter 5 has introduced a new approach to reusing content. Instead of copying and exchanging the files in form of physical learning objects, content is presented by Sharable Content Services (SCS) solving several problems of traditional learning objects mentioned in [POS05]. These SCSs can be combined by means of BPEL4WS documents to build classes or courses. Although the LearnServe Content Provider is still able to handle IMS Simple Sequencing documents to describe the content order, IMS Simple Sequencing is not needed anymore. It is a simple design decision how to describe the content structure in its internal representation. The strict usage of Web service standards enables a reduction of elearning standards. At least the following elearning specifications or standards can be simplified or are obsolete:

1. IMS Simple Sequencing is replaced by BPEL4WS course definitions. Owing to the nature of SCSs, courses can better be compiled by BPEL and corresponding BPEL tools. Internal representations of course structures do not have an effect on other platform implementations.

2. IMS Content Packaging is not needed anymore because content is not reused in a physical form.

3. IMS Question and Test Interoperability Specification [IMS05b] is used to exchange definitions of tests and examinations. Both of them are offered in the new organization as SCSs. There is no need to exchange files with test definitions.

4. IMS Learner Information Packaging Specification is not needed anymore because learner information can be access on the remote system if a Web service front-end is available. The IMS already specified interfaces to exchange user data with other systems.

5. IMS Sharable State Persistence[1] addresses the storage of state information of content objects. As they are handled on the content provider machine, information can be stored after each SCS call in a proprietary way.

6. Specifications like ULF (Universal Learning Format [Sab00]) that are based on IMS specifications can be made simpler or are obsolete.

7. The SCORM philosophy to combine the best standards and specifications still gives hope to choose the best definitions when implementing a platform or server. However, SCORM can now be made simpler because it uses some of the specifications mentioned above. Some of the concerns against the realization of the SCORM RTE specification disappeared since tests are not evaluated on the client but on the server of the service provider.

It goes without saying that now several related definitions and standards are also obsolete owing to the service-orientation. Other standards like IEEE LOM are still important to enable a discovery of learning content. The IEEE LTSA standard gives a good orientation and proofs that the implementation of the services still realizes a full-fledged elearning environment.

The use of elearning Web services in an open style on the Web can only be successful if the elearning community will be able to agree on a couple of realization aspects. The latter include particularly the CDSSO mechanism, the interfaces of the provisioning server to enable tracking from any other service, the use of presentation-oriented services, or a common message structure that can be interpreted by all consumer applications, as well as security aspects. All of the latter are covered in the "L" in Figure 4.33 by the blue-colored layers. If the community will not be able to agree about those aspects, implementation efforts are needed each time a new provider joins the environment. Hopefully the elearning community will learn from the problem of many competing standards and specifications in former times and will adapt standards like WSRP already established for Web services. First approaches to create guidelines for a use of Web services in elearning have started under the supervision of the IMS in the working group about general Web services[2] [IMS05a]. Currently, they are working at lower levels of the stack (e.g., versions of SOAP,

---

[1]http://www.imsglobal.org/ssp/sspv1p0/imsssp_bestv1p0.html
[2]http://www.imsglobal.org/gws/index.html

WSDL, HTTP) which a peer has to implement in order to establish interoperability. For the higher levels, this thesis adapted or used models of existing standards that could provide the foundation for the interoperability needed in elearning. Further research within the LearnServe project should address the interoperability of LearnServe offerings with the platforms and Web services that will be developed by other manufacturers. In addition, mobile clients have to be tested within the LearnServe environment. Although WSRP can conceptually run on these devices, there are currently no powerful WSRP implementations for PDAs (Personal Digital Assistants) or mobile phones.

A problem that addresses the definition of metadata is already mentioned (but not solved) in the SCORM specification [ADL04b]. In principle, the full LOM metadata set can be used at each level within a Manifest document. This means that metadata can be defined for the entire document, for each SCO included, for each Asset used, and again for each Submanifest within the original Manifest document. There is a huge lack of recommendations of how to use metadata annotations in elearning in general. This concerns, on the one hand, the use of metadata presented to learners, and, on the other hand, the set of metadata presented to authors who want to reuse SCOs or SCSs, Assets, or entire courses. It goes without saying that metadata for authors ought to be different from metadata used for learners. SCORM also does not address an intelligent creation of profiling information based on tracking data. Algorithms for the creation of profiles have to be developed in order to provide content that match exactly the learners' needs. These algorithms can also obtain help to allocate content on the foundation of tracking data that is not part of learner profiles.

The selection of Web services is crucial for the creation of an information system. It is even more important in the field of elearning, where learners ought to select content services on their own. This situation is even worse having the problem of LOM annotations described above in mind. There is a clear lack of research on the selection and combination process of services; however, a first step in the elearning community has already been done [MH04]. The semantic Web gives hope that even metadata descriptions can be used by automatic software agents to support the selection of services both for functionality and for the population of content checklists. A first research system [ABD+05] addresses the automatic combination of courses by means of BPEL4WS in combination with Virtual Web services (VWS). The latter are implemented in form of agents that enable a late binding of course resources to BPEL definitions based on OWL-S service descriptions. A lot of problems with the automatic selection of Web services in general are not solved. Consequently, the semantic combination of elearning content is still far away from becoming reality.

Bibliography

[Aal03] Aalst, W.M.P. van der (2003): *Don't go with the flow: Web services composition standards exposed.* In IEEE Intelligent Systems Jan/Feb 2003 issue, Web Services - Been there done that? Trends & Controversies.

[AB04] Allamaraju, S.; Brooks, R. (2004): *Web Services for Remote Portlets 1.0 Primer.* Committee Draft 1.00, 03. December 2004. Online: http://www.oasis-open.org/committee/wsrp/ (2005-05-25).

[ABD+05] Anane, R.; Bordbar, B.; Deng, F.; Hendley, R. J. (2005): *A Web Services Approach to Learning Path Composition.* In Proc. of 5th IEEE International Conference on Advanced Learning Technologies (ICALT'05), pp. 628-632, July 2005. Kaoshiung, Taiwan.

[ABF+04] Austin, D.; Barbir, A.; Ferris, C.; Garg, S. (2004): *Web Services Architecture Requirements.* W3C Working Group Note, 11. February 2004. Online: http://www.w3.org/TR/2004/NOTE-wsa-reqs-20040211/ (2005-05-25).

[ACD+03] Andrews, T.; Curbera, F.; Dholakia, H.; Goland, Y.; Klein, J.; Leymann, F.; Liu, K.; Roller, D.; Smith, D.; Thatte, S.; Trickovic, I.; Weerawarana, S. (2003): *Specification: Business Process Execution Language for Web Services Version 1.1..* Online: http://www-106.ibm.com/developerworks/library/ws-bpel/ (2004-05-28).

[ACK+04] Alonso, G.; Casati, F.; Kuno, H.; Machiraju, V. (2004): *Web Services. Concepts, Architectures and Applications.* Springer-Verlag Berlin, Germany.

[ACP02] Adelsberger, H. H.; Collis, B.; Pawlowski, J. M. (eds.) (2002): *Handbook on Information Technologies for Education and Training.* Springer-Verlag Berlin Heidelberg, Germany.

[ADL02a] Advanced Distributed Learning (ADL) (2002): *Advanced Distributed Learning Emerging and Enabling Technologies for the Design of Learning Object Repositories Report*, Version 1.0.

[ADL04a] Advanced Distributed Learning (ADL) (2004): *Sharable Content Object Reference Model (SCORM®) 2004 2nd Edition*, Overview, 2004, 22. July 2004.

[ADL04b] Advanced Distributed Learning (ADL) (2004): *Sharable Content Object Reference Model (SCORM®) Content Aggregation Model*, Version 1.3.1, 2004.

[ADL04c] Advanced Distributed Learning (ADL) (2004): *Sharable Content Object Reference Model (SCORM®) Run-Time Environment*, Version 1.3.1, 2004.

[ADL04d] Advanced Distributed Learning (ADL) (2004): *Sharable Content Object Reference Model (SCORM®) Sequencing and Navigation*, Version 1.3.1, 2004.

[AIC01] Aviation Industry CBT Committee (AICC) Computer Managed Instruction (CMI) (2001): *Guidelines for Interoperability*, Version 3.5., April 2, 2001.

[AK99] Arapis, C.; Konstantas, D. (1999): *Design and Implementation of a Teleteaching Environment*. In Proc. 9. DELOS Workshop Digital Libraries for Distance Learning, pp.79-84, Brno, Czech Republic, 15-17. April 1999.

[AK04] Apostolopoulos, T. K.; Kefala, A. (2004): *An XML-Based E-learning Service Management Framework*. In Proc. fourth IEEE International Conference on Advanced Learning Technologies (ICALT'04), Joensuu, Finland. pp. 850-851.

[ALF+01] Anido, L.; Llamas, M.; Fernández, M. J.; Rodríguez, J.; Santos, J.; Caeiro, M. (2001): *A Conceptual Modelling Framework for Standards-Driven Web-Based Distance Learning*. In Proc. ER2001, LNCS2224, pp. 585-598, 2001, Springer-Verlag Berlin Heidelberg, Germany.

[AFL+01] Anido-Rifón, L.; Fernández-Iglesias, M. J.; Llamas-Nistal, M.; Caeiro-Rodríguez, M.; Santos-Gago, J.; Rodríguez-Estévez, J. S. (2001): *A Component Model for Standardized Web-Based Education*. In ACM Journal of Educational Resources in Computing, Vol. 1, No. 2, Summer 2001, Article #1.

[All03] Allmann, M. (2003): *An Evaluation of XML-RPC*. ACM Performance Evaluation Review, March 2003.

[ALN00] Allen, R.; Lowe-Norris, A. G. (2000): *Active Directory*. O'Reilly, Beijing and Cambridge.

[AP02] Adelsberger, H. H.; Pawlowski, J. M. (2002): *Kontinuierlicher Zuwachs, E-Learning und Standardisierung von Lerntechnologien*. ESSENER UNIKATE 18/2002, pp. 8-18.

[Ark02] Arkin, A. (2002): *Business Process Modeling Language. Last Call Draft of the BPML specification.* BPMI.org and Intalio Corp. Online: http://www.bpmi.org/bpmi-downloads/BPML1.0.zip (2004-07-18).

[Asa04] Asaduzzaman, A. (2004): *Web Services for K-12 Education Systems.* Dev Articels 2004-02-18. Online: http://www.devarticles.com/c/a/Web-Services/Web-Servoices-for-Education-Systems/ (2005-08-22).

[ASF05] Arroyo, S.; Sung-Kook, H.; Feistel, D. (2005): *Searching for Semantic Web Services - A Google based Approach.* In Proc. 2nd International Conference on Information Technology, pp. 393-403, Amman, Jordan, May 2005.

[ASN02] ASN (2002): *Abstract Syntax Notation One (ASN.1),* Specification of Basic Notation, ITU-T Rec. X.680 (2002), ISO/IEC 8824-1:2002. Online: http://asn1.elibel.tm.fr/en/ (2004-08-21).

[AT01] Alessi, S. M.; Trollip, S. R. (2001): *Multimedia for Learning. Methods and Development.* Allyn and Bacon, London. 3. Edition 2001.

[Atw04] Atwood, S. (2004): *Opening Up Online Education.* MIT Technology Review December 2003/January 2004. Online: http://www.technologyreview.com/articles/print_version/atwood1203.asp (2004-01-25).

[Bab01] Babich, Y. (2001): *Entwurf und Realisierung einer verteilten Lernsoftware für ein Hochofenmodell.* Studienarbeit, Lehrstuhl für Informatik 4, Friedrich-Alexander-Universität Erlangen-Nürnberg, Germany, November 2001.

[Bac03] Backroad Connections Pty Ltd (2003): *Definition of key terms used in e-learning (Version 1.00).* Australian Flexible Learning Framework Quick Guides Series, Australian National Training Authority, April 2003. Online: http://flexiblelearning.net.au/guides/keyterms.pdf (2004-07-08).

[Bar02] Barker, P. (2002): *Authoring Systems.* In [ACP02].

[BBB+01] Banerji, A.; Bartolini, C.; Beringer, D.; Chopella, V.; Govindarajan, K.; Karp, A.; Kuno, H.; Lemon, H.; Pogossiants, G.; Sharma, S.; Williams, S. (2001): *Web Services Conversation Language (WSCL).* Online: http://www.w3.org/TR/wscl10/ (2004-05-29).

[BBS04] Boles, D.; Boles, C.; Schmees, M. (2004): *Erlösformen für Web-Content und -Services.* In Informatik Forsch. Entw. (2004)18, pp. 165-173.

[BBZ04] Balzert, H.; Balzert, H.; Zwintzscher, O. (2004): *Die E-Learning-Plattform W3L, Anforderungen, Didaktik, Ergonomie, Architektur, Entwicklung, Einsatz.* In Wirtschaftsinformatik 46(2004) 2, pp129-138.

[BCC+02] Brunner, R.; Cohen, F.; Curbera, F.; Govoni, D.; Haines, S.; Kloppmann, M.; Marchal, B.; Morrison, S.; Ryman, A.; Weber, J.; Wutka, M. (2002): *Java Web Services Unleashed.* Sams Publishing, Indiana, USA.

[BDF+01] Benatallah, B.; Dumas, M.; Fauvet, M.-C.; Rabhi, F. A. (2001): *Towards Patterns of Web Services Composition.* School of Computer Science, University of New South Wales, Sydney NSW 2052, November 2001.

[BDF+02] Benatallah, B.; Dumas, M.; Fauvet, M.-C.; Rabhi, F. A.; Sheng, Q. Z. (2002): *Overview of Some Patterns for Architecting and Managing Composite Web Services.* ACM SIGecom Exchanges, Vol. 3, No. 3, August 2002, pp 9-16.

[Ber93] Bernstein, P. A. (1993): *Middleware: an architecture for distributed system services.* Technical Report, Compaq and DEC Cambridge Research Lab CRL-93-6, March 1993.

[Ber96] Bernstein, P. A. (1996): *Middleware: A Model for Distributed System Services.* In Communication of the ACM Vol. 39 No. 2, February 1996, pp. 86-98.

[BES03] Bry, F.; Eisinger, N.; Scheemayer, G. (2003): *Web Services for Teaching: A Case Study.* In Proc. First International Conference on Web Services (ICWS‘03), Las Vegas, USA, 23-26. June 2003, pp. 402-408.

[BFH+03] Bultan, T.; Fu, X.; Hull, R.; Su, J. (2003): *Conversation Specification: A New Approach to Design and Analysis of E-Service Composition.* In Proc. of 12th International World Wide Web Conference (WWW03), Budapast, Hungary, pp. 403-410.

[BFM98] Berners-Lee, T.; Fielding, R.; Masinter, L. (1998): *Uniform Resource Identifiers (URI): Generic Syntax.* RFC 2396, MIT/LCS, U.C. Irvine, Xerox Corporation, August 1998.

[BH03a] Brown, A.; Haas, H. (2003): *Web Services Glossary.* W3C Working Draft 14. May 2003.

[BH03b] Burghardt, M.; Hagenhoff, S. (2003): *Konzeption eines Abrechnungsmodells für Web Services.* In Matthias Schumen (Ed.): Arbeitsbericht Nr. 26/2003, Institut für Wirtschaftsinformatik, Georg-August-Universität Göttingen.

[BH03c] Brücher, J.; Hugo, M. (2003): *Flash MX ActionScript*. Addison-Wesley, Harlow UK.

[BHB+03] Beneken, G.; Hammerschall, U.; Broy, M.; Cengarle, M. V.; Jürjens, J.; Rumpe, B.; Schoenmkers, M. (2003): *Componentware - State of the Art 2003*. Background paper in *CUE-Workshop*, Venice.

[BHM+04] Booth, D.; Haas, H.; McCabe, F.; Newcomer, E.; Champion, M.; Ferris, C.; Orchard, D. (2004): *Web Services Architecture*. Working Group Note of the W3C Web Services Architecture Working Group.

[Bir03] Biramen, E. (2003): *Web Services. Aktueller Entwicklungsstand und Zukunftsaussichten*. Master Thesis University of Vienna, Austria, 2003.

[BL00] Barritt, C.; Lewis, D. (2000): *Reusable Learning Object Strategy: Definition, Creation Process, and Guidelines for Building, Version 3.1*. Whitepaper published by Cisco Systems. Online: http://www.reusablelearning.org/Docs/Cisco_rlo_roi_v3-1.pdf (2004-08-05).

[BL04] Brocke, J. vom; Lindner, M. A. (2004): *Service portfolio Measurement - A Framework for Evaluating the Financial Consequences of Out-tasking Decisions*. In Proc. of ACM 2nd International Conference on Service Oriented Computing, New York City, NY, USA, November 15-19, 2004, pp. 203-211.

[Blo92] Bloomer, J. (1992): *Power Programming with RPC*. O'Reilly and Associates, Bejing and Cambridge.

[BN04] Brase, J.; Nejdl, W. (2004): *Ontologies and Metadata for eLearning*. In Staab, S. & R. Studer (Eds.): Handbook on Ontologies. International Handbooks on Information Systems Springer 2004, pp. 555-574.

[BN84] Birell, A. D.; Nelson, B. J. (1984): *Implementing remote procedure calls*. ACM Transactions on Computer Systems, (2)1, February 1984, pp. 39-59.

[BNT03] Bouras, C.; Nani, M.; Tsiatsos, T. (2003): *A SCORM-conformant LMS*. In Proc. ED-MEDIA 2003, Honolulu, Hawaii, USA, June 23 - 28 2003, pp. 10-13.

[BPS+04] Bray, T.; Paoli, J.; Sperberg-McQueen, C. M.; Maler, E.; Yergeau, F.; Cowan, J. (2004): *Extensible Markup Language (XML) 1.1*. W3C Recommendation 15 April 2004. Online: http://www.w3.org/TR/2004/REC-xml11-20040204/ (2005-02-12).

[BR02] Barron, A. E.; Rickelman, C. (2002): *Management Systems*. In [ACP02].

[BR03] Blackmon, W. H.; Rehak, D. R. (2003): *Customized Learning: A Web Services Approach*. In Proc. World Conference on Educational Multimedia, Hypermedia and Telecommunications (EDMEDIA), Volume 2003, Issue 1, 2003, pp. 6-9, Honolulu, USA.

[BRE+02] Buckingham Shum, S.; Roure, D. De; Eisenstadt, M.; Shadbolt, N.; Tate, A. (2002): *CoAKTinG: Collaborative Advanced Knowledge Technologies in the Grid*. In Proc. of the 2nd Workshop on Advanced Collaborative Environments, Eleventh IEEE Int. Symposium on High Performance Distributed Computing (HPDC-11), July 24-26, 2002, Edinburgh, Scotland.

[Bri02] Brittenham, P. (2002): *An overview of the Web Services Inspection Language. An update on distributed Web service discovery using WS-Inspection documents*. Online: ftp://www6.software.ibm.com/software/developer/library/ws-wsilover.pdf (2004-04-23).

[BSW02] Bohl, O.; Schellhase, J.; Winand, U. (2002): *Standards für Web-basiertes E-Learning*. In: Eicker, Stefan (ed.): E-Learning: Modelle, Instrumente und Erfahrungen. Tagungsband der Teil-Konferenz E-Learning im Rahmen der Multi-Konferenz Wirtschaftsinformatik (MKWI02), Nürnberg, Germany, 09.-11. September 2002. pp. 93-109.

[BVV+04] Bote-Lorenzo, M. L.; Vaquero-González, L. M.; Vega-Gorgojo, G.; Dimitriadis, Y.; Asensio-Pérez, J.I.; Gómez-Sánchez, E.; Hernández-Leo, D. (2004): *A Tailorable Collaborative Learning System that Combines OGSA Grid Services and IMS-LD Scripting*. Proceedings of the X International Workshop on Groupware, CRIWG 2004, Springer-Verlag, LNCS 3198, 305-321, San Carlos, Costa Rica, September 2004.

[BWM04] Bailetti, T.; Weiss, M.; McInnis, M. (2004): *A Service-Oriented Architecture for Creating Customized Learning Environments*. SWIG 04 Papers. Online: http://www.cscsi.org/home/CSCSI/Members/swig/swig04papers/bailetti-weiss-mcinnis.pdf (2005-08-29).

[Cas05] Castle, B. (2005): *Introduction to Web Services for Remote Portlets. Use WSRP in a Service-Oriented Architecture*. IBM developerWroks. Online: http://www-128.ibm.com/developerworks/webservices/ws-wsrp/ (2005-07-26).

[CCC+02] Cabrera, F.; Copeland, G.; Cox, B.; Freund, T.; Klein, J.; Storey, T.; Thatte, S. (2002): Web Services Transaction (WS-Transdaction). Online: http://www.ibm.com/developersworks/library/ws-transpec/ (2005-08-23).

[CCM+01] Christensen, E.; Curbera, F.; Meredith, G.; Weerawarana, S. (2001): *Web Services Description Language (WSDL) 1.1*. Online: http://www.w3.org/TR/wsdl (2004-04-24).

[CD02] Casati, F.; U. Dayal (eds.) (2002): *Special Issue on Web Services*. IEEE Bulletin of the Technical Committee on Data Engineering, 25(4), December 2002.

[CDK02a] Coulouris, G.; Dollimore, J.; Kindberg, T. (2002): *Verteilte Systeme, Konzepte und Design*. 3. Edition, Pearson Studium, Munich, Germany.

[CDK02b] Coulouris, G.; Dollimore, J.; Kindberg, T. (2002): *Distributed Systems: Concept and Design*. 2. Edition, Addison-Wesley, Harlow, UK.

[CER01] Curbera, F.; Ehnebuske, D.; Roger, D. (2001): *Using WSDL in a UDDI Registry, Version 1.07*. Online: http://www.uddi.org/pubs/wsdlbestpractices-V1.07-Open-20020521.pdf (2004-11-27).

[CET04] CETIS, the centre for educational technology interoperability standards (2004): *Learning Technology Standards: An Overview, January 02, 2004*. Online: http://www.cetis.ac.uk/static/standards.html (2004-07-15).

[Che02] Chen, W. (2002): *Web Services - What Do They Mean to Web-based Education*. In Proc. International Conference on Computers in Education (ICCE2002), pp. 707-708, Auckland, New Zealand, December 2002.

[CHR04] Clement, L.; Hately, A.; Riegen, C. von; Rogers, T. (2004): *UDDI Version 3.0.2, UDDI Spec. Technical Committee Draft, Dated 20041019*. Online: http://uddi.org/pubs/uddi_v3.htm (2005-02-28).

[CHY+97] Chung, P. E.; Huang, Y.; Yajnik, S. Liang, D.; Shih, J. C.; Wang, C.-Y.; Wang, Y.-M. (1997): *DCOM and CORBA Side by Side, Step by Step, Layer by Layer*. In C++ Report, September 1997. Online: http://research.microsoft.com/ ymwang/papers/HTML/DCOMnCORBA/S.html (2005-08-29).

[Coe01] Coenraets, C. (2001): *Web Service: Building the Next Generation of E-Business Applications*. Macromedia White Paper. Online: http://www.macromedia.com/software/jrun/whitepapers/web_services/pdf/web_services.pdf (2005-08-29).

[Col02] Collis, B. (2002): *Information Technologies for Education and Training*. In [ACP02].

[CSM+00] Cass, A. G.; Staudt Lerner, B.; McCall, E. K.; Osterweil, L. J.; Sutton, J.; Stanley, M.; Wise, A. (2000): *Little-JIL/Juliette: A Process Definition Language and Interpreter.* In Proc. of the 22nd International Conference on Software Engineering. 4-11 June 2000. Limerick, Ireland. pp. 754-757.

[CT03] Chappell, D.; Jewell, T. (2003): *Java Web Services.* 1. Edition, O'Reilly, Beijing and Cambridge.

[CWD00] Curbera, F.; Weerawarana, S.; Duftler, M. J. (2000): *Network Accessible Service Specification Language: An XML Language for Describing Network Accessible Services.* Online: http://www.cs.mu.oz.au/eas/subjects/654/nassl.pdf (2004-02-20).

[DHS91] Dark, P. J.; Hutchison, D.; Shepherd, W. D. (1991): *Remote Procedure Calls and Distributed Multimedia Systems.* Lancaster University, Report No. MPG-91-27, October 1991.

[Dit03] Dittler U. (Ed.) (2003): *E-Learning, Einsatzkonzepte und Erfolgsfaktoren des Lernens mit interaktiven Medien.* Oldenbourg Verlag, Munich, 2. Edition.

[DLW+03] Dumke, R.; Lother, M.; Wille, C.; Zbrog, F. (2003): *Web Engineering.* Pearson Studium, Munich 2003. 1. Edition.

[DNW+01] Dhraief H.; Nejdl, W.; Wolf W.; Wolpers M. (2001). *Open Learning Repositories and Metadata Modeling.* In Proc. International Semantic Web Working Symposium (SWWS), pp. 495-514, Stanford University, California, USA.

[DOH+01] Dumas, M.; O'Sullivan, J.; Heravizadeh, M.; Hofstede, A. ter; Edmond, D. (2001): *Towards a Semantic Framework for Service Description.* In Proc. of the IFIP Conference on Database Semantics, pages 277-291, Hong Kong, China, April 2001. Kluwer Academic Publishers.

[EDI05] United Nations Directories for Electronic Data Interchange for Administration, Commerce and Transport (2005): Electronic Data Interchange. http://www.unece.org/trade/untdid/welcome.htm (2005-01-21).

[Emm00] Emmerich, W. (2000): *Software Engineering and Middleware: A Roadmap.* In Proc. of 22nd International Conference on Software Engineering (ISCE2000), pp. 117-129, Limerick, Ireland.

[ES05] Ehlers, D.; Schenkel, P. (eds.) (2005): *Bildungscontrolling im E-Learning. Erfolgreiche Strategien und Erfahrungen jenseits des ROI.* 1. Edition 2005, Springer-Verlag Berlin Heidelberg, Germany.

[ESW05] Euler, D.; Seufert, S.; Wirth, M. (2005): *Gestaltung des Qualitätsmanagement zur Zertifizierung von E-Learning-Programmen.* In: Euler, D; Seufert, S. (Eds.): *E-Learning in Hochschulen und Bildungszentren.* 1. Edition 2005, Oldenbourg Verlag München Wien, pp. 453-472.

[FFE+03] Fuller, J; Fuecks, K. E.; Waters, B.; Solin, D.; Stephens, J.; Reynolds, L. (2003): *Professional PHP Web Services.* Wrox Press, Birmingham, UK.

[FGK02] Florescu, D.; Grünhagen, A.; Kossmann, D. (2002): *XL: An XML Programming Language for Web Service Specification and Composition.* In Proc. of WWW2002, International World Wide Web Conference, pp. 65-76, May 7-11, 2002, Honolulu, HI, USA.

[Fra99] Frank, U. (1999): *Component Ware - Software-technische Konzepte und Perspektiven für die Gestaltung betrieblicher Informationssysteme.* In Information Management & Consulting, 14(2), 1999, pp 11-18.

[Fre91] Ferenczi, S. (1991): *Concepts for a Modular and Distributed Prolog Language.* In J. Maluszynski and M. Wirsing (Eds.): Programming Language Implementation and Logic Programming, Proc. of the 3rd International Symposium, PLILP'91, 26-28 August 1991, Passau, Germany, Lecture Notes in Computer Science 528, pp. 158-170.

[Fu03] Fu, Y. (2003): *E-learning as Knowledge Construction: An online courseware design facilitated by web services.* Dissertation, Faculty of Science, The University of Reading, December 2003.

[GBB04] Grob, H. L.; Brocke, J. vom; Bensberg, F. (2004): *Bewertung von Geschäftsmodellen im E-Learning — Konzeption, Methoden und Perspektiven.* In Proc. of the E-Learning Workshop Hannover "Einsatzkonzepte und Geschäftsmodelle", September 27-28, 2004, Hannover, Germany.

[GBD+04] Grob, H. L.; Bensberg, F.; Dewanto, B. L.; Düppe, I. (2004): *Controlling von Learning Management-Systemen - ein kennzahlenorientierter Ansatz.* In: Campus 2004 (Tagungsband), Kommen die digitalen Medien an den Hochschulen in die Jahre? In Carstensen, D.; Barrios, B. (eds.): Band 29 der Gesellschaft für Medien in der Wissenschaft (GMW), Münster, Germany,pp. 46-56.

[GDB04a] Grob, H. L.; Bensberg, F.; Dewanto, B. L. (2004): *Developing, Deploying, Using and Evaluating an Open Source Learning Management System.* In Proc. of the 26th International Conference on Information Technology Interfaces (ITI 2004), Zagreb, Croatia, pp. 387-393..

[GDB04b] Grob, H. L.; Bensberg, F.; Dewanto, B. L. (2004): *Model Driven Architecture (MDA): Integration and Model Reuse for Open Source eLearning Platforms*. Online: http://eleed.campussource.de/archiv/81/ (2005-08-29).

[GFH+03] Guangzuo, C.; Fei, C.; Hu, C; Jiuling, C.; Shengqing, W.; Shufang, L. (2003): *OntoEdu: A Kind of Instructional Support Platform based on Ontology*. In Proc. Conference Report at Annual Conference of CETA, China, December 2003.

[GGM04] Gütl, C.; Garcia Barrios, V. M.; Mödritscher, F. (2004): *Adaptation in E-Learning Environments through the Service-Based Framework and its Application for AdeLE*. In Proc. ELEARN 2004, pp. 1891 - 1898, Washington, USA.

[GHM+03] Gudgin, M.; Hadley, M.; Mendelsohn, N.; Moreau, J.-J.; Nielsen, H. F. (2003): *SOAP Version 1.2*. W3C Recommendation 24 June 2003.

[GL05] Graf, S.; List, B. (2005): *An Evaluation of Open Source E-Learning Platforms Stressing Adaptation Issus*. In Proc. of 5th IEEE International Conference on Advanced Learning Technologies (ICALT'05), pp. 163-165, July 2005. Kaoshiung, Taiwan.

[GNR00] Gibbons, A. S.; Nelson, J.; Richards, R. (2000): *The nature and origin of instructional objects*. In D. A. Wiley (Ed.), The Instructional Use of Learning Objects.

[Gri98] Griffel, F. (1998): *Componentware. Konzepte und Techniken eines Softwareparadigmas*. 1. Edition, Dpunkt Verlag, Heidelberg, Germany.

[Gro93] Grob, H. L.(1993): *Capital Budgeting with Financial Plans. An Introduction*. Gabler, Wiesbaden, Germany.

[Gro95] Grob, H. L. (1995): *Multimediale Lehre an der Universität*. In Forschungsjournal der Westfälischen Wilhelms-Universität Münster, Heft 1, 4. Jg. 1995, S. 38-42, Germany.

[Gro01] Grosso, W. (2001): *Java RMI*. O'Reilly, Beijing and Cambridge.

[Gru93] Gruber, T. R. (1993): *A Translation Approach to Portable Ontology Specifications*. Knowledge Acquisition, 5(2), 1993: pp. 199-220.

[GSW03] Gardner, L.; Sheridan, D.; White, D. (2003): *Computer Supported Learning: A Large-Scale, Web-based Learning and Assessment System to Support Flexible Education*. In Proc. 34th Annual Hawaii International Conference on System Sciences (HICSS-34)-Volume 1, Maui, Hawaii, USA.

[GT00] Gruhn, V.; Thiel, A. (2000): *Komponentenmodelle*. Addison Wesley Publishing Company, Boston, USA.

[Hal05] Hall, B. (2005): *The Directory of E-Learning Providers 2005*. To appear in December 2005, brandon-hall.com.

[Han02] Hanimann, S. (2002): *Einbindung von e-Learning in den universitären Lehrbetrieb*. Diplomarbeit, Universität Zürich. Online: http://www.ifi.unizh.ch/ifiadmin/staff/rofrei/DA/DA_Arbeiten_2002/Hanimann_Sabine.pdf (2004-07-07).

[Han04] Hanisch, F. (2004): *Highly Interactive Web-Based Courseware*. Dissertation der Eberhard-Karls-Universität Tübingen. Online: http://w210.ub.uni-tuebingen.de/dbt/volltexte/2004/1167/pdf/hanisch.pdf (2004-06-08)

[HB03] Hoppe, G.; Breitner, M. H. (2003): *Business Models for E-Learning*. Discussion Paper No. 287, October 2003, Hannover, Germany.

[Her64] Hertz, D. B. (1964): *Risk Analysis in Capital Investment*. In: Harvard Business Reviews 1964, pp 95-106.

[HG03] Hilliger von Thile, A.; Göres, J. (2003): *Ersetzung von CORBA durch Message-oriented Middleware und Web-Services in einem existierenden Unternehmensportal*. In Proc. 10. Conference on Database Systems For Business, Technology and Web (BTW2003), Springer-Verlag, Leipzig, Germany, February 2003, pp. 3-5.

[Hip03] Hipfl, I. (2003): *Handbuch eLearning in den Geisteswissenschaften, Projekt "EMIL", Elektronische Medien in der Lehre der Geisteswissenschaften*. Institut für Informationsverarbeitung in den Geisteswissenschaften, Karl-Franzens Universität Graz. Online: http://grips.uni-graz.at/material/emil_handbuch.pdf (2004-07-07).

[HK03] Hettrich, A.; Koroleva, N. (2003): *Marktstudie Learning Management Systeme (LMS) und Learning Content Management Systeme (LCMS) - Fokus deutscher Markt*. Fraunhofer IOA, Stuttgart, Germany.

[HLV+02] Hüsemann, B.; Lechtenbörger, J.; Vossen, G.; Westerkamp, P. (2002): *XLX - A Platform for Graduate-Level Exercises*. In Proc. International Conference on Computers in Education (ICCE2002), Auckland, New Zealand, December 2002, pp. 1262-1266.

[HM02] Hallam-Baker, P.; Maler, E. (2002): *Assertions and Protocol for the OASIS Security Assertion Markup Language (SAML)*. OASIS, 2002. Online: http://www.oasis-open.org/committees/security/docs/cs-sstc-core-01.pdf (2004-07-07).

[Hof02] Hofman, J. (2002): *Peer-to-peer: the next hot trend in e-learning.* In Learning Circuits, ASTD's Online Magazine, February 2002.

[HS00] Herzum, P.; Sims, O. (2000): *Business Component Factory: A comprehensive Overview of Component-Based Development for the Enterprise.* Wiley & Sons, Hoboken, NJ, USA.

[HY05] Hsu, K. C.; Yang, F.-C. O. (2005): *OEPortal: an Open, Unified, and Interoperable Presentation-Preserving e-Learning Portal.* In Proc. of 5th IEEE International Conference on Advanced Learning Technologies (ICALT'05), pp. 628-632, July 2005. Kaoshiung, Taiwan.

[IEE02] The IEEE Learning Technology Standards Committee (LTSC) (2002): *Draft Standard for Learning Object Metadata,* IEEE 1484.12.1-2002, 15 July 2002. Online: http://ltsc.ieee.org.

[IEE03] The IEEE Learning Technology Standards Committee (LTSC) (2003): *Draft Standard for Learning Technology - Learning Technology Systems Architecture (LTSA).* IEEE P1484.1/D9, 2001-11-30. Online: http://ltsc.ieee.org.

[IEE04] The IEEE Learning Technology Standards Committee (LTSC) (2004): *Draft Standard for Learning Technology - Data Model for Content Object Communication.* IEEE 1484.11.1 Draft 5. July 13, 2004. Online: http://ltsc.ieee.org.

[IM02] Innes, J.; McGreal, R. (2002): *Metadata Specifications.* In [ACP02].

[IMC01] Ip, A.; Morrison, I.; Currie, M.(2001): *What is a learning object, technically?* In Proceedings of WebNet 2001 - World Conference on the WWW and Internet, Orlando, Florida, October 23-27, 2001. AACE 2001, pp. 580-586.

[IMS01a] IMS Global Learning Consortium, Inc. (2001): *IMS Content Packaging Best Practices Guide.* Version 1.1.2, August 2001.

[IMS01b] IMS Global Learning Consortium (2001): *IMS Content Packaging Information Model.* Version 1.1.2.

[IMS01c] IMS Global Learning Consortium (2001): *IMS Learning Resource Meta-Data Information Model.* Version 1.2.1.

[IMS01d] IMS Global Learning Consortium (2001): *IMS Learner Information Packaging Information Model Specification.* Final Specification. Version 1.0.

[IMS03a] IMS Global Learning Consortium (2003): *IMS Simple Sequencing Information and Behavior Model.* Version 1.0 Final Specification.

[IMS03b] IMS Global Learning Consortium (2003): *IMS Simple Sequencing Best Practice and Implementation Guide*. Version 1.0 Final Specification.

[IMS03c] IMS Global Learning Consortium (2003): *IMS Simple Sequencing XML Binding*. Version 1.0 Final Specification.

[IMS03d] IMS Global Learning Consortium (2003): *IMS Abstract Framework: White Paper* . Version 1.0, 01. July 2003.

[IMS04a] IMS Global Learning Consortium (2004): *IMS Meta-Data*. Version 1.3 Public Draft Specification, March 2004.

[IMS04b] IMS Global Learning Consortium (2004): *IMS Enterprise Services Specification*. Version 1.0 Public Draft, 12. January 2004.

[IMS05a] IMS Global Learning Consortium (2005): *IMS General Web Services Base Profiles*. Version 1.0 Public Draft Specification, 31. January 2005.

[IMS05b] IMS Global Learning Consortium (2005): *IMS Question and Test Interoperability Overview*. Version 2.0 Final Specification, 24. January 2005.

[Jec04] Jeckle, M. (2004): *Web services*. Online: http://www.jeckle.de/webServices/index .html (2004-04-24).

[Jon02a] Jong, I. de (2002): *Web Services/SOAP and CORBA*. OMG Whitepaper. Online: http://www.omg.org/whitepapers (2004-03-19).

[Jon02b] Jones, E. R. (2002): *Implications of SCORM and Emerging E-learning Standards on Engineering Education*. In Proc. of the 2002 ASEE Gulf-Southwest Annual Conference, March 20-22, 2002.

[JOV03] Jaeschke, P.; Oberweis, A.; Vossen, G. (2003): *Web-basiertes Lernen: Eine Übersicht über Stand und Entwicklungen*. In [RV03].

[JP00] Jansen, B. J.; Pooch, U. (2000): *Web user studies: A review and framework for future work*. Journal of the American Society of Information Science and Technology. 52(3), pp. 235-246.

[Kai01] Kaiser, R. (2001): *Analyse und Anwendung von Standards für e-Learning-Umgebungen unter besonderer Berücksichtigung des SCORM Modells*. Diplomhausarbeit, Hochschule für Technik und Wirtschaft Dresden (FH) Fachbereich Informatik/-Mathematik.

[Kay00] Kay, M. (2000): *XSLT Programmers's Reference*. Wrox Press LTD, Birmingham, UK.

[KB03] Karastoyanova, D.; Buchmann, A. (2003): *Components, Middleware and Web Service*. In Proc. IADIS International Conference WWW/Internet 2003, Algarve, Portugal, pp. 5-9.

[KBS03] KBSt - Koordinierungs- und Beratungsstelle der Bundesregierung für Informationstechnik in der Bundesverwaltung im Bundesministerium der Inneren (2003): *SAGA. Standards und Architekturen für eGovernment-Anwendungen*. Version 1.1. Schriftenreihe der KBSt, Band 56, Februar 2003.

[Ker01a] Kerres, M (2001): *Multimediale und telemediale Lernumgebungen, Konzeption und Entwicklung*. 2. Edition 2001, Oldenbourg Verlag Munich, Germany.

[KKR03] Klein, M.; König-Ries, B. (2003): *A Process and a Tool for Creating Service Descriptions Based on DAML-S*. In Proc. of the 4th VLDB Workshop on Technologies for E-Services, TES 2003: 143-154.

[KKS+03] Keidl, M.; Kemper, A.; Seltzsam, S.; Stocker, K. (2003); *Web Services*. In [RV03].

[Kle01] Klein, S. (2001): *Electronic commerce: the flip side of a buzzword*. The Journal of Information Technology Theory and Application (JITTA), 3:4, 2001, pp. 23-26.

[KLR+95] Kappel, G.; Lang, P.; Rausch-Schott, S.; Retschitzegger, W. (1995): *Workflow Management Based on Objects, Rules, and Roles*. IEEE Data Engineering Bulletin 18(1), pp. 11-18, March 1995.

[KLT03] Kropp, A.; Leue, C.; Thompson, R. (2003): *Web Services for Remote Portlets Specification*. OASIS Standard Version 1.0, August 2003.

[KNS92] Keller, G.; Nüttgens, M.; Scheer, A.-W. (1992): *Semantische Prozessmodellierung auf der Grundlage "Ereignisgesteuerter Prozeßketten (EPK)"*. In: Scheer, A.-W. (Hrsg.): Veröffentlichungen des Instituts für Wirtschaftsinformatik, Heft 89, Saarbrücken, 1992.

[Kre01b] Kreger, H. (2001): *Web Services Conceptual Architecture (WSCA 1.0)*. International Business Machines Corporation (IBM Software Group).

[KSK+03] Keidl, M.; Seltzsam, S.; König, C.; Kemper, A. (2003): *Kontext-basierte Personalisierung von Web Services*. In Proc. 10. Conference on Database Systems For Business, Technology and Web (BTW2003), Leipzig, Germany, Feburary 2003, pp. 344-363.

[KT05] Koper, R.; Tattersall, C. (eds.): *Learning Design. A Handbook on Modelling and Delivering Networked Education and Training.* 1. Edition, Springer-Verlag Berlin Heidelberg, Germany.

[LCC+01] Levine, P.; Clark, J.; Casanave, C.; Kanaskie, K.; Harvey, B.; Clark, J.; et al. (2001): *ebXML Business Process Specification Schema Version 1.01.* Online: http://www.ebxml.org/specs/ebBPSS.pdf (2004-05-27).

[Leu99] Leuthold, J.H. (1999): *Is Computer-Based Learning Right for Everyone?* In Proc. of the 32nd Hawaii International Conference on System Sciences HICSS-32, Volume 1, pp. 1015-1022, 05-08. January, 1999, Los Alamitos, CA, USA.

[Ley01] Leymann, F. (2001): *Web Services Flow Language (WSFL 1.0).* Online: http://www-306.ibm.com/software/solutions/webservices/pdf/WSFL.pdf (2004-05-26).

[Ley03] Leymann, F. (2003): *Web Services: Distributed Applications without Limits - An Outline.* In Proc. 10. Conference on Database Systems For Business, Technology and Web (BTW2003), Springer-Verlag, Leipzig, Germany.

[LG02] Lee, Y.; Geller, J. (2002): *A Component-Based Architecture for Adaptive, Collaborative Web-Based Learning.* In J. Fong et al. (Eds): ICWL 2002, LNCS 2436, pp. 203-215, 2002, Springer-Verlag Berlin Heidelberg, Germany.

[LH03] Li, L.; Horrocks, I. (2003): *A software framework for matchmaking based on semantic web technology.* In Proc. of the Twelfth International World Wide Web Conference (WWW 2003), ACM 2003, pp 331-339.

[LHS+03] Lin, J.; Ho, C.; Sadiq, W.; Orlowska, M. E. (2002): *Using Workflow Technology to Manage Flexible e-Learning Services.* In Educational Technology and Society 5(4) 2002.

[LHW+01] Lin, J; Ho, C.; Sadiq, W.; Orlowska, M. E. (2001): *On Workflow enabled e-Learning Services.* In Proc. IEEE International Conference on Advanced Learning Technologies, ICELT2001, 6-8 August 2001, Madison, USA.

[LR04] Leymann, F.; Roller, D. (2004): *Modeling Business Processes with BPEL4WS.* In: M. Nüttgens, J. Mendling (eds.): Proc. of the 1st GI Workshop XML4BPM - XML Interchange Formats for Business Process Management at Modellierung 2004, Marburg, Germany, March 2004, pp.7-24.

[LS04] Lattermann, C.; Sandrock, J. (2004): *Ableitung von Geschäftsmodellen im E-Learning — exemplarische Darstellung am Beispiel Projekt Impuls EC*. In Proc. of First Potsdamer Mulitmedia Conference. Potsdam, Germany, 2004.

[LSD03] Liu, X.; Saddik, A. El; Georganas, N. D. (2003): *An Implementable Architecture Of an E-Learning System*. In Proc. Electrical and Computer Engineering CCECE 2003, pp. 717-720, Montreal, Canada, 2003.

[LW05] Libbrecht,   P.;   Winterstein,   S.   (2005):   *The   Service   Architecture in   the   ActiveMath   Learning   Environment*.   In   Proc.   ELeGI   Conference   2005,   Kaleidoscope   Workshop   E-Learning   Architectures.   Online: http://www.activemath.org/p̃aul/copy_left/Libbrecht-ServiceArch_in_ActiveMath-ElegiKaleido05.pdf (2005-08-29).

[Mar04] Marshall, S. (2004): *E-learning standards: Open enablers of learning or compliance strait jackets?* In Atkinson, R.; McBeath, C.; Jonas-Dwyer, D.; Phillips, R. (eds.): Beyond the comfort zone: Proceedings of the 21st ASCILITE Conference. Perth, 5-8 December, pp. 596-605.

[Mas05] Massey, J. (2005): *Study of the e-learning suppliers' "market" in Europe*. Final Report. Directorate-General for Education and Culture. European Union. Online: http://europa.eu.int/comm/education/programmes/elearning/doc/studies/market _study _en.pdf (2005-08-09).

[MB02] Metros, S. E.; Bennett, K. (2002): *Learning Objects in Higher Education*. EDU-CASE Center for Applied Research, Research Bulletin Volume 2002, Issue 19, 1. October 2002. Online: http://www.educause.edu/ir/library/pdf/ERB0219.pdf (2005-08-29).

[McI68] McIlroy, M. D. (1968): *Mass Produced Software Components*. In Report of NATO Conference on Software Engineering, NATO Science Committee, Garmisch, Germany, pp. 138-155.

[Mef00] Meffert,   H.   (2000):   *Marketing.   Grundlagen   marktorientierter Unernehmensführung.   Konzepte - Instrumente - Praxisbeispiele*. 9th Edition. Gabler, Wiesbaden, Germany.

[Meh99] Mehuron, W. (1999): *FEDERAL INFORMATION PROCESSING STANDARDS PUBLICATION FIPS PUB 46-3, Data Encryption Standard (DES)*. U.S. DEPARTMENT OF COMMERCE/National Institute of Standards and Technology. Online: http://csrc.nist.gov/publications/fips/fips46-3/fips46-3.pdf (2005-02-25).

[Mer02] Mertens, P. (Ed.) (2002): *Lexikon der Wirtschaftsinformatik*. 4. Edition, Springer-Verlag Berlin, Germany.

[MH04] Moor, A. de; Heuvel, W.-J. van den (2004): *Web Service Selection in Virtual Communities*. In Proc. of the 37th Hawaii International Conference on System Sciences (HICSS), Hawaii,USA, Track 7 - Volume 7, Page: 70197.

[Mic95] Microsoft Corporation (1995): *The Component Object Model Specification*. Version 0.9. Redmond, WA, USA.

[Mic96] Microsoft Corporation (1995): *DCOM Technical Overview. Redmond, WA, USA*. Online: http://msdn.microsoft.com/library/default.asp?url=/library/en-us/dndcom/html/msdn_dcomtec.asp (2004-04-29).

[Mon97] Montgomery, J. (1997): *Distributed Components*. In Byte Magazine, April 1997, pp 93-95, 98.

[Mor04] Morrison, D. (2004): *E-Learning Flexible Framework and Tools: Is it too Late? - the Director's Cut*. In Proc. 11th International Conference of Association for Learning Technology (ALT-C). University of Exeter, Devon, UK, September 2004.

[MPW92] Milner, R.; Parrow, J.; Walker, D. (1992): *A calculus of mobile processes (Part I and II)*. Information and Computation, 100(1):1-77, September 1992.

[NCW00] Nagy, W. A. ; Curbera, F.; Weerawaranna, S. (2000): *The Advertisement and Discovery of Services (ADS) protocol for Web services*. Online: http://www-106.ibm.com/developerworks/library/ws-ads.html (2004-04-24).

[NG04] Neumann, F.; Geys, R. (2004): *SCORM and the Learning Grid*. In Proc. of 4th International LeGE-WG Workshop - Towards a European Learning Grid Infrastructure: Processing with a European Learning Grid, Suttgard, Germany, 27-28. April 2004.

[NIS02] National Institute of Standards and Technology (2002): *Federal Information Processing Standards Publication 180-2 Specifications for the SECURE HASH STANDARD*. August 2002. Online: http://csrc.nist.gov/publications/fips/fips180-2/fips180-2.pdf (2005-02-25).

[NPB03] Nilsson, M.; Palmér, M.; Brase, J. (2003): *The LOM RDF binding - principles and implementation*. In Proc. of the 3rd annual ARIADNE conference, Katholieke Universiteit Leuven, Belgium, November 2003. Online: http://kmr.nada.kth.se/papers/SemanticWeb/LOMRDFBinding-ARIADNE.pdf (2005-08-28).

[NR04] Nielsen, H. F.; Ruellan H. (2004): *SOAP 1.2 Attachment Feature*. W3C Working Group Note 8 June 2004.

[NSD+05] Navarro, L. I.; Such, M. M.; Diaz, A. S.; Martin, M. D.; Peco, P. P. (2005): *Learning Units Design based in Grid Computing*. In Proc. 5th IEEE International Conference on Advanced Learning Technologies 2005 (ICALT2005), Kaohsiung, Taiwan, 5-8. July 2005.

[NWQ+02] Nejdl, W.; Wolf, B.; Qu, C.; Decker, S.; Sintek, M. (2002): *Edutella: A P2P Networking Infrastructure Based on RDF*. In Proc. 11th International World Wide Web Conference (WWW2002), pp. 604-615, Hawaii, USA, May 2002.

[NWS+02] Nejdl, W.; Wolf, B.; Staab, S.; Tane, J. (2002): *EDUTELLA: Searching and Annotating Resources within an RDF-based P2P Network*. In Proc. International Workshop on the Semantic Web (part of WWW2002), Hawaii, USA, May 2002.

[Oas04] OASIS (Organization for the Advancement of Structured Information Standards) (2004): *Web Services Security: SOAP Message Security 1.0 (WS-Security 2004)*. OASIS Standard 200401, March 2004. Online: http://docs.oasis-open.org/wss/2004/01/oasis-200401-wss-soap-message-security-1.0.pdf (2005-02-28).

[Off00] Off, T. (2000): *Überblick über DCOM als Komponenteninfrastruktur*. Online: http://home.arcor.de/thomas_off/sofftwaretechnik2004/download/SWT_Werkzeuge_Einfuehrung_DCOM_V0_1.pdf (2004-05-04).

[OKI02] Eduworks Corporation White Paper (2002): *What is the Open Knowledge Initiative?* 20. September 2002 Online: http://web.mit.edu/oki/learn/whtpapers/OKI_white_paper_120902.pdf (2005-08-29).

[OMG04] OMG (2004): *Common Object Request Broker Architecture: Core Specification*. Version 3.0.3 March 2004.

[Ora05] Oracle Corporation (2005): *Oracle Certification Program Candidate Guide. Oracle Certified Professional Internet Application Developer, Oracle Forms Developer Rel. 6/6i*. January 2005. Online: http://www.oracle.com/education/download/appd6_cg.pdf (2005-08-10).

[OWL03] OWL Service Coalition (2003): *OWL-S: Semantic Markup for Web Services*. http://www.daml.org/services/owl-s/1.0/owl-s.pdf (2004-04-04).

[Pan03] Pankratius, Victor (2003): *E-Learning Grids: Einsatz von Grid Computing im elektornischen Lernen*. Diplomhausarbeit, Westf. Wilhelms-Universität Münster, August 2003.

[Paw01] Pawlowski, J.M. (2001): *Das Essener-Lern-Modell (ELM): Ein Vorgehensmodell zur Entwicklung computerunterstützter Lernumgebungen.* Dissertation University of Essen, December 2001.

[Paw05] Pawlowski, J.M. (2005): *E-Learning Standards: Chancen und Potenzial für die Hochschule der Zunkunft.* In: Euler, D; Seufert, S. (Eds.): *E-Learning in Hochschulen und Bildungszentren.* 1. Edition 2005, Oldenbourg Verlag München Wien, pp. 453-472.

[PH02] Pawlowski, J. M.; Adelsberger, H. H. (2002): *Electronic Business and Education.* In [ACP02].

[Phl83] Phlips, L.(1983): *The Economics of Price Discrimination.* Cambridge Univ. Press.

[Por85] Porter M. E. (1985): *Competitive Advantage.* Collier Macmillan Publishers, London.

[POS05] Pankratius, V.; Oberweis, A.; Stucky, W. (2005): *Lernobjekte im E-Learning - Eine kritische Beurteilung zugrunde liegender Konzepte anhand eines Vergleichs mit komponentenbasierter Software-Entwicklung.* In Proc. 9. Workshop Multimedia in Bildung und Wirtschaft. 22-23. September, TU Ilmenau, Germany.

[PV03] Pankratius, V.; Vossen, G. (2003): *Towards E-Learning Grids: Using Grid Computing in Electronic Learning.* In Proc. IEEE Workshop on Knowledge Grid and Grid Intelligence (in conjunction with 2003 IEEE/WIC International Conference on Web Intelligence / Intelligent Agent Technology), pp. 4-15. Saint Mary's University, Halifax, Nova Scotia, Canada, October, 2003.

[QJ04] Qui, X.; Jooloor, A. (2004): *Web Service Architecture for e-Learning.* In Proc. International Conference on Education and Information Systems: Technologies and Applications (EISTA 2004), 21-25. July 2004, Orlando, USA.

[Rei01] Reisig W. (1991): *Petri-Netze, Eine Einführung.* Springer-Verlag Berlin, Germany.

[RFP05] Rust, M.; Flach, G.; Petersdorff-Campen, R. von (2005): *Content Sharing - Probleme und Lösungen bei der Föderation von Lernmoduldatenbanken.* In Stefan Brass, Christian Goldberg (Eds.): Proc 17th GI-Workshop on the Foundations of Databases. Institute of Computer Science, Martin-Luther-University Halle-Wittenberg, Wörlitz, Germany, May 2005, pp. 107-111.

[Riv92a] Rivest, R. L. (1992): *The MD5 Message-Digest Algorithm.* IETF RFC 1321.

[Riv92b] Rivest, R. L. (1992): *The RC4 Encryption Algorithm*. RSA Data Security Inc., March 1992.

[RLT97] Reichl, P.; Linnhoff-Popien, C.; Thißen, D. (1997): *Einbeziehung von Nutzerinteressen bei der QoS-basierten Dienstvermittlung unter CORBA*. In Proc. Kommunikation in Verteilten Systemen, GI/ITG-Fachtagung, Braunschweig 19.-21. Februar 1997. Springer-Verlag, 1997. pp. 236-251.

[Rol03] Rolls, D. (2003): *Service Provisioning Markup Language (SPML)*. Version 1.0., OASIS, 2003. Online: http://www.oasis-open.org/committees/download.php/4137/os-pstc-spml-core-1.0.pdf (2004-04-04).

[RSA78] Rivest, R.; Shamir, A.; Adleman, L. (1978): *A Method for Obtaining Digital Signatures and Public-Key Cryptosystems*. Communications of the ACM, 21 (2), pp. 120-126, February 1978.

[RSB04] Roman, E.; Sriganesh, R. P.; Brose, G. (2004): *Mastering Enterprise JavaBeans*. John Wiley & Sons, 3rd Edition, December 2004, Hoboken, NJ, USA.

[RV03] Rahm, E.; Vossen, G. (Eds.) (2003): *Web & Datenbanken. Konzepte, Architekturen, Anwendungen*. Dpunkt.Verlag, Heidelberg, Germany.

[Sab00] Saba (2000): Universal Learning Format. Technical Specification Version 1.0. 23. October 2003. Online: http://xml.coverpages.org/ulfSpecification20001204.pdf (2005-09-02).

[Sch98] Scheer, A. W. (1998): *Wirtschaftsinformatik. Referenzmodelle für industrielle Geschäftsprozesse*. 2. Edition, Springer-Verlag Berlin, Germany.

[Sch02a] Schank, R.C. (2002): *Designing World-Class E-Learning. How IBM, GE, Harvard Business School, & Columbia University are Succeeding at e-Learning*. 1st Edition, McGraw-Hill, New York, USA.

[Sch02b] Schollmeier, R. (2002): *Peer-to-Peer Networking. Applications for and Impacts on Future IP-Based Networks*. In Proc. 3. ITG Fachtagung Netze und Anwendungen "Neue Kommunikationsanwendungen in modernen Netzen", Duisburg, Germany, February 28-March 1, 2002.

[Sch02c] Schmees, M. (2002): *Kostenpflichtige Web-Services. Integration von Zahlungs- und Abrechnungsmechanismen in Web-Services*. Diplomhausarbeit, Carl von Ossietzky Universität Oldenburg, Germany.

[Sch02d] Schneemayer, G. (2002): *Contextual Web Services for Teaching*. Diplomhausarbeit, Ludwig-Maximilians-Universität München, Germany.

[Sch03] Schemm, J. W. (2003): *Semantisches Discovery von Web Services*. Diplomhausarbeit, Institut für Wirtschaftsinformatik, Westfälische Wilhelms-Universität Münster, Germany, December 2003.

[SCL+03] Shih, T. K.; Chang, W.-C.; Lin, N. H.; Lin, L. H.; Hsu, H.-H.; Hsieh, C.-T. (2003): *Using SOAP and .NET Web Service to Build SCORM RTE and LMS*. In Proc. 17 th International Conference on Advanced Information Networking and Applications (AINA'03), Xi'an, China S.A.R, p. 408.

[SH02] Stahlknecht, P.; Hasenkamp, U. (2002): *Einführung in die Wirtschaftsinformatik*. 10. Edition, Springer-Verlag, Berlin 2002.

[Ski54] Skinner, B. F. (1954): *The science of learning and the art of teaching*. Harvard Educational Review, Vol. 24, No. 2, pp 86-97.

[SMA+05] Simon, B.; Massart, D.; Assche, F. van ; Ternier, S.; Duval, E.; Brantner, S.; Olmedilla, D.; Miklós, Z. (2005): *A Simple Query Interface for Interoperable Learning Repositories*. In Proc. Workshop on Interoperability of Web-Based Educational Systems in conjunction with 14th International World Wide Web Conference (WWW'05). May, 2005, Chiba, Japan.

[SMD94] Simon, B.; Massart, D.; Duval, E. (2004): *Simple Query Interface Specification*. Public Draft, Version 0.8 (2004-06-17). Online: http://nm.wu-wien.ac.at/e-learning/interoperability/sqi/sqi.pdf (2005-08-02)

[SMH94] Seiya, M. M.; Michirou, Y.; Hiroshi, K. (1994): *RpC (Remote predicate Call)*. IPSJ SIGNotes Artificial Intelligence No. 095-003, 1994.

[SPD03] Suciu, A.; Pusztai, K.; Diaconu, A (2003): *Enhanced Prolog Remote Predicate Call Protocol*. In Proc. of 2nd International RoEduNet Conference, Iasi, Romania, 2003.

[SPM02] Suciu, A.; Pusztai, K.; Muresan, T. (2002): *A Prolog Remote Predicate Call Protocol*. In Proc. of ECIT 2002, Second European Conference on Intelligent Systems and Technologies, Iasi, Romania, July 17-20, 2002.

[Sri95] Srinivasan, R. (1995): *RFC1831, RPC: Remote Procedure Call Protocol Specification*. Version 2, Sun Microsystems, August 1995.

[Sta03] Stallings, W. (2003): *Betriebssysteme, Prinzipien und Umsetzung*. 4. Edition, Prentice-Hall, Munich 2003.

[Ste90] Stevens, W. R. (1990): *UNIX Network Programming*. Prentice-Hall, Munich 1990.

[Ste04] The Stencil Group (2002): *The Evolution of UDDI*. UDDI.org White Paper. Online: http://xml.coverpages.org/UDDIWhitePaper20020724.pdf. (2004-04-24).

[Ste05] Steinemann, M.-A. (2005): *Distributed Architectures for Laboratory-Based E-Learning*. Inauguraldissertation der Philosophisch-naturwissenschaftlichen Fakultät der Universität Bern. June 2005.

[Sun03] Sun Corporation (2003): *E-Learning Framework*. Technical White Paper, February 2003. Online: http://www.sun.com/products-n-solutions/ edu/whitepapers/pdf/framework.pdf (2005-09-02).

[SVW05] Schwieren, J.; Vossen, G.; Westerkamp, P. (2005): *Efficient Handling of Programming Exercises in a Scalable E-Learning Platform*. To appear in Proc. 4th European Conference on E-Learning (ECEL) 2005, Amsterdam, November 2005.

[Szy97] Szyperski, C. (1997): *Component Software - Beyond Object-Oriented Programming*. Addison Wesley Publishing Company, Boston, USA.

[TBG01] Trastour, D.; Bartolini, C.; Gonzalez-Castillo, J. (2001): *A Semantic Web Approach to Service Description for Matchmaking of Services*. In Proc. International Semantic Web Working Symposium (SWWS) 2001, pp. 447-461.

[TCA+05] Hoel, T.; Campbell, L.; Arnaud, M.; Pawlowski, J. (2005): *A Service Oriented Approach to Learning in Europe - the need for a common framework*. Position paper to the CEN/ISSS WS-LT, Oslo meeting of 24-25. January 2005.

[TDB97] Tarau, P.; Dahl, V.; Bosschere, K. De (1997): *Remote Execution, Mobile Code and Agents in BinProlog*. In Proc. WWW6 – Logic Programming Workshop, Santa Clara, April 7, 1997.

[TF02] Tanigawa, T; Fuji, T. (2002): *The Methodology for Reuse of E-Learning Resources*. In Proc. World Conference on E-Learning in Corp., Govt., Health., & Highe Ed. (ELEARN) 2002, Volume 2002, Issue 1, Montreal, Canada, pp. 154-161.

[Tha01] Thatte, S. (2001): *XLANG: Web Services for Business Process Design*. Microsoft Corp. Online: http://www.gotdotnet.com/team/xml_wsspecs/xlang-c/default.htm (2004-05-27).

[Tim98] Timmers, P. (1998): *Business Models for Electronic Markets*. Journal on Electronic Markets, 8 (2): pp. 3-8.

[Tim00] Timmers, P. (2000): *Electronic Commerce: Strategies and Models for Business-to-Business Trading*. Wiley, Chichester.

[TS02] Tanenbaum, A. S.; Steen, M. van (2002): *Distributed Systems: Principles and Paradigms*. 1st Edition, Prentice Hall, Munich, Germany.

[TS03] Tanenbaum, A. S.; Steen, M. van (2003): *Verteilte Systeme: Grundlagen und Paradigmen*. 1. Edition, Pearson Education, Munich, Germany.

[Var89] Varian, H. R. (1989): *Price discrimination*. In R. Schmalensee and R. D. Willig (eds): Handbook of Industrial Organization, Volume I, pp. 597-654. Elsevier.

[VH04] Vollmer, J; Hickernell, T. (2004): *E-learning comes to CRM*. Tech Trend, August 7, 2002. Online: http://techupdate.zdnet.com/techupdate/stories/main/0,14179,2875894-1,00.html (2005-08-24)

[VHL01] Vossen, G.; Hüsemann, B.; Lechtenbörger, J. (2001): *XLX - Eine Lernplattform für den universitären Übungsbetrieb*. In Arbeitsberichte des Instituts für Wirtschaftsinformatik, Universität Münster, Germany, Arbeitsbericht Nr. 79, August 2001.

[VJ02] Vossen, G.; Jaeschke, P. (2002): *Towards a Uniform and Flexible Data Model for Learning Objects*. In Proc. 30th Annual Conference of the International Business School Computing Association (IBSCA), Savannah, Georgia, USA, July 2002, pp. 99-129.

[VJO02] Vossen, G.; Jaeschke, P.; Oberweis, A. (2002): *Flexible Workflow Management as a Central E-Learning Support Paradigm*. In Proc. 1st European Conference on E-Learning, Uxbridge, UK, November 2002, pp. 253-267.

[Vos00] Vossen, G. (2000): *Datenbankmodelle, Datenbanksprachen und Datenmanagementsysteme*. 4th Edition, Oldenbourg Verlag, Munich, Germany.

[Vos04] Voskamp, J. (2004): *Learning Management System - Referenzmodell*. Dissertation an der Fakultät für Informatik und Elektrotechnik der Universität Rostock, Germany, March 2004.

[VP03] Vantroys, T.; Peter, Y. (2003): *COW, a Flexible Platform for the Enactment of Learning Scenarios*. In Favela, J; Decouchant, D. (eds.): Groupware: Design, Implementation, and Use, 9th International Workshop, CRIWG 2003, Autrans, France,

September 28 - October 2, 2003, Proceedings. Lecture Notes in Computer Science 2806 Springer 2003, pp. 168-182.

[VW04] Vossen, G.; Westerkamp, P. (2004): *XLX and L2P - Web-Based Platforms for Blended Learning*. In EMISA Forum 2/2004 Jahrgang 24, pp. 18-20.

[W3C01] World Wide Web Consortium (2001): *SOAP Security Extensions: Digital Signature*. W3C Note, 06 February 2001.

[W3C02] World Wide Web Consortium (2002): *XML Encryption Syntax and Processing*. W3C Recommendation, 10 December 2002. Online: http://www.w3.org/TR/xmlenc-core/ (2005-06-22)

[Was02] Wasznicky, Martin (2002): *Using Web Services Instead of DCOM*. Online: http://msdn.microsoft.com/library/default.asp?url=/library/en-us/dndotnet/html/webservicesdcom.asp (2004-11-16).

[WCL05] Weerawarana, S.; Curbera, F.; Leymann, F. (2005): *Web Services Platform Architecture*. Prentice Hall PTR, Munich, Germany.

[WG05] Wolpers, M.; Grohmann, G. (2005): *PROLEARN: technology-enhanced learning and knowledge distribution for the cooperate world*. Int. J. Knowledge and Learning, Vol. 1, Nos. 1/2, pp.44-61.

[WGG+05] Wills, G.B.; Gilbert, L.; Gee, Q.; Davis, H.C.; Miles-Board, T.; Millard, D.E.; Carr, L.A.; Hall, W.; Grange, S. (2005): *Towards Grid Services for a Virtual Research Environment*. In Proc. of 5th IEEE International Conference on Advanced Learning Technologies (ICALT'05), July 2005, Kaoshiung, Taiwan, pp. 163-165.

[Wil00] Wiley, D. A. (2000): *Connecting learning objects to instructional design theory: A definition, a metaphor, and a taxonomy*. In D. A. Wiley (Ed.), The Instructional Use of Learning Objects, pp. 1-35.

[Wir01] Wirtz, B. (2001): *Electronic Business*. Gabler, Wiesbaden, Germany.

[WV02] Weikum, G.; Vossen, G. (2002): *Transactional Information Systems: Theory, Algorithms, and the Practice of Concurrency Control and Recovery*. Morgan Kaufmann Publishers, San Francisco, USA.

[WWW00] Weitzel, T.; Wendt, O. ; Westarp, F. von (2000): *Reconsidering Network Effect Theory*. In Proc. of the 8th European Conference on Information Systems (ECIS 2000), Vienna, Austria, pp. 484-491.

[WZ04] Wu, J.; Zhang, S. (2004): *Broadband Multimedia e-learning system using Web Service*. In Proc. APAN Network Research Workshop 2004, Cairns, Australia.

[XYS03] Xu, Z.; Yin, Z.; Saddik, A. El (2003): *A Web Service Oriented Framework for Dynamic E-Learning Systems*. In Proc. CCECE 2003 - CCGEI 2003, Montreal, Canada, 2003.

Appendix A

Appendix

In the following the WSDL document for each service is listed. The descriptions use WSDL 1.1. The Maltus Email Web service document is shown on behalf of elearning communication services.

A.1 Third Party Email WSDL Files

Listing A.1: WSDL Document of the Maltus Email Web service.

```
<?xml version="1.0"?>
<definitions xmlns="http://schemas.xmlsoap.org/wsdl/"
        xmlns:xs="http://www.w3.org/2001/XMLSchema"
        name="IEmailServiceservice"
        targetNamespace="http://www.borland.com/soapServices/"
        xmlns:tns="http://www.borland.com/soapServices/"
        xmlns:soap="http://schemas.xmlsoap.org/wsdl/soap/"
        xmlns:soapenc="http://schemas.xmlsoap.org/soap/encoding/">
  <message name="SendMailRequest">
    <part name="ToAddress" type="xs:string"/>
    <part name="FromAddress" type="xs:string"/>
    <part name="ASubject" type="xs:string"/>
    <part name="MsgBody" type="xs:string"/>
  </message>
  <message name="SendMailResponse">
    <part name="return" type="xs:int"/>
  </message>
  <portType name="IEmailService">
    <operation name="SendMail">
```

```
        <input  message="tns:SendMailRequest"/>
        <output  message="tns:SendMailResponse"/>
      </operation>
    </portType>
    <binding name="IEmailServicebinding"  type="tns:IEmailService">
      <soap:binding  style="rpc"
            transport="http://schemas.xmlsoap.org/soap/http"/>
      <operation  name="SendMail">
        <soap:operation
            soapAction="urn:EmailIPortTypeInft-IEmailService#SendMail"
            style="rpc"/>
        <input>
          <soap:body  use="encoded"
                encodingStyle="http://schemas.xmlsoap.org/soap/encoding/"
                namespace="urn:EmailIPortTypeInft-IEmailService"/>
        </input>
        <output>
          <soap:body  use="encoded"
                encodingStyle="http://schemas.xmlsoap.org/soap/encoding/"
                namespace="urn:EmailIPortTypeInft-IEmailService"/>
        </output>
      </operation>
    </binding>
    <service name="IEmailServiceservice">
      <port name="IEmailServicePort"  binding="tns:IEmailServicebinding">
        <soap:address  location=
              "http://webservices.matlus.com/scripts/emailwebservice.dll/
                        soap/IEmailservice"/>
      </port>
    </service>
  </definitions>
```

A.2   LearnServe Repository WSDL Files

Listing A.2: WSDL Document of the LearnServe Repository.

```xml
<?xml version="1.0" encoding="UTF-8"?>
<wsdl:definitions
    name="Repository"
    targetNamespace="http://www.westerkamp.info/Repository.wsdl"
    xmlns:import1="http://ltsc.ieee.org/xsd/LOM"
    xmlns:import2="http://www.imsglobal.org/xsd/imscp_v1p1"
    xmlns:soap="http://schemas.xmlsoap.org/wsdl/soap/"
    xmlns:tns="http://www.westerkamp.info/Repository.wsdl"
    xmlns:wsdl="http://schemas.xmlsoap.org/wsdl/"
    xmlns:xsd="http://www.w3.org/2001/XMLSchema"
    xmlns:xsd1="http://www.westerkamp.info/Repository.xsd1"
    xmlns:xsd2="http://www.westerkamp.info/Repository.xsd2">
    <wsdl:documentation xmlns:wsdl="http://schemas.xmlsoap.org/wsdl/">
      Created using Cape Clear Studio SOA Editor - http://www.capeclear.com
    </wsdl:documentation>
    <wsdl:types>
        <xsd:schema
            targetNamespace="http://www.westerkamp.info/Repository.xsd1"
            xmlns:SOAP-ENC="http://schemas.xmlsoap.org/soap/encoding/"
            xmlns:xsd="http://www.w3.org/2001/XMLSchema"
            xmlns:xsd1="http://www.westerkamp.info/Repository.xsd1">
            <xsd:complexType name="searchresults">
                <xsd:sequence>
                    <xsd:element maxOccurs="1" minOccurs="1"
                                 name="Title" type="xsd:string"/>
                    <xsd:element maxOccurs="1" minOccurs="0"
                                 name="Language" type="xsd:string"/>
                    <xsd:element maxOccurs="1" minOccurs="0"
                                 name="Description" type="xsd:string"/>
                    <xsd:element maxOccurs="1" minOccurs="0"
                                 name="Version" type="xsd:string"/>
                    <xsd:element
                        maxOccurs="1"
                        minOccurs="0"
                        name="Contribute.Entry"
                        type="xsd:string"/>
                    <xsd:element maxOccurs="1" minOccurs="1"
                                 name="Location" type="xsd:anyURI"/>
                    <xsd:element
                        maxOccurs="1"
                        minOccurs="0"
                        name="TypicalAgeRange"
```

```
                            type="xsd:string"/>
                    <xsd:element maxOccurs="1" minOccurs="0"
                                        name="Difficulty" type="xsd:string"/>
                    <xsd:element
                        maxOccurs="1"
                        minOccurs="0"
                        name="TypicalLearningTime"
                        type="xsd:string"/>
                    <xsd:element maxOccurs="1" minOccurs="0"
                                        name="Cost" type="xsd:decimal"/>
                </xsd:sequence>
            </xsd:complexType>
            <xsd:import
                namespace="http://ltsc.ieee.org/xsd/LOM"
                schemaLocation="http://dbms.uni-muenster.de/
                                staff/westerkamp/wsdl/lom.xsd"/>
            <xsd:import
                namespace="http://www.imsglobal.org/xsd/imscp_v1p1"
                schemaLocation="http://www.imsglobal.org/xsd/imscp_v1p1.xsd"/>
        </xsd:schema>
    </wsdl:types>
    <wsdl:message name="AdvancedSearchResponse">
        <wsdl:part name="return_value" type="import1:lom"/>
    </wsdl:message>
    <wsdl:message name="SearchRequest">
        <wsdl:part name="keywords" type="xsd:string"/>
    </wsdl:message>
    <wsdl:message name="AdvancedSearchRequest">
        <wsdl:part name="ID" type="xsd:string"/>
        <wsdl:part name="lom" type="import1:lom"/>
    </wsdl:message>
    <wsdl:message name="DeleteContentReferenceRequest">
        <wsdl:part name="ID" type="xsd:string"/>
    </wsdl:message>
    <wsdl:message name="RegisterNewContentRequest">
        <wsdl:part name="Manifest" type="import2:manifestType"/>
    </wsdl:message>
    <wsdl:message name="SearchResponse">
        <wsdl:part name="return_value" type="xsd1:searchresults"/>
    </wsdl:message>
    <wsdl:message name="RegisterNewContentResponse">
        <wsdl:part name="return_value" type="xsd:string"/>
    </wsdl:message>
    <wsdl:message name="UpdateContentDataResponse">
        <wsdl:part name="return_value" type="xsd:string"/>
    </wsdl:message>
```

```
<wsdl:message name="DeleteContentReferenceResponse">
    <wsdl:part name="return_value" type="xsd:string"/>
</wsdl:message>
<wsdl:message name="UpdateContentDataRequest">
    <wsdl:part name="ID" type="xsd:string"/>
    <wsdl:part name="manifest" type="import2:manifestType"/>
</wsdl:message>
<wsdl:portType name="RepositoryPortType">
    <wsdl:operation name="Search">
        <wsdl:input message="tns:SearchRequest"/>
        <wsdl:output message="tns:SearchResponse"/>
    </wsdl:operation>
    <wsdl:operation name="UpdateContentData">
        <wsdl:input message="tns:UpdateContentDataRequest"/>
        <wsdl:output message="tns:UpdateContentDataResponse"/>
    </wsdl:operation>
    <wsdl:operation name="DeleteContentReference">
        <wsdl:input message="tns:DeleteContentReferenceRequest"/>
        <wsdl:output message="tns:DeleteContentReferenceResponse"/>
    </wsdl:operation>
    <wsdl:operation name="RegisterNewContent">
        <wsdl:input message="tns:RegisterNewContentRequest"/>
        <wsdl:output message="tns:RegisterNewContentResponse"/>
    </wsdl:operation>
    <wsdl:operation name="AdvancedSearch">
        <wsdl:input message="tns:AdvancedSearchRequest"/>
        <wsdl:output message="tns:AdvancedSearchResponse"/>
    </wsdl:operation>
</wsdl:portType>
<wsdl:binding name="RepositoryBinding" type="tns:RepositoryPortType">
    <soap:binding style="rpc"
            transport="http://schemas.xmlsoap.org/soap/http"/>
    <wsdl:operation name="Search">
        <soap:operation soapAction="learnserve:Repository:
                                RepositoryPortType#Search"/>
        <wsdl:input>
            <soap:body parts="keywords" use="literal"/>
        </wsdl:input>
        <wsdl:output>
            <soap:body parts="return_value" use="literal"/>
        </wsdl:output>
    </wsdl:operation>
    <wsdl:operation name="UpdateContentData">
        <soap:operation soapAction="learnserve:Repository:
                        RepositoryPortType#UpdateContentData"/>
        <wsdl:input>
```

```
                    <soap:body parts="ID manifest" use="literal"/>
                </wsdl:input>
                <wsdl:output>
                    <soap:body parts="return_value" use="literal"/>
                </wsdl:output>
            </wsdl:operation>
            <wsdl:operation name="DeleteContentReference">
                <soap:operation soapAction="learnserve:Repository:
                            RepositoryPortType#DeleteContentReference"/>
                <wsdl:input>
                    <soap:body parts="ID" use="literal"/>
                </wsdl:input>
                <wsdl:output>
                    <soap:body parts="return_value" use="literal"/>
                </wsdl:output>
            </wsdl:operation>
            <wsdl:operation name="RegisterNewContent">
                <soap:operation soapAction="learnserve:Repository:
                            RepositoryPortType#RegisterNewContent"/>
                <wsdl:input>
                    <soap:body parts="Manifest" use="literal"/>
                </wsdl:input>
                <wsdl:output>
                    <soap:body parts="return_value" use="literal"/>
                </wsdl:output>
            </wsdl:operation>
            <wsdl:operation name="AdvancedSearch">
                <soap:operation soapAction="learnserve:Repository:
                            RepositoryPortType#AdvancedSearch"/>
                <wsdl:input>
                    <soap:body parts="ID lom" use="literal"/>
                </wsdl:input>
                <wsdl:output>
                    <soap:body parts="return_value" use="literal"/>
                </wsdl:output>
            </wsdl:operation>
        </wsdl:binding>
        <wsdl:service name="Repository">
            <wsdl:port binding="tns:RepositoryBinding" name="RepositoryPort">
                <soap:address location="http://repository..uni-muenster.de"/>
            </wsdl:port>
        </wsdl:service>
    </wsdl:definitions>
```

A.3   LearnServe Content Provider WSDL File

Listing A.3: WSDL Document of the LearnServe Content Provider (This listing does not cover the WSRP functions. They are shown in Appendix A.5).

```xml
<?xml version="1.0" encoding="UTF-8"?>
<wsdl:definitions
    name="ContentProvider"
    targetNamespace="http://www.westerkamp.info/ContentProvider.wsdl"
    xmlns:soap="http://schemas.xmlsoap.org/wsdl/soap/"
    xmlns:tns="http://www.westerkamp.info/ContentProvider.wsdl"
    xmlns:wsdl="http://schemas.xmlsoap.org/wsdl/"
    xmlns:xsd="http://www.w3.org/2001/XMLSchema"
    xmlns:xsd1="http://www.westerkamp.info/ContentProvider.xsd1">
    <wsdl:documentation xmlns:wsdl="http://schemas.xmlsoap.org/wsdl/">
    Created using Cape Clear Studio SOA Editor </wsdl:documentation>
    <wsdl:types>
        <xsd:schema
            targetNamespace="http://www.westerkamp.info/ContentProvider.xsd1"
            xmlns:SOAP-ENC="http://schemas.xmlsoap.org/soap/encoding/"
            xmlns:xsd="http://www.w3.org/2001/XMLSchema"
            xmlns:xsd1="http://www.westerkamp.info/ContentProvider.xsd1">
            <xsd:complexType name="Bank">
                <xsd:sequence>
                    <xsd:element maxOccurs="1" minOccurs="0"
                                 name="AccountNumber" type="xsd:string"/>
                    <xsd:element maxOccurs="1" minOccurs="0"
                                 name="Bank" type="xsd:string"/>
                    <xsd:element maxOccurs="1" minOccurs="0"
                                 name="Name" type="xsd:string"/>
                    <xsd:element maxOccurs="1" minOccurs="0"
                                 name="CardNumber" type="xsd:string"/>
                    <xsd:element maxOccurs="1" minOccurs="0"
                                 name="CardType" type="xsd:string"/>
                    <xsd:element maxOccurs="1" minOccurs="0"
                                 name="CardDate" type="xsd:string"/>
                </xsd:sequence>
            </xsd:complexType>
        </xsd:schema>
    </wsdl:types>
    <wsdl:message name="NewMessageResponse">    </wsdl:message>
    <wsdl:message name="accreditationResponse">
        <wsdl:part name="return_value" type="xsd:string"/>
    </wsdl:message>
    <wsdl:message name="NewMessageRequest">
```

```
        <wsdl:part name="arg1" type="xsd:string"/>
    </wsdl:message>
    <wsdl:message name="accreditationRequest">
        <wsdl:part name="SCS" type="xsd:string"/>
        <wsdl:part name="review" type="xsd:string"/>
    </wsdl:message>
    <wsdl:message name="bookContentRequest">
        <wsdl:part name="SCS" type="xsd:string"/>
        <wsdl:part name="bank" type="xsd1:Bank"/>
    </wsdl:message>
    <wsdl:message name="bookContentResponse">
        <wsdl:part name="license" type="xsd:string"/>
    </wsdl:message>
    <wsdl:portType name="ContentProviderPortType">
        <wsdl:operation
            name="accreditation"
            <wsdl:input message="tns:accreditationRequest"/>
            <wsdl:output message="tns:accreditationResponse"/>
        </wsdl:operation>
        <wsdl:operation name="bookContent">
            <wsdl:input message="tns:bookContentRequest"/>
            <wsdl:output message="tns:bookContentResponse"/>
        </wsdl:operation>
    </wsdl:portType>
    <wsdl:binding name="ContentProviderBinding"
                type="tns:ContentProviderPortType">
        <soap:binding style="rpc" transport=
                "http://schemas.xmlsoap.org/soap/http"/>
        <wsdl:operation name="accreditation">
            <soap:operation
                soapAction="capeconnect:ContentProvider:
                            ContentProviderPortType#accreditation"/>
            <wsdl:input>
                <soap:body use="literal"/>
            </wsdl:input>
            <wsdl:output>
                <soap:body use="literal"/>
            </wsdl:output>
        </wsdl:operation>
        <wsdl:operation name="bookContent">
            <soap:operation
                soapAction="capeconnect:ContentProvider:
                            ContentProviderPortType#bookContent"/>
            <wsdl:input>
                <soap:body use="literal"/>
            </wsdl:input>
```

```
            <wsdl:output>
                <soap:body use="literal"/>
            </wsdl:output>
        </wsdl:operation>
    </wsdl:binding>
    <wsdl:service name="ContentProvider">
        <wsdl:port binding="tns:ContentProviderBinding"
                    name="ContentProviderPort">
            <soap:address location=
                "http://localhost:8000/ccx/ContentProvider"/>
        </wsdl:port>
    </wsdl:service>
</wsdl:definitions>
```

A.4   LearnServe Provisioning Server WSDL Files

Listing A.4: WSDL Document of the LearnServe Provisioning Server.

```
<?xml version="1.0" encoding="UTF-8"?>
<wsdl:definitions
    name="ProvisioningServer"
    targetNamespace="http://www.westerkamp.info/ProvisioningServer.wsdl"
    xmlns:soap="http://schemas.xmlsoap.org/wsdl/soap/"
    xmlns:tns="http://www.westerkamp.info/ProvisioningServer.wsdl"
    xmlns:wsdl="http://schemas.xmlsoap.org/wsdl/"
    xmlns:xsd="http://www.w3.org/2001/XMLSchema"
    xmlns:xsd1="http://www.westerkamp.info/ProvisioningServer.xsd1"
    xmlns:xsd2="http://www.westerkamp.info/ProvisioningServer.xsd2">
    <wsdl:documentation xmlns:wsdl="http://schemas.xmlsoap.org/wsdl/">
    Created using Cape Clear Studio SOA Editor </wsdl:documentation>
    <wsdl:types>
        <xsd:schema
            targetNamespace="http://www.westerkamp.info/
                             ProvisioningServer.xsd1"
            xmlns:SOAP-ENC="http://schemas.xmlsoap.org/soap/encoding/"
            xmlns:xsd="http://www.w3.org/2001/XMLSchema"
            xmlns:xsd1="http://www.westerkamp.info/
                             ProvisioningServer.xsd1">
        <xsd:complexType name="authenticate">
            <xsd:sequence>
                <xsd:element maxOccurs="1" minOccurs="1"
                            name="UID" type="xsd:string"/>
                <xsd:element maxOccurs="1" minOccurs="1"
                            name="password" type="xsd:string"/>
            </xsd:sequence>
        </xsd:complexType>
        <xsd:complexType name="artifact">
            <xsd:sequence>
                <xsd:element maxOccurs="1" minOccurs="1"
                            name="uri" type="xsd:anyURI"/>
                <xsd:element maxOccurs="1" minOccurs="1"
                            name="token" type="xsd:string"/>
            </xsd:sequence>
        </xsd:complexType>
        <xsd:complexType name="User">
            <xsd:sequence>
                <xsd:element maxOccurs="1" minOccurs="1"
                            name="Lastname" type="xsd:string"/>
                <xsd:element maxOccurs="1" minOccurs="1"
```

```
                              name="Firstname" type="xsd:string"/>
        <xsd:element maxOccurs="1" minOccurs="1"
                              name="Email" type="xsd:string"/>
        <xsd:element maxOccurs="1" minOccurs="1"
                              name="Password" type="xsd:string"/>
        <xsd:element maxOccurs="1" minOccurs="0"
                              name="Street" type="xsd:string"/>
        <xsd:element maxOccurs="1" minOccurs="0"
                              name="City" type="xsd:string"/>
        <xsd:element maxOccurs="1" minOccurs="0"
                              name="Country" type="xsd:string"/>
        <xsd:element maxOccurs="1" minOccurs="0"
                              name="ZipCode" type="xsd:string"/>
        <xsd:element maxOccurs="1" minOccurs="0"
                              name="AccountNumber" type="xsd:string"/>
        <xsd:element maxOccurs="1" minOccurs="0"
                              name="Bank" type="xsd:string"/>
        <xsd:element
            maxOccurs="1"
            minOccurs="0"
            name="CreditCardNumber"
            type="xsd:string"/>
        <xsd:element
            maxOccurs="1"
            minOccurs="0"
            name="CreditCardType"
            type="xsd:string"/>
        <xsd:element
            maxOccurs="1"
            minOccurs="0"
            name="CreditCardDate"
            type="xsd:string"/>
        <xsd:element maxOccurs="1" minOccurs="0"
                              name="Audiolevel" type="xsd:string"/>
        <xsd:element maxOccurs="1" minOccurs="0"
                              name="Language" type="xsd:string"/>
        <xsd:element maxOccurs="1" minOccurs="0"
                              name="DeliverySpeed" type="xsd:string"/>
        <xsd:element
            maxOccurs="1"
            minOccurs="0"
            name="AudioCaptioning"
            type="xsd:string"/>
        <xsd:element maxOccurs="1" minOccurs="0"
                              name="LearningStyle" type="xsd:string"/>
    </xsd:sequence>
```

```
        </xsd:complexType>
        <xsd:complexType name="Performance">
            <xsd:sequence>
                <xsd:element maxOccurs="1" minOccurs="1"
                             name="SCS" type="xsd:string"/>
                <xsd:element maxOccurs="1" minOccurs="1"
                             name="SuccessStatus" type="xsd:string"/>
            </xsd:sequence>
        </xsd:complexType>
    </xsd:schema>
</wsdl:types>
<wsdl:message name="UserLogoutResponse">
    <wsdl:part name="return_value" type="xsd:string"/>
</wsdl:message>
<wsdl:message name="setValueResponse">
    <wsdl:part name="return_value" type="xsd:string"/>
</wsdl:message>
<wsdl:message name="GetLastStringRequest">
    <wsdl:part name="SCS" type="xsd:string"/>
</wsdl:message>
<wsdl:message name="setValueExeRequest">
    <wsdl:part name="SCS" type="xsd:string"/>
    <wsdl:part name="element" type="xsd:string"/>
    <wsdl:part name="value" type="xsd:string"/>
    <wsdl:part name="UID" type="xsd:string"/>
</wsdl:message>
<wsdl:message name="getValueRequest">
    <wsdl:part name="SCS" type="xsd:string"/>
    <wsdl:part name="element" type="xsd:string"/>
</wsdl:message>
<wsdl:message name="RegisterUserRequest">
    <wsdl:part name="user" type="xsd1:User"/>
    <wsdl:part name="return_value" type="xsd:string"/>
</wsdl:message>
<wsdl:message name="setValueRequest">
    <wsdl:part name="SCS" type="xsd:string"/>
    <wsdl:part name="element" type="xsd:string"/>
    <wsdl:part name="value" type="xsd:string"/>
</wsdl:message>
<wsdl:message name="getUserPerformanceResponse">
    <wsdl:part name="performance" type="xsd1:Performance"/>
</wsdl:message>
<wsdl:message name="setValueExeResponse">
    <wsdl:part name="return_value" type="xsd:string"/>
</wsdl:message>
<wsdl:message name="getUserPerformanceRequest">
```

```
</wsdl:message>
<wsdl:message name="UserLoginRequest">
    <wsdl:part name="user" type="xsd1:authenticate"/>
</wsdl:message>
<wsdl:message name="CommitResponse">
    <wsdl:part name="return_value" type="xsd:string"/>
</wsdl:message>
<wsdl:message name="CommitRequest">
    <wsdl:part name="SCS" type="xsd:string"/>
</wsdl:message>
<wsdl:message name="UserLoginResponse">
    <wsdl:part name="return_value" type="xsd1:artifact"/>
</wsdl:message>
<wsdl:message name="GetLastErrorResponse">
    <wsdl:part name="error_code" type="xsd:string"/>
</wsdl:message>
<wsdl:message name="getValueResponse">
    <wsdl:part name="return_value" type="xsd:string"/>
</wsdl:message>
<wsdl:message name="GetDiagnosticResponse">
    <wsdl:part name="diagnostic" type="xsd:string"/>
</wsdl:message>
<wsdl:message name="GetDiagnosticRequest">
    <wsdl:part name="SCS" type="xsd:string"/>
    <wsdl:part name="value" type="xsd:string"/>
</wsdl:message>
<wsdl:message name="GetLastErrorRequest">
    <wsdl:part name="SCS" type="xsd:string"/>
</wsdl:message>
<wsdl:message name="RegisterUserResponse">   </wsdl:message>
<wsdl:message name="UserLogoutRequest">   </wsdl:message>
<wsdl:message name="GetLastStringResponse">
    <wsdl:part name="error_string" type="xsd:string"/>
</wsdl:message>
<wsdl:portType name="ProvisioningServerPortType">
    <wsdl:operation name="UserLogin">
        <wsdl:documentation
            xmlns:wsdl="http://schemas.xmlsoap.org/wsdl/">
            User Login to CDSSO.</wsdl:documentation>
        <wsdl:input message="tns:UserLoginRequest"/>
        <wsdl:output message="tns:UserLoginResponse"/>
    </wsdl:operation>
    <wsdl:operation name="UserLogout">
        <wsdl:documentation
            xmlns:wsdl="http://schemas.xmlsoap.org/wsdl/">
            UserLogout from CDSSO mechanism.</wsdl:documentation>
```

```
        <wsdl:input message="tns:UserLogoutRequest"/>
        <wsdl:output message="tns:UserLogoutResponse"/>
</wsdl:operation>
<wsdl:operation name="getValue">
        <wsdl:documentation
            xmlns:wsdl="http://schemas.xmlsoap.org/wsdl/">
            Gets tracking data from the LearnServe Provisioning Server.
                </wsdl:documentation>
        <wsdl:input message="tns:getValueRequest"/>
        <wsdl:output message="tns:getValueResponse"/>
</wsdl:operation>
<wsdl:operation name="setValue">
        <wsdl:documentation
            xmlns:wsdl="http://schemas.xmlsoap.org/wsdl/">
            Stores data on the LearnServe Provisioning Server
                    </wsdl:documentation>
        <wsdl:input message="tns:setValueRequest"/>
        <wsdl:output message="tns:setValueResponse"/>
</wsdl:operation>
<wsdl:operation name="GetLastError">
        <wsdl:input message="tns:GetLastErrorRequest"/>
        <wsdl:output message="tns:GetLastErrorResponse"/>
</wsdl:operation>
<wsdl:operation name="GetLastString">
        <wsdl:input message="tns:GetLastStringRequest"/>
        <wsdl:output message="tns:GetLastStringResponse"/>
</wsdl:operation>
<wsdl:operation name="GetDiagnostic">
        <wsdl:input message="tns:GetDiagnosticRequest"/>
        <wsdl:output message="tns:GetDiagnosticResponse"/>
</wsdl:operation>
<wsdl:operation name="Commit">
        <wsdl:input message="tns:CommitRequest"/>
        <wsdl:output message="tns:CommitResponse"/>
</wsdl:operation>
<wsdl:operation name="RegisterUser">
        <wsdl:input message="tns:RegisterUserRequest"/>
        <wsdl:output message="tns:RegisterUserResponse"/>
</wsdl:operation>
<wsdl:operation name="setValueExe">
        <wsdl:input message="tns:setValueExeRequest"/>
        <wsdl:output message="tns:setValueExeResponse"/>
</wsdl:operation>
<wsdl:operation name="getUserPerformance">
        <wsdl:input message="tns:getUserPerformanceRequest"/>
        <wsdl:output message="tns:getUserPerformanceResponse"/>
```

```
        </wsdl:operation>
    </wsdl:portType>
    <wsdl:binding
        name="ProvisioningServerBinding"
        type="tns:ProvisioningServerPortType">
        <soap:binding style="rpc"
            transport="http://schemas.xmlsoap.org/soap/http"/>
        <wsdl:operation name="UserLogin">
            <soap:operation
                soapAction="learnserve:ProvisioningServer:
                            rovisioningServerPortType#UserLogin"/>
            <wsdl:input>
                <soap:body use="literal"/>
            </wsdl:input>
            <wsdl:output>
                <soap:body use="literal"/>
            </wsdl:output>
        </wsdl:operation>
        <wsdl:operation name="UserLogout">
            <soap:operation
                soapAction="learnserve:ProvisioningServer:
                            ProvisioningServerPortType#UserLogout"/>
            <wsdl:input>
                <soap:body use="literal"/>
            </wsdl:input>
            <wsdl:output>
                <soap:body use="literal"/>
            </wsdl:output>
        </wsdl:operation>
        <wsdl:operation name="getValue">
            <soap:operation
                soapAction="learnserve:ProvisioningServer:
                            ProvisioningServerPortType#getValue"/>
            <wsdl:input>
                <soap:body use="literal"/>
            </wsdl:input>
            <wsdl:output>
                <soap:body use="literal"/>
            </wsdl:output>
        </wsdl:operation>
        <wsdl:operation name="setValue">
            <soap:operation
                soapAction="learnserve:ProvisioningServer:
                            ProvisioningServerPortType#setValue"/>
            <wsdl:input>
                <soap:body use="literal"/>
```

```
        </wsdl:input>
        <wsdl:output>
            <soap:body use="literal"/>
        </wsdl:output>
</wsdl:operation>
<wsdl:operation name="GetLastError">
        <soap:operation
            soapAction="learnserve:ProvisioningServer:
                        ProvisioningServerPortType#GetLastError"/>
        <wsdl:input>
            <soap:body use="literal"/>
        </wsdl:input>
        <wsdl:output>
            <soap:body use="literal"/>
        </wsdl:output>
</wsdl:operation>
<wsdl:operation name="GetLastString">
        <soap:operation
            soapAction="learnserve:ProvisioningServer:
                        ProvisioningServerPortType#GetLastString"/>
        <wsdl:input>
            <soap:body use="literal"/>
        </wsdl:input>
        <wsdl:output>
            <soap:body use="literal"/>
        </wsdl:output>
</wsdl:operation>
<wsdl:operation name="GetDiagnostic">
        <soap:operation
            soapAction="learnserve:ProvisioningServer:
                        ProvisioningServerPortType#GetDiagnostic"/>
        <wsdl:input>
            <soap:body use="literal"/>
        </wsdl:input>
        <wsdl:output>
            <soap:body use="literal"/>
        </wsdl:output>
</wsdl:operation>
<wsdl:operation name="Commit">
        <soap:operation
            soapAction="learnserve:ProvisioningServer:
                        ProvisioningServerPortType#Commit"/>
        <wsdl:input>
            <soap:body use="literal"/>
        </wsdl:input>
        <wsdl:output>
```

```
                    <soap:body use="literal"/>
                </wsdl:output>
            </wsdl:operation>
            <wsdl:operation name="RegisterUser">
                <soap:operation
                    soapAction="capeconnect:ProvisioningServer:
                                ProvisioningServerPortType#RegisterUser"/>
                <wsdl:input>
                    <soap:body use="literal"/>
                </wsdl:input>
                <wsdl:output>
                    <soap:body use="literal"/>
                </wsdl:output>
            </wsdl:operation>
            <wsdl:operation name="setValue">
                <soap:operation
                    soapAction="capeconnect:ProvisioningServer:
                                ProvisioningServerPortType#setValue"/>
                <wsdl:input>
                    <soap:body use="literal"/>
                </wsdl:input>
                <wsdl:output>
                    <soap:body use="literal"/>
                </wsdl:output>
            </wsdl:operation>
            <wsdl:operation name="getUserPerformance">
                <soap:operation
                    soapAction="capeconnect:ProvisioningServer:
                                ProvisioningServerPortType#getUserPerformance"/>
                <wsdl:input>
                    <soap:body use="literal"/>
                </wsdl:input>
                <wsdl:output>
                    <soap:body use="literal"/>
                </wsdl:output>
            </wsdl:operation>
        </wsdl:binding>
        <wsdl:service name="ProvisioningServer">
            <wsdl:port binding="tns:ProvisioningServerBinding"
                        name="ProvisioningServerPort">
                <soap:address location="http://provserver.uni-muenster.de"/>
            </wsdl:port>
        </wsdl:service>
</wsdl:definitions>
```

A.5   WSRP WSDL Files

The following definitions cover only a part of the entire WSDL definitions of the WSRP standardizations. The latter can be found on http://www.oasis-open.org/committees/tc_home.php?wg_abbrev=wsrp.

Listing A.5: Bindings of WSRP WSDL Document.

```
<?xml version="1.0" encoding="UTF-8"?>
<wsdl:definitions targetNamespace="urn:oasis:names:tc:wsrp:v1:bind"
                  xmlns:bind="urn:oasis:names:tc:wsrp:v1:bind"
                  xmlns:intf="urn:oasis:names:tc:wsrp:v1:intf"

                  xmlns="http://schemas.xmlsoap.org/wsdl/"

                  xmlns:wsdl="http://schemas.xmlsoap.org/wsdl/"
                  xmlns:soap="http://schemas.xmlsoap.org/wsdl/soap/">

<!-- This file reflects v1.0 of the specification -->


  <import namespace="urn:oasis:names:tc:wsrp:v1:intf"
          location="wsrp_v1_interfaces.wsdl"/>

  <wsdl:binding name="WSRP_v1_Markup_Binding_SOAP"
                type="intf:WSRP_v1_Markup_PortType">
    <soap:binding style="document"
                  transport="http://schemas.xmlsoap.org/soap/http"/>

      <wsdl:operation name="getMarkup">
        <soap:operation soapAction="urn:oasis:names:tc:wsrp:v1:getMarkup"/>
        <wsdl:input name="getMarkup">
          <soap:body use="literal"/>
        </wsdl:input>
        <wsdl:output name="getMarkupResponse">
          <soap:body use="literal"/>
        </wsdl:output>
        <wsdl:fault name="AccessDenied">
          <soap:fault name="AccessDenied" use="literal"/>
        </wsdl:fault>
        <wsdl:fault name="InvalidUserCategory">
          <soap:fault name="InvalidUserCategory" use="literal"/>
        </wsdl:fault>
        <wsdl:fault name="InconsistentParameters">
          <soap:fault name="InconsistentParameters" use="literal"/>
        </wsdl:fault>
```

```
<wsdl:fault name="InvalidRegistration">
  <soap:fault name="InvalidRegistration" use="literal"/>
</wsdl:fault>
<wsdl:fault name="MissingParameters">
  <soap:fault name="MissingParameters" use="literal"/>
</wsdl:fault>
<wsdl:fault name="OperationFailed">
  <soap:fault name="OperationFailed" use="literal"/>
</wsdl:fault>
<wsdl:fault name="InvalidHandle">
  <soap:fault name="InvalidHandle" use="literal"/>
</wsdl:fault>
<wsdl:fault name="InvalidCookie">
  <soap:fault name="InvalidCookie" use="literal"/>
</wsdl:fault>
<wsdl:fault name="InvalidSession">
  <soap:fault name="InvalidSession" use="literal"/>
</wsdl:fault>
<wsdl:fault name="UnsupportedMode">
  <soap:fault name="UnsupportedMode" use="literal"/>
</wsdl:fault>
<wsdl:fault name="UnsupportedWindowState">
  <soap:fault name="UnsupportedWindowState" use="literal"/>
</wsdl:fault>
<wsdl:fault name="UnsupportedLocale">
  <soap:fault name="UnsupportedLocale" use="literal"/>
</wsdl:fault>
<wsdl:fault name="UnsupportedMimeType">
  <soap:fault name="UnsupportedMimeType" use="literal"/>
</wsdl:fault>
</wsdl:operation>

<wsdl:operation name="performBlockingInteraction">
  <soap:operation soapAction="urn:oasis:names:tc:
                          wsrp:v1:performBlockingInteraction"/>
  <wsdl:input name="performBlockingInteraction">
    <soap:body use="literal"/>
  </wsdl:input>
  <wsdl:output name="performBlockingInteractionResponse">
    <soap:body use="literal"/>
  </wsdl:output>
  <wsdl:fault name="AccessDenied">
    <soap:fault name="AccessDenied" use="literal"/>
  </wsdl:fault>
  <wsdl:fault name="InvalidUserCategory">
    <soap:fault name="InvalidUserCategory" use="literal"/>
```

```
    </wsdl:fault>
    <wsdl:fault name="InconsistentParameters">
      <soap:fault name="InconsistentParameters" use="literal"/>
    </wsdl:fault>
    <wsdl:fault name="InvalidRegistration">
      <soap:fault name="InvalidRegistration" use="literal"/>
    </wsdl:fault>
    <wsdl:fault name="MissingParameters">
      <soap:fault name="MissingParameters" use="literal"/>
    </wsdl:fault>
    <wsdl:fault name="OperationFailed">
      <soap:fault name="OperationFailed" use="literal"/>
    </wsdl:fault>
    <wsdl:fault name="InvalidHandle">
      <soap:fault name="InvalidHandle" use="literal"/>
    </wsdl:fault>
    <wsdl:fault name="PortletStateChangeRequired">
      <soap:fault name="PortletStateChangeRequired" use="literal"/>
    </wsdl:fault>
    <wsdl:fault name="InvalidCookie">
      <soap:fault name="InvalidCookie" use="literal"/>
    </wsdl:fault>
    <wsdl:fault name="InvalidSession">
      <soap:fault name="InvalidSession" use="literal"/>
    </wsdl:fault>
    <wsdl:fault name="UnsupportedMode">
      <soap:fault name="UnsupportedMode" use="literal"/>
    </wsdl:fault>
    <wsdl:fault name="UnsupportedWindowState">
      <soap:fault name="UnsupportedWindowState" use="literal"/>
    </wsdl:fault>
    <wsdl:fault name="UnsupportedLocale">
      <soap:fault name="UnsupportedLocale" use="literal"/>
    </wsdl:fault>
    <wsdl:fault name="UnsupportedMimeType">
      <soap:fault name="UnsupportedMimeType" use="literal"/>
    </wsdl:fault>
  </wsdl:operation>

<wsdl:operation name="releaseSessions">
  <soap:operation soapAction="urn:oasis:names:tc:
                              wsrp:v1:releaseSessions"/>
  <wsdl:input name="releaseSessions">
    <soap:body use="literal"/>
  </wsdl:input>
  <wsdl:output name="releaseSessionsResponse">
```

```
        <soap:body use="literal"/>
      </wsdl:output>
      <wsdl:fault name="AccessDenied">
        <soap:fault name="AccessDenied" use="literal"/>
      </wsdl:fault>
      <wsdl:fault name="InvalidRegistration">
        <soap:fault name="InvalidRegistration" use="literal"/>
      </wsdl:fault>
      <wsdl:fault name="MissingParameters">
        <soap:fault name="MissingParameters" use="literal"/>
      </wsdl:fault>
      <wsdl:fault name="OperationFailed">
        <soap:fault name="OperationFailed" use="literal"/>
      </wsdl:fault>
    </wsdl:operation>

    <wsdl:operation name="initCookie">
      <soap:operation soapAction="urn:oasis:names:tc:
                                  wsrp:v1:initCookie"/>
      <wsdl:input name="initCookie">
        <soap:body use="literal"/>
      </wsdl:input>
      <wsdl:output name="initCookieResponse">
        <soap:body use="literal"/>
      </wsdl:output>
      <wsdl:fault name="AccessDenied">
        <soap:fault name="AccessDenied" use="literal"/>
      </wsdl:fault>
      <wsdl:fault name="InvalidRegistration">
        <soap:fault name="InvalidRegistration" use="literal"/>
      </wsdl:fault>
      <wsdl:fault name="OperationFailed">
        <soap:fault name="OperationFailed" use="literal"/>
      </wsdl:fault>
    </wsdl:operation>
  </wsdl:binding>


<wsdl:binding name="WSRP_v1_ServiceDescription_Binding_SOAP"
              type="intf:WSRP_v1_ServiceDescription_PortType">
  <soap:binding style="document"
              transport="http://schemas.xmlsoap.org/soap/http"/>

  <wsdl:operation name="getServiceDescription">
    <soap:operation soapAction="urn:oasis:names:tc:
                                wsrp:v1:getServiceDescription"/>
```

```
      <wsdl:input name="getServiceDescription">
        <soap:body use="literal"/>
      </wsdl:input>
      <wsdl:output name="getServiceDescriptionResponse">
        <soap:body use="literal"/>
      </wsdl:output>
      <wsdl:fault name="InvalidRegistration">
        <soap:fault name="InvalidRegistration" use="literal"/>
      </wsdl:fault>
      <wsdl:fault name="OperationFailed">
        <soap:fault name="OperationFailed" use="literal"/>
      </wsdl:fault>
    </wsdl:operation>
  </wsdl:binding>

<wsdl:binding name="WSRP_v1_PortletManagement_Binding_SOAP"
                type="intf:WSRP_v1_PortletManagement_PortType">
    <soap:binding style="document"
                transport="http://schemas.xmlsoap.org/soap/http"/>

    <wsdl:operation name="getPortletDescription">
      <soap:operation soapAction="urn:oasis:names:tc:
                                    wsrp:v1:getPortletDescription"/>
      <wsdl:input name="getPortletDescription">
        <soap:body use="literal"/>
      </wsdl:input>
      <wsdl:output name="getPortletDescriptionResponse">
        <soap:body use="literal"/>
      </wsdl:output>
      <wsdl:fault name="AccessDenied">
        <soap:fault name="AccessDenied" use="literal"/>
      </wsdl:fault>
      <wsdl:fault name="InvalidUserCategory">
        <soap:fault name="InvalidUserCategory" use="literal"/>
      </wsdl:fault>
      <wsdl:fault name="InconsistentParameters">
        <soap:fault name="InconsistentParameters" use="literal"/>
      </wsdl:fault>
      <wsdl:fault name="InvalidRegistration">
        <soap:fault name="InvalidRegistration" use="literal"/>
      </wsdl:fault>
      <wsdl:fault name="MissingParameters">
        <soap:fault name="MissingParameters" use="literal"/>
      </wsdl:fault>
      <wsdl:fault name="OperationFailed">
        <soap:fault name="OperationFailed" use="literal"/>
```

```
      </wsdl:fault>
      <wsdl:fault name="InvalidHandle">
        <soap:fault name="InvalidHandle" use="literal"/>
      </wsdl:fault>
  </wsdl:operation>

  <wsdl:operation name="clonePortlet">
      <soap:operation
        soapAction="urn:oasis:names:tc:wsrp:v1:clonePortlet"/>
      <wsdl:input name="clonePortlet">
        <soap:body use="literal"/>
      </wsdl:input>
      <wsdl:output name="clonePortletResponse">
        <soap:body use="literal"/>
      </wsdl:output>
      <wsdl:fault name="AccessDenied">
        <soap:fault name="AccessDenied" use="literal"/>
      </wsdl:fault>
      <wsdl:fault name="InvalidUserCategory">
        <soap:fault name="InvalidUserCategory" use="literal"/>
      </wsdl:fault>
      <wsdl:fault name="InconsistentParameters">
        <soap:fault name="InconsistentParameters" use="literal"/>
      </wsdl:fault>
      <wsdl:fault name="InvalidRegistration">
        <soap:fault name="InvalidRegistration" use="literal"/>
      </wsdl:fault>
      <wsdl:fault name="MissingParameters">
        <soap:fault name="MissingParameters" use="literal"/>
      </wsdl:fault>
      <wsdl:fault name="OperationFailed">
        <soap:fault name="OperationFailed" use="literal"/>
      </wsdl:fault>
      <wsdl:fault name="InvalidHandle">
        <soap:fault name="InvalidHandle" use="literal"/>
      </wsdl:fault>
  </wsdl:operation>

  <wsdl:operation name="destroyPortlets">
      <soap:operation
        soapAction="urn:oasis:names:tc:wsrp:v1:destroyPortlets"/>
      <wsdl:input name="destroyPortlets">
        <soap:body use="literal"/>
      </wsdl:input>
      <wsdl:output name="destroyPortletsResponse">
        <soap:body use="literal"/>
```

```
    </wsdl:output>
    <wsdl:fault name="InconsistentParameters">
      <soap:fault name="InconsistentParameters" use="literal"/>
    </wsdl:fault>
    <wsdl:fault name="InvalidRegistration">
      <soap:fault name="InvalidRegistration" use="literal"/>
    </wsdl:fault>
    <wsdl:fault name="MissingParameters">
      <soap:fault name="MissingParameters" use="literal"/>
    </wsdl:fault>
    <wsdl:fault name="OperationFailed">
      <soap:fault name="OperationFailed" use="literal"/>
    </wsdl:fault>
  </wsdl:operation>

  <wsdl:operation name="setPortletProperties">
    <soap:operation
       soapAction="urn:oasis:names:tc:wsrp:v1:setPortletProperties"/>
    <wsdl:input name="setPortletProperties">
      <soap:body use="literal"/>
    </wsdl:input>
    <wsdl:output name="setPortletPropertiesResponse">
      <soap:body use="literal"/>
    </wsdl:output>
    <wsdl:fault name="AccessDenied">
      <soap:fault name="AccessDenied" use="literal"/>
    </wsdl:fault>
    <wsdl:fault name="InvalidUserCategory">
      <soap:fault name="InvalidUserCategory" use="literal"/>
    </wsdl:fault>
    <wsdl:fault name="InconsistentParameters">
      <soap:fault name="InconsistentParameters" use="literal"/>
    </wsdl:fault>
    <wsdl:fault name="InvalidRegistration">
      <soap:fault name="InvalidRegistration" use="literal"/>
    </wsdl:fault>
    <wsdl:fault name="MissingParameters">
      <soap:fault name="MissingParameters" use="literal"/>
    </wsdl:fault>
    <wsdl:fault name="OperationFailed">
      <soap:fault name="OperationFailed" use="literal"/>
    </wsdl:fault>
    <wsdl:fault name="InvalidHandle">
      <soap:fault name="InvalidHandle" use="literal"/>
    </wsdl:fault>
  </wsdl:operation>
```

```
<wsdl:operation name="getPortletProperties">
  <soap:operation
     soapAction="urn:oasis:names:tc:wsrp:v1:getPortletProperties"/>
  <wsdl:input name="getPortletProperties">
    <soap:body use="literal"/>
  </wsdl:input>
  <wsdl:output name="getPortletPropertiesResponse">
    <soap:body use="literal"/>
  </wsdl:output>
  <wsdl:fault name="AccessDenied">
    <soap:fault name="AccessDenied" use="literal"/>
  </wsdl:fault>
  <wsdl:fault name="InvalidUserCategory">
    <soap:fault name="InvalidUserCategory" use="literal"/>
  </wsdl:fault>
  <wsdl:fault name="InconsistentParameters">
    <soap:fault name="InconsistentParameters" use="literal"/>
  </wsdl:fault>
  <wsdl:fault name="InvalidRegistration">
    <soap:fault name="InvalidRegistration" use="literal"/>
  </wsdl:fault>
  <wsdl:fault name="MissingParameters">
    <soap:fault name="MissingParameters" use="literal"/>
  </wsdl:fault>
  <wsdl:fault name="OperationFailed">
    <soap:fault name="OperationFailed" use="literal"/>
  </wsdl:fault>
  <wsdl:fault name="InvalidHandle">
    <soap:fault name="InvalidHandle" use="literal"/>
  </wsdl:fault>
</wsdl:operation>

<wsdl:operation name="getPortletPropertyDescription">
  <soap:operation soapAction="urn:oasis:names:tc:
                  wsrp:v1:getPortletPropertyDescription"/>
  <wsdl:input name="getPortletPropertyDescription">
    <soap:body use="literal"/>
  </wsdl:input>
  <wsdl:output name="getPortletPropertyDescriptionResponse">
    <soap:body use="literal"/>
  </wsdl:output>
  <wsdl:fault name="AccessDenied">
    <soap:fault name="AccessDenied" use="literal"/>
  </wsdl:fault>
  <wsdl:fault name="InvalidUserCategory">
```

```
        <soap:fault name="InvalidUserCategory" use="literal"/>
      </wsdl:fault>
      <wsdl:fault name="InconsistentParameters">
        <soap:fault name="InconsistentParameters" use="literal"/>
      </wsdl:fault>
      <wsdl:fault name="InvalidRegistration">
        <soap:fault name="InvalidRegistration" use="literal"/>
      </wsdl:fault>
      <wsdl:fault name="MissingParameters">
        <soap:fault name="MissingParameters" use="literal"/>
      </wsdl:fault>
      <wsdl:fault name="OperationFailed">
        <soap:fault name="OperationFailed" use="literal"/>
      </wsdl:fault>
      <wsdl:fault name="InvalidHandle">
        <soap:fault name="InvalidHandle" use="literal"/>
      </wsdl:fault>
    </wsdl:operation>
</wsdl:binding>

<wsdl:binding name="WSRP_v1_Registration_Binding_SOAP"
              type="intf:WSRP_v1_Registration_PortType">
  <soap:binding style="document"
              transport="http://schemas.xmlsoap.org/soap/http"/>

  <wsdl:operation name="register">
    <soap:operation soapAction="urn:oasis:names:tc:wsrp:v1:register"/>
    <wsdl:input name="register">
      <soap:body use="literal"/>
    </wsdl:input>
    <wsdl:output name="registerResponse">
      <soap:body use="literal"/>
    </wsdl:output>
    <wsdl:fault name="MissingParameters">
      <soap:fault name="MissingParameters" use="literal"/>
    </wsdl:fault>
    <wsdl:fault name="OperationFailed">
      <soap:fault name="OperationFailed" use="literal"/>
    </wsdl:fault>
  </wsdl:operation>

  <wsdl:operation name="deregister">
    <soap:operation
        soapAction="urn:oasis:names:tc:wsrp:v1:deregister"/>
    <wsdl:input name="deregister">
      <soap:body use="literal"/>
```

```
      </wsdl:input>
      <wsdl:output name="deregisterResponse">
        <soap:body use="literal"/>
      </wsdl:output>
      <wsdl:fault name="InvalidRegistration">
        <soap:fault name="InvalidRegistration" use="literal"/>
      </wsdl:fault>
      <wsdl:fault name="OperationFailed">
        <soap:fault name="OperationFailed" use="literal"/>
      </wsdl:fault>
    </wsdl:operation>

    <wsdl:operation name="modifyRegistration">
      <soap:operation
        soapAction="urn:oasis:names:tc:wsrp:v1:modifyRegistration"/>
      <wsdl:input name="modifyRegistration">
        <soap:body use="literal"/>
      </wsdl:input>
      <wsdl:output name="modifyRegistrationResponse">
        <soap:body use="literal"/>
      </wsdl:output>
      <wsdl:fault name="InvalidRegistration">
        <soap:fault name="InvalidRegistration" use="literal"/>
      </wsdl:fault>
      <wsdl:fault name="MissingParameters">
        <soap:fault name="MissingParameters" use="literal"/>
      </wsdl:fault>
      <wsdl:fault name="OperationFailed">
        <soap:fault name="OperationFailed" use="literal"/>
      </wsdl:fault>
    </wsdl:operation>
  </wsdl:binding>
</wsdl:definitions>
```

Bisher erschienene und geplante Bände der Reihe
Advances in Information Systems and Management Science

ISSN 1611-3101

Bd. 1: Lars H. Ehlers

Content Management Anwendungen.

Spezifikation von Internet-Anwendungen
auf Basis von Content Management Systemen

ISBN 3-8325-0145-2   40.50 €
285 Seiten, 2003

Content Management Anwendungen stellen für Unternehmen die Chance einer attraktiven und einfach zu pflegenden Präsenz im Internet dar. Umfangreiche Inhalte auf den Web-Seiten und regelmäßige Aktualisierungen lassen sich so realisieren. Dabei stellen Content Management Systeme (CMS) die technologische Basis zum Aufbau dieser Anwendungen dar.

Dieses Buch verdeutlicht dem Leser wichtige Internet-Grundlagen und die Eigenschaften von Content Management Systemen. Darauf aufbauend liefert Lars H. Ehlers umfangreiche Gestaltungsempfehlungen für die fachkonzeptionelle Modellierung von Content Management Anwendungen.

Aus dem Inhalt:

- Internet: Grundlagen des Hypertextes, Möglichkeiten von HTML sowie client- und serverseitigen Skriptsprachen, Übersicht von Planungsansätzen für Internet-Anwendungen

- Content Management Systeme: Komponenten, Erweiterungsmöglichkeiten, Metamodell; Fragebogen zur Systemauswahl

- Content Management Anwendungen: Erstellung, enthaltene Dimensionen, Modellierung von Präsentation, Navigation und Content

Bd. 2: Stefan Neumann

Workflow-Anwendungen in technischen Dienstleistungen.

Eine Referenz-Architektur für die Koordination
von Prozessen im Gebäude- und Anlagenmanagement

ISBN 3-8325-0156-8   40.50 €
310 Seiten, 2003

Technische Dienstleistungen werden von Unternehmen, die sich auf ihre Kernkompetenzen konzentrieren, in zunehmendem Maße an externe Anbieter vergeben. Aufgrund der Komplexität, Variantenvielfalt und zwischenbetrieblichen Ausrichtung dieser Leistungen stoßen heutige Anwendungssysteme zur Unterstützung der Auftragsabwicklung an ihre Grenzen. Vor diesem Hintergrund stellen Workflowmanagementsysteme viel versprechende Lösungsmöglichkeiten bereit.

Stefan Neumann analysiert am Beispiel der Bewirtschaftung von Gebäuden und technischen Einrichtungen (Facility Management) umfassend die besonderen Anforderungen technischer Dienstleistungen an die Gestaltung von Informationssystemen. Darauf aufbauend entwirft er eine neuartige Systemarchitektur, die basierend auf dem Workflow-Ansatz eine verbesserte, durchgängig integrierte Definition, Planung, Steuerung und Kontrolle technischer Dienstleistungen ermöglicht.

Das Buch richtet sich an Dozenten und Studenten der Wirtschaftsinformatik und der Betriebswirtschaftslehre sowie an Organisations- und Anwendungssystemgestalter im Servicemanagement.

Aus dem Inhalt:

- Informationssysteme in technischen Dienstleistungen: Charakterisierung technischer Dienstleistungen und des technischen Facility Management, Referenz-Ordnungsrahmen für Dienstleistungs-Informationssysteme, verfügbare Systeme und Referenzmodelle

- Workflowmanagement: Grundlagen, Architekturen, Nutzen, Integration von Workflow- und Fachkomponenten

- Architektur Workflow-basierter Anwendungen im technischen Facility Management: Fachkonzepte für Workflow-Komponenten, Leistungs- und Prozessgestaltung, Anlagenmanagement, Projektplanung und -steuerung, Serviceauftragsabwicklung.

Bd. 3: Christian Probst

Referenzmodell für IT-Service-Informationssysteme.

ISBN 3-8325-0161-4   40.50 €

315 Seiten, 2003

IT-Service-Informationssysteme werden in Unternehmen zur Unterstützung des IT-Service-Managements eingesetzt. Sie sind unabdingbare Voraussetzung, um Beratung, Entwicklung, Einführung, Betrieb, Unterstützung und Stilllegung zu bzw. von IT-Services effektiv und effizient zu realisieren. Hierfür müssen neben der Komplexität und Kompliziertheit der Komponenten eines IT-Services (Hardware, Software und Carrier-Services) sowohl die hohe Innovationsgeschwindigkeit in der IT als auch eine variable Leistungstiefe flexibel und ökonomisch beherrscht und durch geeignete Systeme unterstützt werden. Obschon heute de facto jede größere Organisation essenziell von IT-Dienstleistungen abhängig ist, kann ein beachtliches Theoriedefizit hinsichtlich der Gestaltung von IT-Service-Informationssystemen festgestellt werden.

Hier setzt Christian Probst in seiner Dissertation an, in der er Literatur und bestehende Ansätze der Referenzmodellierung im Umfeld des IT-Service-Managements (u. A. ITIL, eTOM und DMTF DMI/ CIM) analysiert und daraus praktische Gestaltungsempfehlungen in Form eines ganzheitlichen Ordnungsrahmens ableitet, der durch über 200 Prozess-, Funktions- und Datenmodelle umfassend detailliert wird.

Das Buch richtet sich an Dozenten und Studenten der Wirtschaftsinformatik und der Betriebswirtschaftslehre sowie an IT-Service-Manager, Organisations- und Anwendungssystemgestalter im IT-Service-Management.

Bd. 4: Jan vom Brocke

Referenzmodellierung.

Gestaltung und Verteilung von Konstruktionsprozessen

ISBN 3-8325-0179-7 40.50 €
424 Seiten, 2003

Referenzmodelle sind der Schlüssel zur wirtschaftlichen Konstruktion leistungsfähiger Informationssysteme. Wie Informationsmodelle so zu konstruieren sind, dass sie der angestrebten Referenzfunktion in Theorie und Praxis gerecht werden, zeigt die vorliegende Arbeit.

Jan vom Brocke entwickelt hierzu das Konzept der Verteilten Referenzmodellierung (VRM), in dem er innovative Ansätze des Software Engineering (z. B. Open Source und Component Based Software Engineering) für die Referenzmodellierung erschließt. Die Arbeit gibt umfangreiche Gestaltungsempfehlungen, nach denen Referenzmodelle im Netzwerkverbund verteilt agierender Akteure komponentenorientiert entwickelt und in Austausch- und Diskursprozessen flexibel an neue Anforderungen angepasst werden können. Als Basis schafft Jan vom Brocke konzeptionelle Grundlagen zur Gestaltung von Konstruktionsprozessen und liefert eine differenzierte Analyse des State-of-the-Art der Referenzmodellierung.

Die Arbeit von Jan vom Brocke ist mit einem Dissertationspreis der Universität Münster ausgezeichnet worden. Die innovativen Forschungsergebnisse werden als richtungsweisend für die wissenschaftliche Entwicklung der Referenzmodellierung eingestuft. Durch die Konstruktion von Metamodellen und die Implementierung der Internetplattform referenzmodelle.de sind die Ergebnisse unmittelbar in der Praxis einsetzbar. Die umfassende Aufbereitung des Themengebiets und dessen strukturierte Darstellung machen das Buch zu einem Standardwerk für Dozenten und Studenten der Wirtschaftsinformatik.

Bd. 5: Holger Hansmann

Architekturen Workflow-gestützter PPS-Systeme.

Referenzmodelle für die Koordination von Prozessen
der Auftragsabwicklung von Einzel- und Kleinserienfertigern

ISBN 3-8325-0282-3 40.50 €
299 Seiten, 2003

Die Komplexität der Produktionsplanung und -steuerung (PPS) stellt hohe Anforderungen an Anwendungssysteme. Heutige PPS-Systeme bieten zwar eine umfassende Unterstützung einzelner PPS-Funktionen, weisen jedoch eine Reihe von Defiziten auf. Insbesondere erlauben sie keine ganzheitliche und unternehmensindividuell spezifizierbare Prozessgestaltung, -steuerung und -kontrolle und unterstützen nur in eingeschränktem Maße eine flexible Integration zusätzlich benötigterAnwendungssysteme. Einen Ansatz, diesen Defiziten zu begegnen, stellt die Integration von PPS-Systemen mit dar, die eine automatisierte und individuell anhandvon Prozessmodellen spezifizierbare Prozesskoordination ermöglichen.

In diesem Buch vermittelt Holger Hansmann dem Leser essentielle Grundlagen der PPS und des Workflow-Managements und analysiert umfassend die spezifischen Anforderungen der industriellen Auftragsabwicklung an die Gestaltung von Workflow-Anwendungen. Darauf aufbauend entwirft er eine neuartige Systemarchitektur für Workflow-gestützte PPS-Systeme, die eine effizientere und durchgängig integrierte Definition, Planung, Steuerung und Kontrolle industrieller Geschäftsprozesse ermöglicht.

Bd. 6: Michael zur Muehlen

Workflow-based Process Controlling.

Foundation, Design, and Application of workflow-driven Process Information Systems

ISBN 3-8325-0388-9   40.50 €
315 Seiten, 2004

Workflow-based Process Controlling Systems provide companies with the ability to measure the operational performance of their business processes in a timely and accurate fashion. The combination of workflow audit trails with data warehouse technology and operational business data allows for complex analyses that can support managers in their assessment of an organization?s performance. The increasing maturity of business process management and data warehouse systems enables the design and development of advanced process-oriented management information systems.

Michael zur Muehlen discusses the integration of workflow audit trail data with existing data warehouse structures and develops a reference architecture for process-oriented management information systems. Starting with an organizational and technical analysis of process organizations, this book provides a comprehensive documentation of business process management, workflow technology, and existing standardization efforts The proposed reference architecture is validated in an industry context. A prototypical implementation of the reference architecture and its integration with a commercial business process management system are demonstrated as well.

This book is directed at both practitioners and academics in the fields of business process management, management accounting, and information systems research.

Bd. 7: Martin B. Schultz

Anreizorientiertes   Investitionscontrolling   mit vollständigen Finanzplänen.

Ein Referenzprozessmodell für Inverstment Center

ISBN 3-8325-0420-6   40.50 €
380 Seiten, 2005

Am Investitionsprozess in dezentralisierten Unternehmen sind zahlreiche Akteure mit individuellen und häufig divergierenden Interessen beteiligt. Um die Effektivität und Effizienz des Prozesses sicherzustellen, ist das Investitionscontrolling phasenübergreifend anreizorientiert auszugestalten. Hierzu wird in dem Buch von Martin B. Schultz folgenden Fragen nachgegangen:

Wie ist die Führung als Empfänger von Anreizen begrifflich abzugrenzen und welche Faktoren beeinflussen die Rationalität der Führung?

Wie ist eine zweckmäßige Controllingkonzeption auszugestalten, die die Anreizorientierung integrativ umfasst?

Welche konstituierenden Eigenschaften weist das Investitionscontrolling in Investment Centern auf?

Wie hat ein Ordnungsrahmen für das anreizorientierte Investitionscontrolling in Investment Centern auszusehen, der sowohl die Gestaltung der Instrumente und Informationssysteme als auch deren Nutzung zu strukturieren vermag?

Welche Instrumente sind im Rahmen des anreizorientierten Investitionscontrollings in Investment Centern auf welche Weise einzusetzen?

Wie sollte der Ablauf eines Investitionsprozesses gestaltet sein, der die Aktivitäten des anreizorientierten Investitionscontrollings umfasst und der als Referenzprozessmodell für die Implementierung in Unternehmen dienen kann?

Wie ist ein computergestütztes Controllinginstrument auszugestalten, mit dem der Investitionsprozess in Investment Centern phasenübergreifend begleitet werden kann?

Für die vorliegende Arbeit wurde Martin B. Schultz mit dem Österreichischen Controllerpreis 2004 ausgezeichnet.

Bd. 8: Norman Lahme

Information Retrieval im Wissensmanagement.

Ein am Vorwissen orientierter Ansatz zur Komposition von Informationsressourcen

ISBN 3-8325-0526-1   40.50 €
274 Seiten, 2004

Die Suche nach relevanten Informationsressourcen ist eine regelmäßige Aufgabe für die Mitglieder einer Organisation. Zu ihrer Unterstützung bei dieser Aufgabe können Information Retrieval-Systeme als Werkzeuge des Wissensmanagements zum Einsatz gelangen. Derzeitige Ansätze hierzu lassen jedoch Unterschiede zwischen den Informationsressourcen hinsichtlich ihrer Verstehbarkeit unberücksichtigt.

Norman Lahme entwickelt zur Berücksichtigung dieser Unterschiede eine verstehbarkeitsorientierte Information Retrieval-Methode. Nach dieser wird zu einer Anfrage eines Nachfragers von Informationen eine an dessen Vorwissen orientierte und somit grundsätzlich verstehbare Komposition von Informationsressourcen ermittelt, die im Hinblick auf die zu ihrer Internalisierung durchschnittlich benötigte Zeit optimal ist. Zu seiner Methode erstellt er zudem einen effizienten Algorithmus, der auf Erkenntnissen aus der künstlichen Intelligenz aufbaut, sowie ein Softwareprodukt, das den Algorithmus implementiert und die Anwendung und Erprobung der Methode erlaubt.

Das Buch wendet sich an Dozenten und Studenten der Informatik, der Betriebswirtschaftslehre und der Wirtschaftsinformatik sowie an Praktiker, die sich mit der informationstechnischen Unterstützung des Wissensmanagements befassen.

Bd. 9: Jörg Bergerfurth

Referenz-Informationsmodelle für das Produktionscontrolling.

Nutzerspezifische Analyse- und Auswertungssichten für produktionsbezogene Aufgaben

ISBN 3-8325-0492-3   40.50 €
275 Seiten, 2004

Einer aufgabenspezifischen Versorgung mit betriebswirtschaftlich relevanten Informationen kommt im Rahmen des Produktionscontrollings große Bedeutung zu. Bei der Umsetzung von Konzepten zum Produktionscontrolling in Informationssystemen werden jedoch häufig Mängel bzgl. der nutzerindividuellen Informationsversorgung festgestellt. Die vorhandenen Daten der operativen bzw. datenerzeugenden Systeme werden nicht für eine ganzheitliche Betrachtung controllinggerecht zusammengeführt. Instrumente zur Informationsaufbereitung insbesondere Kennzahlensysteme werden zumeist unzureichend eingesetzt. Zudem sind die Auswertungen nicht aktuell genug und unflexibel, so dass die Transparenz der Produktion gering ist. Die von Jörg Bergerfurth entwickelten

Referenz-Informationsmodelle bieten auf fachkonzeptioneller Ebene eine Grundlage für ein umfassendes **Produktionscontrolling**. Die Modelle ermöglichen neben der breiten Abdeckung der Produktionsbereiche auch sehr flexible und individuelle **Analyse- und Auswertungssichten**. Die dokumentierten Modelle dienen auf fachkonzeptioneller Ebene als Vorlage für die Informationssystemgestaltung, wie bspw. den Aufbau eines Data-Warehouses. Das Buch richtet sich an Dozenten und Studenten der Wirtschaftsinformatik und der Betriebswirtschaftslehre sowie an Anwendungssystemgestalter in den Produktionsbereichen.

Bd. 10: Dominik Kuropka

Modelle zur Repräsentation natürlichsprachlicher Dokumente.

Ontologie-basiertes Information-Filtering und -Retrieval mit relationalen Datenbanken

ISBN 3-8325-0514-8   40.50 €
264 Seiten, 2004

Kostengünstige Massenspeicher und die zunehmende Vernetzung von Rechnern haben die Anzahl der Dokumente, auf die ein einzelnes Individuum zugreifen kann (bspw. Webseiten) oder die auf das Individuum einströmen (bspw. E-Mails), in den letzten Jahren rapide ansteigen lassen. In immer mehr Bereichen der Wirtschaft, Wissenschaft und Verwaltung nimmt der Bedarf an hochwertigen Information-Filtering und -Retrieval Werkzeugen zur Beherrschung der Informationsflut zu. Zur computergestützten Lösung dieser Problemstellung sind Modelle zur Repräsentation natürlichsprachlicher Dokumente erforderlich, um formale Kriterien für die automatisierte Auswahl relevanter Dokumente definieren zu können.

Dominik Kuropka gibt in seiner Arbeit eine umfassende Übersicht über den Themenbereich der Suche und Filterung von natürlichsprachlichen Dokumenten. Es wird eine Vielzahl von Modellen aus Forschung und Praxis vorgestellt und evaluiert. Auf den Ergebnissen aufbauend wird das Potenzial von Ontologien in diesem Zusammenhang eruiert und es wird ein neues, ontologie-basiertes Modell für das Information-Filtering und -Retrieval erarbeitet, welches anhand von Text- und Code-Beispielen ausführlich erläutert wird.

Das Buch richtet sich an Dozenten und Studenten der Informatik, Wirtschaftsinformatik und (Computer-)Linguistik sowie an Systemdesigner und Entwickler von dokumentenorientierten Anwendungssystemen und Werkzeugen.

Bd. 11: Christoph Köster

Kosten- und Prozesscontrolling in der Versicherungswirtschaft.

Ontologie-basiertes Information-Filtering und -Retrieval mit relationalen Datenbanken

ISBN 3-8325-0519-9   40.50 €
272 Seiten, 2004

Kostencontrolling und -management als Instrumente der Unternehmenssteuerung sehen sich in jüngerer Vergangenheit heftiger Kritik ausgesetzt. Insbesondere den traditionellen Methoden der Kostenrechnung wird die Relevanz für rationale Entscheidungsfindungen abgesprochen, weil sie sich nicht den Gegebenheiten aktueller Umwelt- und Rahmenbedingungen angepasst haben. Mit der Ausrichtung der Organisation des Versicherungs-Unternehmens auf die elementaren Geschäftsprozesse und der Gewinnung von kostenrelevanten Daten aus Dokumenten- und Workflow-Management-Systemen (DMS / WfMS) mittels Audit-Trails wird ein überzeugender Lösungsansatz vorgestellt. Besonders in der personalkostenintensiven Versicherungswirtschaft, deren Gemeinkosten im Wesentlichen durch die Sachbearbeitung in Sparten entstehen, ist eine präzise verursachungsgerechte Verrechnung der Kosten für ein erfolgreiches Kostencontrolling von größter Bedeutung. Da im Wesentlichen einzelne Aktivitäten als Bestandteil von Versicherungsvorgängen mit den dazugehörenden Dokumenten Personalkosten auslösen, wird ein Weg aufgezeigt, wie aus DMS / WfMS ermittelte Audit-Trail-Daten zur Etablierung eines effizienten Kosten- und Prozesscontrollings und -monitorings genutzt werden können. Mit Hilfe des kombiniert-integrierten Einsatzes von adäquaten Kostencontrolling- und -managementinstrumenten und Informationstechnologie werden Möglichkeiten geschaffen, der Führungsebene von Versicherungsunternehmen umfassende und zeitnahe Instrumente zur Planung, Überwachung und Kontrolle von Geschäftsprozessen und Kosten an die Hand zu geben.

Bd. 12: Andreas Rottwinkel

Management von Partnerkontakten in Versicherungsunternehmen.

Referenzmodelle für die
Koordination von Partnerkontakten

ISBN 3-8325-0523-7   40.50 €
230 Seiten, 2004

Ein Partnerkontakt dokumentiert den Informationsaustausch zwischen einem Unternehmen und dessen Partner sowie den aktuellen Stand der Bearbeitung dieses Ereignisses. Ausgehend von den Problemstellungen bei der Kontaktbearbeitung in Versicherungsunternehmen stellt Andreas Rottwinkel in seiner Dissertation mit Computer-Supported Cooperative Work, Dokumenten-Management, Workflow-Management und Customer-Relationship-Management bestehende Ansätze vor, die sich bei Versicherern bisher nicht behaupten konnten. Mit dem Management von Partnerkontakten wird ein neuer Ansatz konzipiert, in dem spartenübergreifend nicht nur Kunden, sondern auch Partner wie Makler, Werkstätten oder Rechtsanwälte fokussiert werden.
Mit Referenzmodellen für die Koordination von Partnerkontakten unterstützt Andreas Rottwinkel fachkonzeptuell die Einführung von Partnerkontaktsystemen in Versicherungsunternehmen. Eine Einbettung finden diese Modelle zur Beschreibung von Informationssystemen im Versicherungs-V-Modell einem Ordnungsrahmen für Versicherungsinformationssysteme.
Das Buch richtet sich an Dozenten und Studenten der Wirtschaftsinformatik und der Betriebswirtschaftslehre sowie an IT-Manager, Organisations- und Anwendungssystemgestalter.

Bd. 13: Ulrich Kathöfer

Data Mining mit Genetischen Algorithmen.

ISBN 3-8325-0522-9   40.50 €
280 Seiten, 2004

Die Weiterentwicklung von Hardware und Datenbanken hat in den letzten Jahren zu einer rasanten Steigerung des Interesses an der automatisierten Auswertung von Massendaten geführt. Das Data Mining, dessen Potenzial bisher nur in Ansätzen genutzt wird, soll wissenschaftlich gestützte und praktisch anwendbare Verfahrensweisen dafür liefern. Auch wenn statistische Methoden viele Fragen beantworten können, bleibt doch der Bedarf an innovativen Herangehensweisen, um noch mehr Informationen aus den Daten herauszuholen.

Mit Genetischen Algorithmen, einer Gruppe von Verfahren, die Mechanismen der natürlichen Evolution nachahmen, werden komplexe Optimierungsprobleme oft überzeugend gelöst. Der Anwender eines solchen Algorithmus muss allerdings dafür sorgen, dass Codierung und Auswahl von Parametern zur Problemstellung passen.

Ulrich Kathöfer entwickelt in diesem Buch eine Reihe von Erweiterungen der Standard-Algorithmen, die für spezifische Problemstellungen des Data Mining zu besseren, robusteren oder schneller erreichbaren Ergebnissen führen. Anwendbar sind die Ergebnisse auch für andere Fragestellungen, in denen Optimierung eine Rolle spielt.

Das Buch richtet sich sowohl an Dozenten und Studierende der Mathematik, Informatik und Wirtschaftsinformatik als auch an Praktiker, die Genetische Algorithmen insbesondere im Bereich der Datenanalyse einsetzen wollen.

Bd. 14: Anita Hukemann

Controlling im Onlinehandel.

Ein kennzahlenorientierter Ansatz für Onlineshops

ISBN 3-8325-0540-7   40.50 €
300 Seiten, 2004

Die Erscheinungsformen und Auswirkungen der Internetökonomie werden derzeit vielfältig diskutiert, insbesondere da der prognostizierte Geschäftserfolg vieler Internetunternehmen bis heute ausbleibt. Die euphorischen Vorhersagen aus den Zeiten des New Economy Booms konnten keineswegs erfüllt werden. Studien belegen, dass diejenigen Unternehmen der Internetökonomie, die trotz der wirtschaftlichen Krise inzwischen langfristige wirtschaftliche Erfolge aufweisen, eine systematische Unternehmenssteuerung auf strategischer und operativer Ebene betreiben. Die Bedeutung von Controlling ist den Unternehmen bewusst und die Einrichtung von Controllingsystemen wird von der Unternehmensführung vor allem für den Onlinehandel mit Nachdruck gefordert.

Anita Hukemann präsentiert einen Lösungsansatz für die Etablierung von Controllingsystemen im Onlinehandel. Kennzeichnend für die Arbeit ist die umfassende Katalogisierung und Systematisierung der vielfältigen Controllinginstrumente. Als Basis dient die Datengrundlage des Onlinehandels, die für Controllingzwecke nutzbar gemacht werden muss, um darauf aufbauend originäre Instrumente zu entwickeln. Bei der Gestaltung der Controllinginstrumente wurden sowohl etablierte Methoden des Handelscontrollings berücksichtigt als auch eine Adaption der klassischen Instrumente vorgenommen. Von großem praktischem Nutzen für den Aufbau eines Kennzahlensystems für den Onlinehandel wird die Herleitung und Entwicklung von über 80 spezifischen Controllingkennzahlen angesehen.

Bd. 15: Thomas Serries

Situationsbezogene Informationsversorgung in der industriellen Auftragsabwicklung.

Erweiterte OLAP-Techniken für Workflow-einbeziehende PPS

ISBN 3-8325-0632-2   40.50 €
308 Seiten, 2004

Die Effizienz der industriellen Auftragsabwicklung ist ein entscheidendes Merkmal für den betriebswirtschaftlichen Erfolg auftragsorientierter Einzel- und Kleinserienfertiger. Obwohl mit PPS- bzw. Workflowmanagementsystemen ausgereifte Koordinationsinstrumente vorhanden sind, zeigt die Praxis, dass ihr alleiniger Einsatz keinen reibungslosen Produktionsablauf garantieren kann. Manuelle Eingriffe in die Planungen und Prozessabläufe sind vielfach unumgänglich. PPS- und Workflowmanagementsysteme halten umfangreiche Daten bereit, die zum Treffen einer zielgerichteten Entscheidung notwendig sind. Ihre Auswertungsmöglichkeiten werden den Anforderungen an die benötigten Informationen jedoch nur eingeschränkt gerecht.

Thomas Serries untersucht, inwieweit OLAP-Techniken diese Anforderungen im Sinne einer situationsbezogenen Informationsversorgung in der industriellen Auftragsabwicklung unterstützen können. Für die sich aus den Datenstrukturen zur Abbildung mehrdimensionaler Informationsräume ergebenden Restriktionen werden Erweiterungen an OLAP-Techniken entwickelt, die die domänenspezifischen Datenstrukturen der Workflow-einbeziehenden PPS für mehrdimensionale Auswertungen zugänglich machen und dennoch von der industriellen Auftragsabwicklung unabhängig sind.

Das Buch richtet sich an Dozenten und Studenten der Wirtschaftsinformatik sowie an Anwendungssystemgestalter, insbesondere in produktionsnahen Bereichen, und die Hersteller von OLAP- und Data-Warehouse-Systemen.

Bd. 16: Thomas Zabel

Klassifikation mit Neuronalen Netzen.

CARTE Cooperative Adaptive Resonance Theory Ensembles

ISBN 3-8325-0803-1   40.50 €
220 Seiten, 2005

Für die betriebswirtschaftliche Entscheidungsfindung besteht die Notwendigkeit, bislang unbekannte Zusammenhänge und wertvolle Information aus einer immer größer werdenden Datenbasis zu ermitteln. Dies erfordert eine neue Generation von intelligenten und möglichst automatischen Modellen und Techniken, die den Anwender bei der Analyse der Daten unterstützen. Derzeitige Ansätze zur Klassifikation auf Basis neuronaler Netze weisen Schwächen auf. Die in dieser Arbeit entwickelten Klassifikatoren basieren auf der Adaptiven Resonanz Theorie und der Bildung von Ensembles.

Thomas Zabel entwickelt in diesem Buch eine Methode zur Erstellung von Klassifikatoren auf Basis der Adaptiven Resonanz Theorie. Zu seiner Methode erstellt er zudem einen effizienten Algorithmus, der auf Erkenntnissen der Ensemblebildung aufbaut, sowie ein Softwareprodukt, das den Algorithmus implementiert und die Anwendung und die Erprobung der Methode ermöglicht. Mithilfe des Softwareprodukts wird eine empirische Untersuchung von Versicherungsdaten unter der Fragestellung Erkennung von aktiven bzw. inaktiven Versicherungsagenturen durchgeführt. Die Klassifikationsqualität der verwendeten Methoden erweist sich als zufrieden stellend.

Das Buch wendet sich an Dozenten und Studierende der Mathematik, Informatik, Wirtschaftsinformatik und Betriebswirtschaftslehre sowie an Praktiker, die Neuronale Netze insbesondere im Bereich der Datenanalyse einsetzen wollen.

Bd. 18: Rainer Babiel

Content Management in der öffentlichen Verwaltung.

Ein systemgestaltender Ansatz für die Justizverwaltung NRW

ISBN 3-8325-0927-5   40.50 €
226 Seiten, 2005

Informationsfreiheitsgesetze bilden die rechtliche Grundlage für den Wandel von Amts-geheimnis verpflichteten Behörden zur modernen, transparenten öffentlichen Verwaltung. Die Öffentlichkeit erhält beinahe unbeschränkten Zugang zu allen Unterlagen und Do-kumenten staatlicher Stellen. Mit dieser Transparenz kommen neue Aufgaben auf die Behörden zu, deren Erfüllung durch Content Management als Domäne der Wirtschafts-informatik ohne zusätzlichen Personalaufbau effizient zu gestalten scheint.
Im Rahmen der vorliegenden Arbeit werden die theoretischen und rechtlichen Rahmen-bedingungen für ein effizientes Informationsmanagement öffentlicher Einrichtungen be-leuchtet und anhand der konkreten Systemimplementierung für die Justizverwaltung NRW konkretisiert. Die sich anschließende Wirtschaft-lichkeitsbetrachtung sowie die Er-gebnisse der durchgeführten Nutzerbefragung zeigen den Erfolg des gestalteten System eindruckvoll auf.

Bd. 19: Michael Ribbert

Gestaltung eines IT-gestützten Kennzahlensystems für das Produktivitätscontrolling operativer Handelsprozesse.

Ein fachkonzeptioneller Ansatz am Beispiel des klassischen Lager-geschäfts des Lebensmittelgroßhandels

ISBN 3-8325-0944-5   40.50 €
292 Seiten, 2005

Der Lebensmittelhandel in Deutschland sieht sich einem intensiven Wettbewerb ausge-setzt. Um dauerhaft am Markt bestehen zu können, ist der effiziente Ressourceneinsatz eine unabdingbare Voraussetzung. Die fehlende rechtliche Beschränkung bzgl. der Adap-tion von Betreiberkonzepten gepaart mit einer hohen Umstellungsflexibilität begründen die hohe Bedeutung der internen Unternehmensprozesse, um dauerhaft Wettbewerbsvor-teile erzielen zu können. Die Effizienz von Prozessen lässt sich durch die Betrachtung der erbrachten Leistungen und der dafür eingesetzten Ressourcen beurteilen, was mit einer Bewertung der Produktivität der Prozesse gleichzusetzen ist. Michael Ribbert entwickelt hierzu eine Methode, welche mittels eines Vorgehensmodells und durch die integrierte An-wendung ausgesuchter Controllinginstrumente zur Definition eines Kennzahlensystems für das prozessorientierte und multidimensionale Produktivitätscontrolling im Handel genutzt werden kann. Die Anwendung der Methode am Beispiel von Referenzprozessen des klassischen Lagergeschäfts des Lebensmittelgroßhandels und die Überführung der Ergebnisse in fachkonzeptionelle Modelle ergeben Referenzmodelle, die für die Ableitung und Spezifikation unternehmensindividueller Controllingkonzepte und unterstützender IT-Systeme genutzt werden können. Das Buch richtet sich an Dozenten und Studenten der Wirtschaftsinformatik und der Betriebswirtschaftslehre sowie an Anwendungssystem-gestalter der Handelsdomäne.